The Fabulous Journeys of *Alice* and *Pinocchio*

Exploring Their Parallel Worlds

Laura Tosi
with Peter Hunt

CRITICAL EXPLORATIONS IN
SCIENCE FICTION AND FANTASY, 61

Series Editors Donald E. Palumbo *and* C.W. Sullivan III

McFarland & Company, Inc., Publishers
Jefferson, North Carolina

ISBN (print) 978-1-4766-6543-6
ISBN (ebook) 978-1-4766-3194-3

Library of Congress cataloguing data are available

British Library cataloguing data are available

Front cover imagery adapted from Luisa Simioni & John Tenniel

Printed in the United States of America

McFarland & Company, Inc., Publishers
Box 611, Jefferson, North Carolina 28640
www.mcfarlandpub.com

Table of Contents

Acknowledgments

The idea for this book began to form while Peter Hunt was spending a term as a visiting professor at the University of Venice in 2013, and during the joint writing of the semi-serious book *As Fit As a Fish*. Some of the ideas that developed into chapters had their first outing at a conference on fantasy literature, which we organized in Venice in November 2013, and in other academic conferences and invited lectures (some of which were delivered with Peter). I am grateful for the invitations, as well as for the helpful criticisms and comments that we received from many colleagues on those occasions, including: Maurizio Ascari, Giorgia Grilli, Zoe Jaques, Lindsay Myers, Maria Nikolajeva, Francesca Orestano, Keith O'Sullivan, Fabio Pesaresi, Kimberley Reynolds, Stefania Tondo, and Pádraic Whyte. And, of course, thanks to Peter Hunt for being there at the beginning of this "fabulous journey," for those early brainstorming sessions on Skype, which helped me immensely to clarify my objectives and critical directions, and for reading and commenting on the final manuscript.

I wish to acknowledge a huge debt to the scholar who has gone before me in studying *Pinocchio* and *Alice* together and whose work reassured me that I was not totally insane in trying to compare these books and these characters: Ann Lawson Lucas, who is no doubt the most quoted critic in my book.

This book has been written with the support and encouragement of many friends and colleagues, some of whom have also helped with supplying various bibliographical material: Elena Paruolo, Mariangela Mosca Bonsignore and Pompeo Vagliani (and the amazing collection of the Fondazione Tancredi di Barolo in Turin), Alessandra Petrina, who brought me books from various university libraries in Padua, Cristina Cavecchi who did the same in libraries in Milan, and Maria Truglio, who very kindly let me read in advance a chapter from her book on Italian children's literature and national identity.

I am particularly grateful to Daniela Marcheschi, a scholar who knows Carlo Lorenzini better than anyone else in the world, for reading chapter three and giving me precious advice, thus setting my mind at rest about my adventurous and unconventional comparisons between authors Collodi and Carroll.

I wish to thank a few of my good Venetian friends and colleagues: Loretta Innocenti, who, born and bred in Florence, explained to me the subtleties of Collodi's Tuscanisms in the *Giannettino* series (thus enabling me to improve my translations); Shaul Bassi, who offered his expertise as a postcolonial scholar (among other things) for the adventure story chapter; and Laura Cerasi, who teaches modern Italian history in Venice and whose reading suggestions on Italian colonialism and attitudes to education after the unification were extremely useful.

I owe an enormous debt of gratitude to my very dear friends Adrienne and Alan Gillam, Patrick Spottiswoode, and Morag Styles for opening their lovely houses to me, and for providing much kindness and warmth, as well as delicious meals and intelligent conversations, during my frequent research trips to London and Cambridge.

I have received astute critiques, encouragement, and reassurance, as well as excellent assistance in revising the chapters, from Lindsay Myers. I have benefited from her help more than I can say, so this is a special thanks to a special friend.

I have a policy of never thanking family for my academic output, but this time I want to make an exception and thank my son Francesco, who, good-humoredly and empathetically (rare virtues in a teenager), has welcomed the riotous Pinocchio and the inquiring Alice into our household as guests, even if I am sure that he thought many times that they had overstayed their welcome.

Preface

"The classics are those books which come to us bearing the aura of previous interpretations, and trailing behind them the traces they have left in the culture or cultures (or just in the languages and customs) through which they have passed." Thus said Italo Calvino in *Why Read the Classics?* (2000: 5). The Italian novelist's words appear to encapsulate the essence and the impact of the *Alice* books and *Pinocchio* on readers of all languages and cultures, and I am well aware of the projections of "the aura of previous interpretations" on my own book, and consequently of the challenge posed by the intention to say something new about these classics.

The books I am looking at, Lewis Carroll's *Alice's Adventures in Wonderland* (1865) and *Through the Looking-Glass* (1871) (which will be considered, unless specified otherwise, as a unit, and generally referred to as "the *Alice* books") and Carlo Collodi's *Le avventure di Pinocchio* (1883) are among the most translated works of world literature, with thousands of editions in almost all languages. They are connected to their nations in a way other classics are not and they have refashioned folktale and fantasy traditions in a way that other classics (like *Cuore* in Italy, or *Peter Pan* in England) have not been able to do. There is an abundance of critical works on the *Alice* books and *Pinocchio* as separate entities but there have been, to date, no scholarly books that consider both together. This is a comparative study which goes beyond the restrictions of establishing whether author A read author B's work and therefore integrated B into his/her own work (after the Irish academic Persse McGarrigle was offered a publishing contract for writing a book on the influence of T.S. Eliot on Shakespeare, in David Lodge's *Small World*, such restrictions have become difficult to enforce).

I adhere to the notion that "comparative literature is the replication, under methodologically stringent conditions, of the common reader's experience that crosses all kinds of borders (temporal, spatial, linguistic, cultural, etc.) in order to build meaning" (Domínguez, Saussy and Villanueva xiv). In other words, the *Fabulous Journeys of* Alice *and* Pinocchio is a critical narrative and a parallel reading of two classics, which records mutual interests and avenues of exploration between and across the diverse linguistic, historical, and national borders of England and Italy. It is a way of "rethinking cultural identities beyond national paradigms" (O'Sullivan 2005: 4).

There are currents of mutual interest and serendipity between Italy and *Alice*, and England and *Pinocchio*: England was the first foreign country to publish a translation of *Pinocchio*, in 1892 (Paruolo 2017: 15), by a lady called Alice, and the author of the first translation into Italian of *Alice's Adventures* in 1872 was Pietrocola Rossetti, an Italian patriot during the *Risorgimento* (or, "resurgence," the nineteenth-century political movement for the unification and independence of Italy), who had to escape for his life to England—he died the year *Pinocchio* was published in book form (1883). These books are broadly contemporaneous with each other, and although they were published with radically different political, social and cultural backgrounds, there are unexpected similarities between them and between their authors' perspectives—reading each book through the lens of the other highlights surprising differences in the use of literary sources and attitudes to the child. My book is a parallel reading of texts that are one-offs in their own countries, texts that are very far from—and in many ways in direct opposition to—the didactic turn in children's books. They both started literary traditions of their own, and it is striking how many children's books have been defined in relation to them since their publication. They speak to each other indirectly, through different national and cultural contexts, but they project very similar images in terms of their structure, themes, and the general impact that they have had on the cultures that produced them.

And yet, it was an American who helped these books (and characters) to become international icons: Walt Disney has provided the world with its primary image of *Pinocchio*, and, to a lesser extent, perpetuated the reputation of *Alice*. Most children today, the world over, access these books though the Disney "mediation": what happened to these books in the hands of his animators underlines the extreme adaptability and "portability" of these characters over space and time. The criticisms leveled against the Disney *Pinocchio* are primarily that it eliminated the anarchic and ambivalent features of the original, as well as all connections to Italianness and poverty. Disney (or, at least, his artists) turned *Pinocchio* into a fairy tale in the Grimms' tradition: "the book is demonstrably Italian," Allan Robin writes, "[but] the film is North European in look and specifically German in detail[...]. The precisely modelled toys, clocks and music boxes [...] are German[...]. Geppetto is a German and voiced by an expatriate German actor, Christian Rub" (78). Similarly, largely for narrative reasons, Disney resurrected the Cricket, Pinocchio's conscience, who is squashed early in the book, as Jiminy Cricket, and cut the book's many characters (from over fifty to eight). The fact that Disney's *Pinocchio* as a character does not resemble Collodi's in almost any respect seems to be irrelevant to millions of viewers.

Perhaps it is less known that these two books nearly bankrupted the Disney studio—although they were among the most innovative (technically) that the studio produced. Disney's *Alice*, similarly, was a costly flop, although it has since been recognized as "probably the most ingeniously experimental of all [his] animated features" (Mosley 205). And it almost certainly flopped because Disney allowed (or was forced to allow) his animators to produce a work that *retained* its essentially English nationalistic features. However, as Mosley noted, "Walt did not grasp the subtle Englishness of the book and the fact that it was not one of those stories to which he could add his brilliant but quintessentially American touches of Disney imagination" (206). Other critics, such as Brooker, complained that Disney reduced "the sophisticated address and the dry irony of Carroll's prose to a soppy heroine in a blandly stereotyped English pastoral" (207). *Pinocchio*'s Italianness and *Alice*'s Englishness eluded and probably baffled Disney, but paradoxically—and this is a paradox that has followed these books like a shadow—these world-famous texts have transcended their origins and have become transnational classics despite and because of their national characteristics.

National associations and mutual stereotyping pave the way to the reception of these texts, although it is not always clear what non–English readers make of *Alice* and non–Italian readers make of *Pinocchio*. How and why do we/they relate to them? How far are national stereotypes mutual? Italians are not surprised to see a chapter devoted to a tea party in Alice— and British (or American) readers may expect Pinocchio and his father to be poor or illiterate or insincere. *Alice* and *Pinocchio* have also been absorbed into national and international culture as shorthand for insincerity or general topsy-turvyness: in 2012, an Italian magazine (*Repubblica*, Il Venerdì, 25 March) posed the question, "Il paese di Pinocchio è davvero più bugiardo tanti altri?" [Is the country of Pinocchio more of a liar than other countries?], followed by an analysis of lying in Italian public life. Similarly, British politicians routinely accuse each other of producing "Alice in Wonderland policies"—especially as "Wonderland" does not mean a land of wonders, but a land where one wonders at the stupidity of *other* people. One definition of a classic text is one that has become common property, and can be adapted to the needs of different times or cultures: how far it thus becomes a different creature, through the vagaries of translation, or deliberate localization, is part of the intricate process of national image-making.

It is also very common to find "classics" described as "timeless": but although they may have transcended time, part of the mystery of lasting fame is that they are also locked into a specific time, place and culture. Thus universal and national appeal is a paradox, just as the imagologists' complex flux of cultural pressures, multi-media images, and time, constantly comes up against the popularist essentialism that constructs universal images of nations. I address issues of translation, national stereotypes and cultural associations between these books and characters in the first two chapters. *Pinocchio* and the two *Alice* books are examples of local stories at their most universal—and universal stories at their most local. This is not just a play on words: in pre-globalized societies, every children's book started "locally," especially when it was conceived for a specific child in a specific environment—one needs only to think of the first version of *Alice*, hand-written and illustrated by Lewis Carroll and full of allusions to people in contemporary Oxford. Similarly, Collodi wrote *Le avventure di Pinocchio* for a children's supplement of a newspaper founded in Florence, his hometown (and then transferred to Rome)—and the language, atmosphere, setting and language of his book are often Tuscan rather than Italian. And yet, world culture tends to recognize *Pinocchio* as "quintessentially" Italian, and *Alice* as "quintessentially" English. It seems likely that these characteristics are synthesized through reactions to specific historical moments (in this case the post–*Risorgimento* and the *Pax Britannica*) and crystallized in the fictional figures of their child protagonists. The representation of Englishness that we find in the *Alice* books "is part cultural literacy, part idealized expression of national temperament, and part nostalgic evocation of Eden [...] such a potent force that it reaches out to readers worldwide" who "experience a kind of secondary Englishness" (Knuth 180). As for the Italianness of *Pinocchio*, this character has often been considered (most famously by the contemporary historian Asor Rosa) as a metaphor for a young country that had to grow up and behave like a responsible adult. But the concern about the Italian character, and the notion that Italians needed to absorb the work ethics of the English and the Germans started immediately after the unification (see Patriarca 64), and tirades against laziness and in favor of industry and hard work are common in Collodi's novel. Chapter 3 is devoted to comparing the national and historical contexts in which these authors operated, their personal backgrounds, and their attitudes to literacy and education.

In chapters 4 and 5 I analyze the development of the folktale, fairy tale, and fantasy genres in Italy and England, and the crucial part that the *Alice* books and *Pinocchio* have played in the refashioning of these traditions in their respective countries. Both books have their roots in folktale traditions, and the contrasts between their treatments of tropes illuminate the ways in which "universal" characteristics of folktale and fantasy are modified by specific cultural and personal contexts (while at the same time, national characteristics add piquancy to the appeal of the universal elements). A contrastive analysis of these texts belonging to the same genre configuration, and characterized by the same generic hybridity but deriving from different national settings, affords new insights into the respective cultures that produced them and about the books themselves.

Metamorphosis is the hallmark of *Alice* and *Pinocchio*. As bodies and characters, they undergo radical transformations, in their original books as well as in world culture. In chapter 6 I explore the way Postmodernism has found the Italian puppet and the English little girl fascinating and inspiring in their capacity to jump from page to stage, from artwork to screen. In this chapter I focus on Angela Carter's and Robert Coover's revisions of these books: these authors have exploited the extreme flexibility of the *Alice* books and *Pinocchio*, and refashioned them in versions that explore "adult" issues of fragmentation of identity, gender formation, and general disillusionment about the notion of "growing up."

The last chapter of the book invites comparisons between genres other than fantasy and the folktale. I contrast the characteristics and the ideology of the school and adventure story genres, which became popular in Italy and England (or Britain) in the last decades of the nineteenth century and the first of the twentieth, periods in which both countries were thinking of themselves as nations in relation to the exotic spaces of the Empire. As with the chapters on Carroll and Collodi, I concentrate on the works of specific authors who can be viewed as representative of these genres: for the school story genre, I consider Thomas Hughes's *Tom Brown's Schooldays* (1857) and Edmondo De Amicis's *Cuore* (1886), and for the adventure stories genre, I examine and contrast the personality and output of George Henty, "imperialist boy's writer" (as in the title of Guy Arnold's monograph) and Emilio Salgari, "a post-colonial writer *ante litteram*" (Lawson Lucas 2003: 82).

The first five chapters of the book may be slightly skewed in favor of *Pinocchio*, in a percentage that could be reckoned, very roughly and unscientifically, around 60 percent about *Pinocchio* and 40 percent about *Alice*. This is because in some cases I wished to take account of some of the most interesting scholarship in Italian that may not be immediately available to English readers. Although in the text I quote from the English translation of *Pinocchio* by Ann Lawson Lucas (1996), for those readers who can read Italian I have provided the original versions in the chapter notes (and occasionally, even in the body of the text, when I needed to work on a more literal translation). After all, *Pinocchio* was written in my mother tongue, Italian, so in some cases I needed to go back to the original to make my critical point (perfection does not belong to the world of translation. Or to other worlds, for that matter). On the other hand, as I am a professor of English literature and my critical background and reading is in English, I have more of an English perspective on genres such as the folktale and fantasy than an Italian scholar of Italian literature would probably have. It was extremely interesting to identify and become aware of cultural differences even in what one may believe is basic, common, "transnational" critical terminology.

This book is addressed to scholars and students of Italian as well as English children's literature and culture, and everyone who is interested in taking their reading and literary interests across national, linguistic, and historical borders.

Although this book is the result of a collaborative—and appropriately transnational—venture between two scholars (one Italian and one English), Peter Hunt is the author of the section titled "*Alice* and *Pinocchio* as 'Gendered Books'" in chapter 2, "The Blue Fairy: Collodi, MacDonald, Kingsley, and Carroll" in chapter 4, and of the Appendix: "Strange Meeting in Wonder-Tuscany." Laura Tosi is the author of the rest of the book.

PART ONE

Theories, Choices
and Contexts

1. *Alice* meets *Pinocchio*: Parallel Readings, National Stereotypes and Cultural Associations

Parallel Readings and the International Canon

This book is a parallel reading of two international classics. Or, rather, two readings that intersect with each other and with the societies and the nations that produced them. It is not just a comparison between *Le avventure di Pinocchio* and the *Alice* books, or even a confrontation or juxtaposition: it is looking at each book through the lens of the other. This highlights similarities and differences in terms of universal fantasy and national characteristics, and opens up new critical perspectives. In 1977 Giorgio Manganelli called his critical work on *Pinocchio* "un libro parallelo" [a parallel book], in the knowledge that every critical reading creates a new perception of a literary work, and therefore a new literary work. Both the *Alice* books and *Pinocchio* are texts that appear to have in their DNA an amazing potential for generating new texts and new readings: "a great book," Manganelli argues, "will produce infinite books" (11) and this critical book, in its own humble way, is the result of a cross-generation of two great, and infinitely productive, books.

In his preface, Manganelli discloses the golden rule of the "professional parallelist": "everything arbitrary, everything well documented" (8). Writing a parallel critical book on *Alice* and *Pinocchio* is, similarly and simultaneously, an arbitrary and a well-documented enterprise, and one that needs to deal with the issue of internationalism in relation to children's literature. Can we conceive of an international canon of children's literature (based on translation)? Critics are very wary of generalizations and not too optimistic about this. Maria Nikolajeva, in *Children's Literature Comes of Age* (1996), for example, writes that "with very few exceptions, children's literature in different countries has little in common" (43), universal texts being mostly collections of folktales or adaptations of adult texts such as *Robinson Crusoe* (although she considers *Alice*, very cautiously, as the only example of a "truly universal children's book" [43]). Emer O'Sullivan warns of treating "classics" written in the source language in the same way as classics in translation (and uses *Pinocchio* in German translations as an example of this, in her chapter "World Literature and Children's Classics" [2005: 130–164]). Her conclusion is that a "corpus of so-called classics of international children's literature [...] cannot be equated with a canon of children's literature" (2005: 148). Other authors, such as Klingberg (39), have argued that exchanges can only be identified within countries that belong to the same linguistic and geographical groups, such as Anglophone countries or Southern European countries. Much earlier (and now much more controversially), Paul Hazard in his *Les livres, les enfants et les hommes* (1932), noted in a chapter "Superiority of the North over the South," the "superior" and more prolific children's literature "harvest" (78) of the Northern countries as compared with the Southern. Nothing of interest, he claimed, happens in Spain, and he wondered, for example, why the Italian masterpieces *Pinocchio* and *Cuore* "waited centuries to make themselves known; they date *only from the Risorgimento*" (78) (*my emphasis*). The relationship between children's literature and national identity is indeed crucial, and there are reasons for the fact that these books came out after the unification, as will be discussed later.

National differences can be a source of humor, and Yanko Tsvetkov's *Atlas of Prejudice* (2014) is a typical example of this. In his map sequence, "Tearing Europe Apart: 20 Ways to Slice a Continent," which cuts Europe in two depending on religion, weather, eating habits, working hours, and so on, the only map in which Italy and England are on the same side, is the map about *plumbing* (apparently, England and Italy belong to the same part of Europe that needs a plumber—the other half can repair their sinks). If we take Hazard's and Klingberg's distinctions to extremes, all we are left with is a map of Europe where *Alice* and *Pinocchio* are never on the same side.

So, what can a parallel reading of works as diverse as these, which belong to different literary and linguistic traditions, offer to a comparative study? As O'Sullivan writes in the first overview of comparative children's literature studies, "the peculiarities and the individual features of the various literatures [...] come to light only when they are seen in relation to others" (2005: 4). These texts offer the possibility of analyzing the cross-cultural development of the fantasy mode in countries in which these texts have emerged quite independently of each other. Post-*Risorgimento* Italy and Victorian England have produced texts that are not easy to classify in terms of genre (and gender representations) in their respective countries, but that have changed the history of children's literature in their very different historical, social, and national contexts, with remarkably different conditions of production and reception. And yet these books manage to be universal in several ways: as Benedetto Croce famously wrote: "il legno in cui è intagliato Pinocchio è l'umanità" [the wood *Pinocchio* is carved from is the human race] (331); and as the children's literature historian F.J. Harvey Darton equally famously put it, *Alice's Adventures in Wonderland* was "the spiritual volcano of children's books" (260). Groundbreaking, subversive books, which surprisingly show a certain affinity in their treatment of social and literary themes, *Alice* and *Pinocchio* are among the most famous, most translated books in the world; they are national and international classics. Despite the fact that *Pinocchio* is widely regarded as stereotypically Italian, and *Alice* as stereotypically British, they have transcended their national origins.

In the last few years there has been a growing interest in the representation of nationality in children's literature: "Children's Literature is a key instrument of culture connecting child and nation, and defining their relationship" (Kelen and Sundmark 3). I start from the premise that children's literature is of vast cultural importance in many countries: it shapes the way nations think and what they think. The way nations see and understand the world stems in part from the stories and characters and modes of narrative that are encountered by their children. A nation has been defined as "an imagined community [...] conceived as a deep, horizontal comradeship" (Anderson 7)—it is a human creation, an act of faith in the sense of unity which derives from "the possession in common of a rich legacy of memories" and "the will to perpetuate the value of the heritage that one has received" (Renan 19). Nations, according to Homi Bhabha, can be "narrated" (1), and if we apply Jonathan Gottschall's theory of "life stories," in which we "see ourselves as the striving heroes of our own epics" (171), to nation forming, we can see that the journey towards national awareness or national pride is paved with cultural and political storytelling.

There have been several collections of essays on the issue of children's literature and national identity (see, for example, Lawson Lucas 1997, Webb, Meek). As Kelen and Sundmark have noted, modern nation states and children's literature emerged at the same time—and this is not surprising, as among children's literature's many functions is that it teaches children how to be citizens (1). This of course is one of the reasons why the most famous Italian classics for children were written soon after the formation of an independent nation. After all "it is for the benefit of the child that the adult work of nation-making is undertaken" (Kelen and Sundmark 3).

Like children's literature, nation-making is very much a process of the imagination—and the journey that iconic nation-specific texts and characters such as *Alice* and *Pinocchio* undergo in becoming part of an international canon of children's literature is not entirely dissimilar. Equally obviously, not all national classics—in fact, very few—travel well: the English classic, *The Wind in the Willows* for example, has not been a great success in Italy, despite excellent translations. Much has to be explained to an Italian audience: quintessential Englishness and nostalgia, the attractions of picnics with sardines, cold tongue, and the rest—and perhaps, above all, the issue of class. For Italian readers the riverbank becomes almost as exotic as the jungle in Kipling's works.

How then do the highly culturally-specific worlds of *Alice* and *Pinocchio* transcend these limitations? *Pinocchio* is very local indeed—it is essentially a Tuscan text as well as Italian; the *Alice* books are a detailed exploration of the mind of a Victorian English scholarly eccentric.

Imagology: Perceptions of Nationality and Stereotypes

The process of defining national traits in children's literature has been greatly assisted in recent years by the perspectives offered by imagology, a text-based discipline rooted in comparative literature. Imagology has been invaluable for investigating national self-images and the images of other countries in culture and literature, as well as the manner in which nations are represented in literature once it crosses national borders. The emphasis of imagology is always on *representation*: it highlights the gap between common perceptions and literary representations of nationality and the way in which stereotypical images are produced, disseminated and internalized over time in accordance with developing political and cultural allegiances. As Joep Leerssen, one of the leading scholars in this field, has put it, "imagology [...] furnishes continual proof that it is in the field of imaginary and poetical literature that national stereotypes are first and most effectively formulated" (2007: 26). Ethnotypes (defined as "stereotypical characterizations attributed to ethnicities or nationalities") are regarded as "representative of literary and discursive conventions, not of social realities" (Beller and Leerssen 2007: xiv). Imagologists reject the reality of national characters in favor of a concept of nationality as a literary trope, "a convention, a misunderstanding, a construct" (Leerssen 2007: 22). National identities are studied as internalized self-images which depend on subjective viewpoints rather than on objective conditions (30): "images do not reflect identities, but constitute possible identifications" (22).

Literary sources perpetuate images over time and literature is the ideal field for formulating and transmitting national stereotypes. Canonical texts are often particularly effective vehicles for the transmission of cultural stereotypes not only because they remain current in the culture system for longer than other text types, but also because their authors are considered important and influential within their national context. The study of imagology has revealed that national representations function as powerful tropes within literature and that these tropes interact in a variety of complex ways with genre, literary conventions and historical contextualization. The way in which national tropes were, or are, geared to their target audience, can be highly informative when it comes to understanding the ways in which cultural and national values are transmitted within specific contexts.

Obviously, all this is relevant to the way in which *Pinocchio* and *Alice* are perceived as national icons and representatives of national fantasy modes, as well as being national characters. Emer O'Sullivan has studied the way imagology can be used to research intercultural relations and national images and self-images in children's texts, as children's literature "overtly or latently reflects dominant social and cultural norms, including self-images and images of others" (O'Sullivan 2011: 6). In the case of *Alice* and *Pinocchio*, however, images of foreign nations are not used to instill a sense of national identity as the result of a contrast. These fantasies do not produce images of *other* nations or foreigners: they operate with self-images, and ask the reader to look at their worlds and their respective images of Italianness and Englishness as defamiliarized. (I prefer to use Englishness rather than Britishness when it comes to defining symbolic national associations with *Alice*. However, I am aware that the relationship between these terms is complicated, and in the course of the book I have tried to be as accurate as possible—for the world Alice has probably an Anglo-British identity in which the English element is clearly prevailing. From an Italian perspective, Alice is unambiguously *inglese*—the word *britannico* is far less used in everyday Italian).

Both in Wonderland and in the spaces inhabited by Pinocchio, places are recognizably Italian/Tuscan and English/Oxfordian and at the same time, *other*—simultaneously familiar and foreign, as is the typical case of fantasy, a land "full of wonder but not of information" (Tolkien 9). For example, in the world of *Pinocchio*, children replace animals for work—Pinocchio works as a guard dog and Lucignolo [Candle-Wick], dies of fatigue when working as, and like, a donkey (as in the Italian idiom: *lavorare come un mulo*). This is part of the distortion of fantasy but it is also the very grim reality of Italian poverty in Collodi's time, where children were put to work at a very young age. Similarly, the very English institutions of the tea party or the game of croquet, or even the monarchy, are parodies and perverted versions of reality.

Pinocchio's Italianness and *Alice*'s Englishness are constructions and projections: they triggered associations and responses from their original readers and they continue to draw very similar reactions from contemporary readers—responses that often confirm stereotypes and expectations. There is a lot of imaginative and creative material around national stereotypes—this does not make them any less plausible for readers. If nations are stories with heroes we can identify with, and countries tell stories about themselves (Gottschall), then national classics spin stories about their nations and, inevitably, present their characters as national representatives. Like the stories, national self-representations are historically determined: the representations of Englishness produced by the Ahlbergs in their picturebooks is not the representation of Englishness that we find in *Alice*. Both the time-specific "realistic" settings of books like *Peepo!* (1981), set in c. 1943, and the non-time-specific rural "English fairy-tale" settings of books like *The Jolly Postman* (1986) portray a culturally recognizable and acceptable view of Englishness. On the other hand, in contemporary representations of Englishness, multiculturalism, which is not as relevant to such texts as *Alice* and *Pinocchio*, must be taken into consideration.

In "The Englishness of English Children's Books" (2001) Margaret Meek reflects on the fact that every English book produces its own representation of Englishness, although fantasy seems to be the common denominator of the children's classics that are most famous outside English borders. Are there other recognizable traits that representations of Englishness share from a diachronic perspective, such as the English landscape or the presence of eccentric characters, or recognizable intertextual connections to earlier genres and traditions that are associated with Englishness? Does *Harry Potter* appear English because we recognize the connection to the public school story (that is, stories set in exclusive private schools in England) and the Arthurian references? A certain amount of circular thinking cannot be avoided: children's books produce images of nationhood, which are only recognized because they coincide with the prejudices that readers have already internalized (possibly through children's books!). National stereotyping is clearly reception-oriented, but, as can be expected, it is almost impossible to trace the exact sources of the individual processes of internalizing stereotypes and prejudices concerning national images:

> They [stereotypes and prejudices] are the kind of things we cannot place as to where precisely we have learned them. They were infused into our cultural literacy at an early, informal stage of our socialization process, in early childhood, as part of texts that by themselves are ephemeral and unmemorable (jokes, comic strips, B movies, proverbs or turns of phrase, publicity billboards or television shows). The schemata that remain in our awareness as a residue of all these small, individually unmemorable cultural socialization experiences are therefore clearly source-anchored [Leerssen 2000: 286].

Categories like North and South (or central/peripheral, backward/modern, etc.) are also, according to imagologists, conventional structures of national imagery. Images of nations appear to be configured in binary oppositions: the North/South opposition, in particular, with its set of stereotypes related to temperament, has a long tradition in Europe (Leerssen 1991: 132). It is obvious that any place can be constructed as the South or North of some other space and be depicted in opposition (*pace* Hazard). Since the days of the Grand Tour, when the English began to visit Italy, they have thought, as Kenneth Grahame did in *The Wind in the Willows,* of it as the warm South—a mental landscape representing the Northerners' yearning for the sun. Even if some national or stereotypical traits turn out to be variable according to the historical moment, others tend to linger in the readers' minds. Even now, the headline picture on the official Italian tourist website (at the time of writing) is of beach umbrellas in Rimini (technically in the *Italia Settentrionale,* the Northern half of Italy), and the three pictures in the "Discover Italy" section are of Molise, Calabria, and Puglia (all far South). The Italian image of contemporary England is still very much a combination of London and a landscape of thatched cottages and stone bridges.

"Traditional" associations of Northern countries with democracy, rationality and composure contrast with Southern anarchy, gregariousness, and sensualism, and become part of a nation's imageme (which Leerssen defines as "a blueprint underlying the various concrete, specific actualizations [of a national character] that can be encountered" (2000: 279). In Beller and Leerssen's edited volume, chapters are devoted to the cultural construction of national characters: the chapter on the English emphasizes the nineteenth-century construction of the "gentleman," "known and marketed as typical until this day" (Spiering 146), a character who never loses his temper, has perfect manners and a sense of duty. The chapter on Italians highlights some traits ascribed through the centuries to the national character; among others, that Italians are Machiavellian and scheming, but also lazy, anarchic, and easy going. In fact, one of the characteristics of nation-representation which has turned into a cliché is the idea that "Nation X is a nation of contrasts" (Leerssen 2000: 279): the national imageme is defined by its contradictory nature. For example, it has been commonly said that soccer is a game for gentlemen played by hooligans, and that Rugby football is a game for hooligans played by gentlemen: and so England can be perceived as the nation of gentlemen *and* hooligans.

In this study, the perspectives of imagology will be integrated with contrastive cultural and historical analyses of the two books, and the way the fantasy mode and folktale sources operate within different national identities. An interdisciplinary and intertextual integrated approach is key—with particular reference to other texts in the English/Italian children's literary traditions and to elements of cultural and linguistic "non translatability" (see Sandis 112).

Nation and Character:
Is *Pinocchio* Quintessentially Italian?
Is *Alice* Quintessentially English?

As we have seen, national stereotypes often take the form of personifications—one only needs to think of Uncle Sam for the United States and John Bull for England. Similarly, both Alice and Pinocchio, as books as well as characters, generate endless cultural associations with their nations for readers of their national tradition and language (and for readers from other nations) that can confirm or challenge stereotypes. In what way do these books, and these characters, encapsulate the image of each nation?

Pinocchio is seen by the world (and by the English) as quintessentially Italian: he is all actions and reactions: he is an impetuous, riotous, unstable (male) character—a creature of impulse and passion. Indeed, as Suzanne Stewart-Steinberg suggests in *The Pinocchio Effect*, one aspect of the self-image of Italians after the unification was

> Superficiality [...] and a childlike nature[...]. It was this aspect that answered to the idea that Italians were essentially children, that Italy—and this particularly when compared to the other modern nations—was in a state of perpetual infancy. The childlike Pinocchio as a cultural icon must, therefore, be understood in these terms [31].

Pinocchio's material nature, always escaping, but always a puppet at the mercy of others, is the prototype of the Italian characterized by what the Southern writer Pasquale Turiello, in 1882 called *scioltezza*, that is, a looseness or elasticity of mind and body: "The Italian refuses all civic ties and instead produces personalized relations of power" (Stewart-Steinberg 31). This refusal to be tied to rules would explain the "ungovernability of Italians" in many fields, but this tendency to anarchy must also be related to Pinocchio's intense and passionate family loyalty: he is, at the same time, a rebel and a reactionary. There is, then, a paradox in *Pinocchio*—and in Italy—a simultaneous centrifugal and centripetal impulse, a surface and a subtext often at odds.

There are paradoxes in Carroll, too, that may be taken as being quintessentially English. There is, again, a constant tension between surface and subtext: this may be between Alice's apparent sanity in the face of civilization's (and language's) rule-bound insanity, and her incipient rebellion, or tension between the apparent nonsense of the children's book and serious purposes of the author. Similarly, the *Alice* books are built on English eccentricity—a trait at once unconscious and self-aware.

If the Italians are impulsive, tentative, and unsure of their nationhood, the English, according to the stereotypes, and according to the Italian image of them, seem to be very sure of themselves (or have successfully adopted an impassive persona). As the German journalist Holger Ehling put it: "While Italians are famous for singing and Americans for praying, the English lead the world in keeping mute in the face of adversity" (183). And so, like Noël Coward's emblematic Englishman, out in the mid-day sun with the mad dogs (Day 176–179), Alice is driven by the quiet inner self-confidence that the rest of the world is simply *wrong*.

Both characters, as expressed in their books, seem to confirm the *effet de typique*, which "canonizes salient features into representative propria [and which] will account for the tendency in national characterization to gravitate to the restricted register of caricature" (Leerssen 2000: 284). It is, of course, tempting to extrapolate these features to simplify national contrasts. Alice's world is cold and emotionless; like a Victorian gentlewoman, she is quintessentially English in her calm, self-contained, reserved, polite and stoic attitude, while Pinocchio can be perceived as essentially Italian in that he is virtually the opposite of Alice: wild, hot-blooded, unreliable, and impetuous. He feels inferior and negotiates with every rule. In their respective "grammars of national characterization" (Leerssen 2000: 275) *Alice* and *Pinocchio* employ a combination of rules so that their image of nation appears in a recognizable configuration, a configuration which interacts with the genre configuration and the rules of fantasy. When we compare these books and these characters, their peculiarities appear even more striking.

A parallel reading of these classics as representing national images also needs to take account of their authors' different degrees of awareness in terms of national identity. As will be seen in chapter 3, Collodi was a patriot: on two occasions he interrupted work and (a precarious) financial security to fight in the Wars of Independence to free Italy from foreign domination. He also wrote textbooks for children—after the unification of Italy school manuals were introduced for the first time and school publishing became very successful. His contribution to a unified and free Italy was going to be textbooks that would teach every Italian child, regardless of class (see "Literacy and Education in Late Nineteenth-Century Italy and England" in chapter 3). Dodgson was born in the middle of the middle classes in the century of the *Pax Britannica,* and, although he pursued some low-key verbal political campaigns, England, as it were, had no need of him.

Readers today, however, are more likely to be alert to the "national values" that the books were projecting: Alice's ethnocentric attitude (and her middle-class pride) towards all the eccentric characters she meets, the overt allusions to her Oxford world or the religious and scientific controversies of its time make her books very recognizably "English High Victorian" for their English readers, and for the rest of the world. Italian readers make sense of the nonsense world of *Alice* by attributing it to a very typical English humor (the Italian novelist Stefano Benni (2007) has written that the Cheshire-Cat is an image of English humor). Alice is the protagonist of a text that has captured, as A.S. Byatt has written, "both the British and the world's imagination in something of the same obsessive way as Shakespeare." And this unsentimental Victorian child has been defined by Robert Graves as "the prime heroine of our nation [...] she being of speculative bent [...] with truly British pride" (Graves 49: 1, 15).

Pinocchio may remind today's Italian readers of the extreme poverty, hunger and the illiteracy of many sections of the population of post-unification Italy—both texts reflect images of nationhood, the Victorian and the post–*Risorgimento*, which may evoke precise associations. For Italians, Pinocchio (the character as well as the book) has an ambivalent relationship with the national character—as a prototype of the Italian, he is perhaps too close to the negative stereotype that Italians may want to deny, that of a childish rebel who is incapable of obeying rules (among other things). The literary historian Alberto Asor Rosa has suggested the symbolic equivalence between Pinocchio and Italy, which he interprets as a "puppet-people-Italy that matures through pain and misfortune." He attributes to Collodi "the intuition that Italy, in this post-unification phase was going through the suffering that changes a puppet into a man" and that this pain was necessary for Italy to grow up and change, even if this meant having "to cancel an ancient part of itself" (Asor Rosa 939–940, my translation). Renato Bertacchini, in his *Le avventure Ritrovate* (1983), reported the reactions of several Italian intellectuals and writers to Asor Rosa's thesis that this marionette represents "one of the most authentic searches for national identity" (Bertacchini 1983: 14). The great majority of the authors interviewed agreed with Asor Rosa, many noticing the paradox of seeing *Pinocchio* as paradigmatic of the Italian national character, and at the same time providing a universal human character, as in Croce's apt definition. (It is interesting that the Oscar-winner and one of the most famous Italian "exports," Roberto Benigni, has a parallel career as the disseminator of Italianness through his series of lectures on Dante's *Divine Comedy*, the Italian Constitution, the Italian national anthem, and his sophisticated yet unsuccessful filmic version of *Pinocchio*).

There are no equivalent surveys to Bertacchini's on the English opinions of Alice, but I have carried out some research on this with the British Lewis Carroll Society, and I circulated questionnaires among mainly British children's literature scholars at the biennial conference of the International Research Society for Children's Literature in Worcester in August 2015, and at the Homerton College, University of Cambridge conference celebrating 150 years of *Alice*'s publication in September 2015. One of the questions was: "How do you respond to the idea that Alice is quintessentially English and represents Englishness to the rest of the world?" The responses I received strongly suggest that the English/British are also aware that she is a national icon (but not the only one—somebody mentioned Marmite as being more representative of Englishness) and that she may represent the epitome of Englishness, and not just abroad. Some of the answers showed some problems with the idea of Englishness *per se*, or associated Alice with a kind of an elite idea of Englishness or a specifically

Victorian-nostalgic, and class-based, idea of Englishness. Other scholars associated stereotypically English traits such as eccentricity, politeness, common sense, and restraint with Alice's behavior in the books—and it was pointed out that it could be the heritage merchandising and tourism-related publications of *Alice* that have contributed in recent times to make her representative of the nation. Most answers recognized the fact that Carroll's protagonist as well as the books have transcended a specific nationality, and that Walt Disney was instrumental in the process. The opinions of children's literature experts, once again, appeared to focus on the paradox of a national literary icon (an English anonymous scholar wrote "Everything about her screams English to me") that has become a universal, international child as well as literary figure.

If we compare the ways in which the *Alice* books and *Pinocchio* approach issues of identity and class it soon becomes apparent that they have opposing attitudes towards these: in *Alice*, as in English society, class is endemic. From Alice's worry about being Mabel and living in a poky house, to the Red Queen and her insignificant courtiers, to Bill the Lizard and the Irish gardener (lower class *and* Irish) and the competition between Alice, the Gryphon, and the Mock Turtle as to who went to the best school, class is a fundamental element. In contrast, Italy was conceived as, and remains, a society that, on the whole, does not perceive itself in class terms (throughout *Pinocchio*, Collodi mocks the use of titles to confer a higher status on professionals—as when Pinocchio calls the puppet-master Mangiafoco "Sua Eccellenza"). In much Italian children's literature, especially in the decades after the political unification, interclassism and mutual respect between the classes were important themes and desirable goals (Myers 2012: 39) both in fantasy and realism. In Edmondo De Amicis's *Cuore* (1886), the other classic of Italian nineteenth-century children's literature, as in *Pinocchio*, education is perceived as essential for social improvement. The state day school is described as a utopian space where the privileged children of the middle classes can be friends with the children of the working classes because they sit in the same classroom (see chapter 7). And yet, even though class appears to be more relevant to Carroll than Collodi, the ending of *Pinocchio* seems to suggest that the reward for good behavior for the puppet is not just the final metamorphosis, but also a form of social upgrading. In the last chapter Pinocchio is wearing elegant leather boots and his room has changed into a middle-class parlor: "he saw a lovely bedroom furnished and decorated with an elegant simplicity" (Collodi/Lucas 168).[1] He now owns an ivory purse and even his father's job has been made more genteel—instead of a simple carpenter,

Geppetto has become a "woodcarver." The extreme poverty of the beginning of the book is replaced by a middle-class ideal—very possibly the goal of the illiterate starving peasant after the unification.

Translation and Dissemination

It is commonly supposed that international classics—and especially transnational children's classics—demonstrate how it is possible for cultures to understand each other and exchange ideas about each other, but translation experts suggest that the fate of *Pinocchio* and *Alice* in translation contradicts this. Translation involves localizing or universalizing ("glocalizing") and so some essence of the original is necessarily lost. Questions of translation of children's books have been thoroughly researched elsewhere (see O'Sullivan 2005 and 2006, Lathey 2006 and 2010, and Klingberg, among others, for studies on the reception and influence of translation) and they are not at the center of my discussion, although issues of national representation are, of course, connected to issues arising from translations.

When we address the question of whether there is something in the *national* characteristics of *Alice* and *Pinocchio* that can tell us about how fantasy crosses national boundaries, we must be aware that national traits and cultural markers change in the course of translation, and so, inevitably, does the type of fantasy presented to the readers in the target culture. In O'Sullivan's essay "Does Pinocchio have an Italian passport?," she looks at several translations, and concentrates on what *Pinocchio* has come to represent in popular culture, after a long journey away from its source. "If we reduce what Pinocchio has become in popular culture today to a common denominator, we will find that the only similarities he bears with the original is the fact that he is a wooden puppet with a long nose" (2006: 153). Similarly, *Alice* can be reduced to "the figure of a little girl in a strange fantastic land who is confronted with a medley of peculiar creatures" (158).

A distinction is in order here: there are two very different issues under discussion. The first is about general cultural associations with these books, and the way their main characters have become famous in world culture as icons with very few traits. This is even true of *Pinocchio*—one only needs to think of Disney's Tyrolean Pinocchio, who looks more Austrian than Italian. And in the United States, for example, it appears that not everyone is aware of *Pinocchio*'s nationality. This is not entirely dissimilar to what happens to folktale characters in popular culture, from commercials in which Cinderella is cleaning to advertise a detergent, to cartoons which make fun of Rapunzel's impossibly long hair: the character is taken out of its folk or fairy-tale context, and recycled in another context in which he or she is identified by a few simple qualities. Even if the viewers are not familiar with the Grimms' or Perrault's versions of "Cinderella," they will recognize her as shorthand for a persecuted female hero who spends her days cleaning but gets her reward in the end.

Similarly, Pinocchio and Alice as national icons in culture are necessarily simplified, and in adaptations and appropriations, they may lose everything except a recognizably common essence. Of course Pinocchio and Alice are *not* folktale characters, and unlike folktale characters their literary origins are easily identifiable. However, the fact that several folktale characters have been universally disseminated through Disney, has changed their status for the world—they have become pseudo or virtual universal folktale characters, and we often hear them referred to as Disney's "Cinderella" or Disney's "Rapunzel," and not Perrault's or the Grimms'.

The second issue is the dissemination of these texts through translations. Despite the difficulties presented by linguistic challenges it is possible to find translations that can be both substantially "true" to the original texts and accessible to children. So, Pinocchio and Alice have been able to travel very far, with their Italian and English passports, even if in some of the countries they have visited they may have been refashioned quite radically in order to reach their target audience (see, for example Dedola and Casari for the dissemination of *Pinocchio* in India, China, Iran, Egypt, and Japan). Most recently, the three volumes of *Alice in the World of Wonderlands,* compiled in 2015 in celebration of the 150th anniversary of *Alice's* publication, include analyses of 174 translations of *Alice's Adventures*, as well as back translations and bibliographical essays on world editions of *Alice.*

There are other classics, which, despite excellent translations, have not been able to travel at all—De Amicis's *Cuore,* for example, is hardly known in England. Thus, even if "classics are arbitrarily adapted editions of well-known works" as O'Sullivan puts it (2006: 148) some classics *can* be transplanted into other languages and cultures and media, as in some way their common core and the way they have been translated or refashioned has made them relevant to the target culture.

Pinocchio was first published in English in 1892; *Alice* appeared in translation in Italy in 1872—and since then, the books have become world currency. A quick overview of *Pinocchio's* reception in England and *Alice's* reception in Italy reveals that from the beginning, there was considerable mutual interest, but also difficulties in making each classic enjoyable for a different target audience. *Alice's* first translator, the exiled patriot Pietrocola Rossetti, was a personal friend of Carroll's and a relative of the poet/painter Dante Gabriel Rossetti; he was someone who could be trusted to do justice to the book, but the situation of the publishing market in Italy was very different from that of England. After the *Risorgimento,* in 1861, when Italy was "unified" (with the exception of the Veneto and Rome) illiteracy was widespread and most Italians could only speak dialect, not Italian (see "The Historical Moment: Italian Post-*Risorgimento* and British *Pax Britannica,* Politics and the Nation(s)" in chapter 3). The first edition of *Alice* in Italian (after the 1869 German and French translations, and the Swedish one of 1870) did not do too well. Rossetti replaced references to English history with references to the Italian political situation and used a Tuscan variety of Italian—he opted for Italian poems for the parodies (Cammarata 310). Even Carroll came to realize, after negotiations with Macmillan and the personal interest that he took in the arrangements with the Italian publisher (Loescher from Rome), that it was no longer worthwhile advertising the Italian *Alice* as "the sale does not pay for the advertising" (quoted in Weaver 49).

However, as Vagliani has shown, the influence of translations of English children's books and their illustrations on Italian children's book publishing increased steadily in the following decades, apart from the Fascist period, in which rampant nationalism slowed down the flow of translations. In 1939, at the National Conference for children and juvenile literature [Convegno nazionale per la letteratura infantile e giovanile] which was held in Rome, Nazareno Padellaro, an educationalist who was very active during the Fascist period and beyond, said:

> I think it is damaging, from the educational point of view, to give our children translations and abridgements of foreign books, because they shift their readers' attention away from national concerns and cause them to lose their bearings, superimposing upon them the illusory images and feelings of other races and mindsets, images which can become all too easily lodged in the consciousness of the young, so that they can no longer be eliminated. The book entitled *Alice in Wonderland* has become famous the world over. The nightmarish atmosphere that haunts the story ends up deforming that [...] sound judgement, with which all Italians are gifted. The Anglo-Saxon spirit may enjoy such flights of fancy but I see no reason why our children should be similarly subjected to them [Padellaro 39–40, my translation. On children's literature during the Fascist period see Castoldi].

Alice came to be properly understood and appreciated in Italy only after the Second World War, thanks to "Rodari's revolution" on one hand, and the critical appreciation of *Alice* as a book addressed to a double audience on the other (Vagliani 8).

   Pinocchio was first translated into English in 1892 by Alice Murray. The early translations of both *Pinocchio* and *Alice* in some way tried to find ways to adapt to the cultural context—to localize the texts (Klingsberg 17): for example, Italian translators tried to replace Carroll's parodies with parodies of Italian popular school rhymes, while English translators of *Pinocchio* tried to find English equivalents of Italian cultural markers like food, such as translating "polenta" as "porridge" (see Paruolo 2001). Lathey has analyzed Lawson Lucas's translation of *Pinocchio* (the one I use in this book) and noted that the "anomalies of translation arising from the tension between a dual adult audience [...] and the very 'childness' of the text [...] inherent in Collodi's narrative inevitably exert their influence on the translation process" (Lathey 2010: 172).

   While in the history of *Alice*'s translations it was the poems and the puns that often were expunged, as nation-specific linguistic markers having hardly any relevance to Italian readers, in some of the early English translations of *Pinocchio* it was often the scenes of cruelty towards animals (or children/puppets turned into animals) that were eliminated. The critic Franklin Stych in 1971 wrote that "Italians have a very different attitude towards animals from the English" (44) and argued that Italians' insensitivity to animals "is a national trait—even more notably as Italians are by nature meek, and as a people they don't have any other serious faults" (45).

   In Italy *Pinocchio* was considered little more than an agreeable text until after the First World War, and the first attempt to revaluate Collodi's book did not come from the Italian critical world, but from France (for the critical debate on *Pinocchio* see Traversetti 1993). In contrast, from the very beginning *Alice* was "widely reviewed and earned almost unconditional praise" (Cohen 131). Although the fabulous journeys of *Alice* and *Pinocchio* towards critical approval and acceptance into the adult as well as children's literary canon proceeded at different speeds, they ended up becoming "national institutions" that, paradoxically, have transcended the boundaries of genre, nation and language.

2. Books, Canons and Characters: Pinocchio in Wonderland and Alice in Tuscany

Why *Alice* and *Pinocchio*?

In 1898, one of the earliest American editions of *Pinocchio*, by the Boston publisher Jordan Marsh, was called *Pinocchio's Adventures in Wonderland* (Douglas-Fairhurst 361). It might be argued that any two national icons could fruitfully be given a comparative analysis; and so why does this book not compare *Heidi* and *Pippi Longstocking* or *Babar* and *The Neverending Story*? Putting *Alice* and *Pinocchio* together for a parallel reading is not so arbitrary: although they differ in their literary sources, the intentions of their authors, and their political, social and cultural backgrounds, there are surprising similarities between them. Not quite incidentally, they were both written by eccentric bachelors under *noms de plume*: Collodi's real surname was Lorenzini; Carroll's was Dodgson (see chapter 3). Carlo and Charles, in Stefano's Benni's words, are "authors who know that the world was not made for children" (2007). The books are one-offs in their authors' careers: the calm, linear progress of *Alice* contrasts with the active and reactive story shape of *Pinocchio*, and yet both *Pinocchio* and *Alice's Adventures* have rebellious beginnings and ambiguous, unsettling endings (see chapter 4). Both eponymous characters have irreverent attitudes to education and politics, even though these attitudes have very different origins and consequences.

The books also address two audiences—or have certainly come to do so. They belong to that category of books that *were* for children (Hunt 1997) and now are accessed by children, normally, in an abridged and simplified form, with illustrations dominating. Reading *Le avventure di Pinocchio*, sophisticated (or adult) readers may appreciate its complex language, narrative strategies, its satire on Italian institutions and contemporary Italian professionals, and its deliberate echoes of the classics and various literary traditions. Similarly, the many-layered *Alice* books speak to an adult audience in their topicality, their complex philosophical and mathematical jokes and their pointed contemporary social and political allusions. In terms of literary history, both books broke new ground with their subversive representation of inquisitive children who were very far from being models of virtue, featuring less-than-adequate adults, and offering derisive representations of authority (Lawson Lucas 1999a).

Critics have occasionally noted similarities and connections between these works. Ann Lawson Lucas has written several articles on the relationship between the *Alice* books and *Pinocchio*: in her Oxford University Press edition of *Pinocchio*, for example, she notes similarities in the authors' biographies: both men were the eldest sons in large families, both were raised in the country, both destined for the church (Lawson Lucas 1996). In her essays she explores the way books treat animals (Lawson Lucas 1999b), and the representation of justice and courtroom scenes (Lawson Lucas 1997), conducive to extensive social criticism. Lawson Lucas is not the only one to have investigated the two classics together and found connections and similarities—in 2013 the novelist Stefano Benni gave a famous lecture contrasting these texts, notes of which are now available online (2007), and the Greek critics Panau and Tslimeni discuss the two books together in an essay, "International Classic Characters and National Ideologies: Alice and Pinocchio in Greece." They describe the ways in which the books have transcended their national origins to interact with Greek national culture, and analyze the way they are recycled in a new national context, which is equally distant from both. Other interactions between texts have been explored: for example, *Pinocchio* has been compared to *Huckleberry Finn* (see Rosenthal, and Halliday) and *Wonderland* has been compared to *Neverland* (see Roth).

It is a fact that both *Pinocchio* and *Alice* are staples of any English/ Anglophone version of an international canon. The presence of *Alice* is not surprising, of course, but it is interesting (and should not be taken for granted) that *Pinocchio* is noticeably and consistently part of the most influential Anglophone selections of world literature for children (which have become "classic" in their own right). It is included, for example, in the first Children's Literature Association *Touchstones* volume (edited by

Perry Nodelman in 1985), devoted to children's novels: together with *Heidi*, it is the only non–English language children's book in the collection (out of 28 titles). *Pinocchio* is also present in Fisher's *Classics for Children and Young People* (1986), and in Frey and Griffith's *The Literary Heritage of Childhood* (1987). All these "canonical" lists devote a minority of essays to books not written originally in English, but *Pinocchio* is always there. In more recent times, there have been collections that have adopted a far more global perspective—Beckett and Nicolajeva's *Beyond Babar*, for example, has filled some of the gaps that were left by the first "Touchstone" volume. O'Sullivan, in her work on the translation of world classics in Germany, has often compared *Alice's* and *Pinocchio's* dissemination: "the history of the reception of *Pinocchio* in Germany is structurally parallel to that of *Alice in Wonderland*" (O'Sullivan 2005: 142).

Then there are thematic, structural and cultural connections between the two books. The first has to do with their origins: both books appear to have been written in two phases. *Pinocchio* was not initially conceived as a book but as series of episodes, published in installments in a children's newspaper, *Il giornale per i bambini*, in 1881 (see Loparco). Collodi was composing his story while it was being serialized, which accounts for the fragmentation of the plot and the suspense at the end of several chapters (and there are also some mistakes, as when the narrator tells us that this is the last we see of Lucignolo [Candle-Wick], and then we meet him again a few chapters later, or Pinocchio's hat that gets drenched in chapter 6, a couple of chapters before Geppetto makes it for him). Collodi even killed Pinocchio off, but was persuaded by his publisher to find a way to rescue him and continue the story (the legend goes that Collodi cynically wrote the last chapters of *Pinocchio* because he needed the money to pay his gambling debts, but there is no evidence for this). There was a long hiatus between the two parts of *Pinocchio*, and there are critics who believe that, in fact, *Pinocchio I* (the first part of the book, ending with Pinocchio's death in chapter 15, and with a different title: *Storia di un Burattino* [*Story of a puppet*]) is quite a different book from *Pinocchio II* (*The Adventures*, which includes the first and second part and ends with chapter 36). The former, according to Emilio Garroni, is "the novel of the puppet's postponed death," the second "the novel of a puppet replaced by another person" (99). According to this line of interpretation, *Pinocchio I* would be characterized by ambiguous male creation (or birth) and aggressive relationships with father figures, universal poverty and catharsis ("a fugue towards death"), in which the final catastrophe is already inscribed in the puppet's choices following his very peculiar "education" (Garroni 71).

Pinocchio II, which replaces poverty with more shocking child exploitation, and juxtaposes father figures with the Blue Fairy as the "mother," can be read as a more moralistic text which transforms the protagonist into a stereotype that has learned his lesson and, in the end, has become so different from the original puppet that he is, actually, somebody else (the puppet does not change into a boy, but duplicates: death has been cancelled by displacement). D'Angelo compares the first fifteen chapters of *Pinocchio* to a dream and explains the continuation of *Pinocchio* as a variant of this narrative device: as in (literary) dreams, the character wakes up after apparent death (86)—an interesting connection with the structure of *Alice*.

Similarly, *Alice's Adventures Under Ground* was (it is usually claimed) originally composed as an extempore story told to Alice Liddell and her sisters in 1862, and then hand-lettered and illustrated by Carroll as a present for Christmas 1864. The revised version, the *Alice* we read today, is twice as long and has two of the most famous chapter additions, "Pig and Pepper" and "A Mad tea-party," and was published in 1865. And then of course Carroll added *Through the Looking-Glass* (1871) and later rewrote and simplified the first book as *The Nursery Alice* (1890). Sundmark (1999) has attempted to chart the process of literarization that *Alice's Adventures in Wonderland* has undergone: reading the different versions of *Alice* against folktale morphology, folklore typology and verbal dueling (what he calls "oral epic" 100). He has noticed, for example, that in order to recreate the original storytelling experience of the "golden afternoon," now lost to him, Carroll had to illustrate the book himself in *Under Ground*. The next distancing step was communicating with addressees that he no longer knew, the reading public, when *Under Ground* was reshaped into *Wonderland*. Having realized that his illustrating powers were inadequate, Carroll asked Tenniel to illustrate the second version:

> Carroll's use of pictures answered a need for making up, however poorly, for what was lost in the transition from the original situation, where the simultaneous presence of author and audience made descriptions superfluous. Instead of verbal approximation which would [...] have slowed down the narration, Carroll came to rely on pictures [Sundmark 108].

From the rhetorical/linguistic point of view, Sundmark also remarks that agonistic traits and an aggressive verbal style are more noticeable in the second book (137–138). Most recently Beer has focused, once again, on the storytelling origin of *Alice*:

> It started [...] as spoken dialogue. One can hear the attempt to keep the speaking voice alive in speech tags, indications of mood, and expanded sentences that Carroll

added when he made changes to *Alice's Adventures Under Ground*. The emphasis is on the unknown reader as listener and conversationalist[...]. The baffling withdrawal of her sister into a book without pictures or conversation plunges Alice down into her mind zone, which is distinguished by its oral culture [Beer 2016: 106, 11].

Whereas the relationship to the political and social situation is clear in Collodi, Carroll obscures his ideas with multiple filters. *Alice's Adventures Under Ground* is littered with purely personal jokes and references that only the real Alice Liddell would have recognized—the Duck, the Dodo, the Lory and the Eaglet whom Alice meets in the pool of tears, are respectively Canon Duckworth, Carroll the stutterer himself ("Do-do-dodgson"), and Alice's sisters Lorinda and Edith. In *Alice's Adventures in Wonderland* he added more—for example, the "Drawling Master was an old conger-eel that used to come once a week: he taught us Drawling, Stretching, and Fainting in Coils." (Carroll 2009: 86). This sounds suspiciously like a sly portrait of John Ruskin, Alice's tutor for a time (see Hunt 2009: 270).

But even Collodi may have alluded to real-life situations, places and people that only readers familiar with Florence and life in the immediately surrounding villages would have recognized. For example, a carpenter that Collodi used to be friends (and drink) with was an Antonio Segoni, whose nickname was Mastro Ciliegia (alluding to the red nose of a heavy drinker), like the carpenter in the first chapter of *Pinocchio* (see Garbarino 18, and Rilli). The black rabbits that carry the coffin to take Pinocchio away in chapter 27 may have been inspired by the "volontari della Misericordia," a group of volunteers in Florence, dressed in black and wearing a hood (for anonymity) whose tip would fall on one side so that it looked like a rabbit's ear—they would carry the moribund or the very sick to hospital on a stretcher (Garbarino 38). (But of course when you enter the world of the author's personal associations, there is no end to possible references and allusions).

In terms of structure, as we shall see in chapters 4 and 5, *Alice* and *Pinocchio* are national fantasies with their roots in the folktale/fairy-tale tradition to which they also contribute with a unique reconfiguration of some of the genre conventions. For example, they both owe a lot to the adventure/picaresque tradition, they are very theatrical and structured over a series of "scenes," and they both have a clear connection to the cautionary tradition (even though their main aim is often to subvert it). They are fantasies which have a "national" guise, but which ultimately give a very personal treatment of the "universal" elements of fantasy.

These books have also founded new literary traditions. In the more modest history of Italian children's literature, *Pinocchio* stands out as a landmark and a beacon. It has been identified by Lindsay Myers as the catalyst for the "Monello Fantasy," a sub-genre of Italian fantasy for children that was highly popular during the last decade of the nineteenth century and which was characterized by its criticism of institutional learning and the school system, its subversive and parodic use of anthropomorphized animal characters (often satire of the Italian professions) and its naughty protagonists (Myers 2012: 49–64). The Monello fantasy is a rebellious genre which has more in common with the American "good bad boy" (pseudo-realistic) fantasy genre than any British genre—and has much the same roots and philosophy. "The Good Bad Boy," Leslie Fiedler observed, "is, of course, America's vision of itself, crude and unruly in his beginnings, but endowed by his creator with an instinctive sense of what is right" (Fiedler in Avery 1994: 197). Produced at least in part in reaction to the pious "good boy" stories that had dominated both the British and American markets through the first half of the nineteenth century, this genre celebrated individuality; in direct contrast to the British, who admired obedience and teamwork above all, Americans admired (overtly or covertly) the rogue with a rebellious—republican—spirit. In books such Thomas Bailey Aldrich's *The Story of a Bad Boy* (1870) or Mark Twain's *The Adventures of Tom Sawyer* (1876), boys do wild and naughty things, but are ultimately the hope of the nation (Hunt 2001: 339). The good bad boys of British children's literature are more difficult to find. Stalky, in Rudyard Kipling's *Stalky and Co* (1899) and Richard Jefferies's eponymous *Bevis* (1882) are clearly seen as boys whose ingenuity and rebelliousness are, or will be, channeled to the benefit of Empire. Perhaps the only equivalent in the twentieth century has been Richmal Crompton's William (from *Just-William* [1922]), and even he operates in a solidly safe middle-class environment.

The Monello model enjoyed a great success and inspired a spate of imitations: "The Italian public had developed a voracious appetite for sequels and prequels, and *Pinocchiate* of all kinds had begun to flood the market" (Myers 2012: 55). These *Pinocchiate* have episodic structures, often host characters who are very similar to those found in *Pinocchio*, have scenes that may rework its key scenes, and allude overtly or covertly to Collodi's text (such as Ettore Ghiselli's *Il fratello di Pinocchio* [1898] or Yambo's *Le avventure di Ciuffettino* [1902]). They are permeated by sociopolitical satire and expose the weaknesses of the contemporary Italian state (see Myers 2012: 55–58 and 63–64). Myers also identifies a second wave of *Pinocchiate*: the "Pinocchioesque Fantasy": between 1950 and 1980. These were not particularly innovative, and remarkably similar to the early twentieth-century imitations—but they were different in their postmodernist self-conscious experimental deconstruction of Collodi's text.

Alice, similarly, established a fresh mode of thinking in children's fiction and had many direct imitations. Conventionally, *Alice* marks, as F. J. Harvey Darton put it, "the first unapologetic [...] appearance in print, for readers who sorely needed it, of liberty of thought in children's books" (Darton 200). There is enough truth in that opinion for it to have shaped the way in which generations have seen the map of British children's books. The nineteenth century, was, it is said, dominated by tractarians and evangelicals, empire-builders, social realists, and ersatz fantasists, all packing a moral—and then along comes Carroll, on the child's side against the adults. However, as will be explained in the following chapters, Carroll, for all his individuality, was rooted in his time, and the *Alice* books can equally be seen as part of a continuum of fantasy and the literary fairy tale. As Jan Susina has pointed out, "For far too long, *Wonderland* has been seen as the originator of a genre, while, in fact, it represents an important synthesis of the tradition of literary fairy tales for children" (Susina 73). The imitations of Carroll tended to be cognate, missing Carroll's essential individuality, sharing elements such as an assertive and polite female protagonist, a fantasy dream and episodic structure, nonhuman characters, nonsense verse, and a return to the real world (see Sigler 1997: xvii). But, apart from these structural similarities, while this may add to the paradox of universal appeal, there are other elements that have indirectly infused children's literature from Carroll in the twentieth and twenty-first centuries: the godlessness, the rebelliousness towards education, the irreverence towards adults, and the bond between narrator and audience.

Alice and Pinocchio in *Alice* and *Pinocchio*

As Vermeule has written, "interacting with fictional people turns out to be a central human cognitive preoccupation, one that exposes many aspects of how our mind works" (12). Some of the insights of cognitive criticism can be useful when we compare *Alice* and *Pinocchio* not just as books, but also as characters. They have become transnational icons also because they give an illusion of the human. Alice and Pinocchio, like other characters from world literature, are typically transtextual—spin-offs and afterlives abound, and they appear to have almost a life of their own so that is not difficult to imagine them in other contexts and media (see chapter 6). But how is this achieved? Why do we empathize with these often-unpleasant characters? Gottschall has suggested that storytelling is the way we make sense of the world, a way to revise our position in the story of our life and satisfy "the need to see ourselves as the striving heroes of our own epics" (171). "We spend our lives crafting stories that make us the noble—if flawed—protagonists of first-person dramas. [...] A life story is not, however, an objective account" (Gottschall 161). And just like human beings, (and unlike characters in folktales who are notoriously "flat") Pinocchio and Alice use their fictional brains to produce an uncommon degree of storytelling in order to make sense of reality. But unlike characters in a postmodern fairy tale, they do not know that they are fictional, and so dramatic illusion is not broken. Pinocchio with his insecurity and broken promises, and Alice with her attempt to grasp her meaningless reality, look very familiar to us.

Pinocchio's characteristic mental stance (a form of interior monologue) is that of regret and remorse—this is the way the puppet relates the past to the present, and the future is a future of broken promises. We can see this in Pinocchio's periodical rambling summaries in which he tries to make sense of his experiences, only to repeat the same mistakes over and over again (Vagnoni 53–54). Even if these summaries are also an effective means of reminding the reader of previous events—particularly useful in serial publication—this form of introspection is totally alien to the typical folktale hero's lack of depth (see chapter 4), as in Lüthi's words: "The whole realm of sentiment is absent from folktale characters, and as a result they lack all psychological depth[...]. Nowhere is this internal emotional state expressed, for the folktale shows us flat figures rather than human beings with active inner lives" (Lüthi 13, 14).

There are moments, in *Pinocchio*, in which we see the puppet relive, recapitulate, assess and present his misfortunes and mistakes, providing the reader with insight into the way his "mind" and his memory operate. Readers can compare what they have just read with the experiences that the puppet has registered, re-ordered and offered to the narratee (see Lavagetto 2003). The plot is refashioned as storytelling and even, in a way, as a sort of performance as in most of these summaries Pinocchio is looking for sympathy and justification.

Similarly, Alice talks to herself a lot, trying to make sense of her new experiences and to connect them with what she knows (or thinks she knows). It could be argued that Alice's continual internal monologues, relating almost everything that happens to things that have happened or which might happen are also a form of self-storytelling, which, as Vermeule argues, makes characters who use it more accessible, attractive, and easier to connect with. This is more than simply focalization: it allows us to mind-read through the character's learning experiences expressed in the verbal (and emotional) "human" act of storytelling.

Cognitive studies can also be used to explain why we tend to forget when we read Collodi's work that Pinocchio is, after all, a puppet. As Perella has noted, "Although 'real boys' and 'puppets' are sometimes moralistically posed as opposites in the story, the reader often forgets that Pinocchio is a wooden marionette" (30). Vermeule notes that the human brain has an inclination to animate things: "animation is a mental habit [...] we endow bodies with mental life in the same way as we endow the sights or sounds of words with meaning. [...] Yet the concept of person is incomplete without immersing it in a wider social world" (22–23). Pinocchio may well appear like a boy because we mentally animate him as a human being, and because he *interacts* with other characters/human beings. This is why he appears less real and more of a puppet when he is relating with other puppets in the *Teatro dei burattini*. He also appears to shrink when he is with them and the puppet-master Mangiafoco [literally "Fire-eater"; translated as "Swallow-fire" in Collodi/Lucas]. When he speaks with the puppets, his own language sounds less realistic and more melodramatic—like his fellow puppets who are characters in the improvised scenarios of the *Commedia dell'arte*, he speaks the language of melodrama.

Alice and *Pinocchio* as "Gendered Books"

Alice and *Pinocchio* are not just (typical, imperfect, or symbolic) representatives of their nations; they also seem to be gendered female and male. Both central characters appear to represent a kind of well-defined gendered childhood—Alice appears to have internalized a code of female good manners and common sense (in contrast to the imprudent behaviors of girls in the cautionary tales she so often mentions), which may reflect an English national ideal of girlhood. Pinocchio embodies a form of "childhood on the road" (Cambi 12), a young picaro or a street urchin who moves in a context of extreme poverty which forces boys to grow fast and work hard (sometimes harder than adults) to support their families. Of course, Pinocchio would not fit in with the male-gendering of G.A. Henty's novels, for example, or the public school story—which epitomize English ideals of the masculine (see chapter 7). Carl Ipsen, in *Italy in the Age of Pinocchio*, focuses on the backwardness of Italy in caring about children—

he claims that it was only around 1870 "that Italy awoke to the suffering of children, the moment when it became a general conviction on the part of political and public opinion alike, that Italian society needed to care for its unfortunate, marginalized and poor children" (4)—Pinocchio epitomized the lower-class marginalized child who has to work and is exploited and degraded by adults: the street child. Collodi sketched this character in an article entitled "Il ragazzo di strada" (Collodi 1995a): poverty and transgression are this boy's main features, and he has to grow up quickly— we are miles away from Enrico, the middle-class protagonist of De Amicis's *Cuore* (see chapter 7).

As Cambi notes (34–39), there are two opposed concepts of male childhood at the heart of Italian children's literature: the *ragazzo perbene*, the bourgeois boy who absorbs good manners and adult rules, and *il ragazzo di strada*, the clever resourceful street boy, who rebels against rules and is impervious to education. Pinocchio is the classic example of this archetype, which raised concern because, like the puppet, "the street kid can be prey to assassins and unscrupulous *padroni* [masters] and at the same time a potential beggar, thief, and general subverter of social order" (Ipsen 3). That image tended to be male: a dangerous boy who is in danger. Truglio has suggested that Italian turn-of-the-century children's books contributed to the process of creating a concept of unified nation by establishing a correspondence between the personal development of a male individual and the modernizing development of the nation. She argues that

> the nineteenth-century concept of recapitulation, which held that ontology (the individual's development) repeats phylogeny (the evolution of the species), undergirds the ideological agenda of this body of texts[...]. Many of these children's books establish an implicit correspondence between the personal development of the child and the modernizing development of the nation. These narratives suggest that just as a human individual must grow from a naïve, untamed, and bestial imp into a mature, productive, and rational adult, so too the nation must progress from rural, feudal, and local relations to urban, capitalist, and national structures [Truglio 4].

Alice and Pinocchio engage in complicated and ambivalent ways with their peers—Alice does not meet other girls in the book—and her references to Ada and Mabel (originally Alice Liddell's cousins Gertrude and Florence in *Alice's Adventures Under Ground*) are perfunctory and dismissive. In *Through the Looking-Glass* (rather wistfully) she watches boys from a distance ("I was watching the boys getting in sticks for the bonfire—and it wants plenty of sticks! Only it got so cold, and it snowed so, they had to leave off. Never mind, Kitty, we'll go and see the bonfire tomorrow" [Carroll 2009: 125]). As Beer has noted, "Boys do not enter Alice's worlds; her brother's Latin book has taught her the vocative, 'O Mouse,' but there is no place for him in Wonderland or Looking-Glass Land" (2016: 19). In Alice's world, boys do things and girls sit in "luxurious captivity" and watch—except in her dreams. The Victorian period, as Reynolds and Humble have noted, "began with the fetishist cult of the domestic angel and ended with the 'angels' in bloomers, in offices, in higher education, and driving motorcars" (4–5), and it may well be, as Auerbach and Knoepflmacher have suggested, that "the success of the *Alice* books had licensed female dreaming and liberated aggressive subtexts for women writers" (6). In the same vein, Judith Little argues that the *Alice* books "provide a really hair-raising elevation of consciousness, and ultimately give us, through her actions and criticisms, a very positive 'image' of woman" (195). At the same time, Alice's empowerment—her quizzical attitude to the (mad) adults that she encounters, which builds up to the end of her dream with the powerful gesture of overturning the cards with her feminine skirt (a gesture so well captured by Tenniel's illustration) is contained and resisted by the dream device itself and by "Carroll's nostalgia, his resistance to female growth and female sexuality" (Auerbach and Knoepflmacher 6). Even in fiction, and even when he engaged sympathetically with the plight of the female child, Carroll was sufficiently in touch with the realities of gendering as a potent element of social power to ultimately return Alice to her kitten-surrounded prison. Within Alice's dream, there is plenty of threat and violence (as we shall see in chapter 4 and 5) but in this female-gendered world Alice is always *safe*—and she is always protected by males, however unreliable or eccentric—the Cheshire-Cat and the White Knight. Indeed, stupidity and eccentricity are generally male (and academic) attributes, while the most frightening characters—the Queen of Hearts, the Duchess, and the Red Queen are (perhaps not by accident) females. However, like Alice, even they are ultimately powerless.

If Alice doesn't engage with boys of her own age, Pinocchio does not meet any girls (apart from one of the early incarnations of the fairy as the dead *bella bambina*). And far from having good manners and common sense, he gets into fights with other boys and almost kills one with a book: his progress is violent and erratic. The Land of Toys can be interpreted as a male utopia, which soon enough turns into a dystopia (see chapter 5). Pinocchio is watched over by the Blue Fairy—but, as is appropriate to a male-gendered book, is also harried and persecuted by her. Ultimately,

Pinocchio the street boy becomes a "ragazzo perbene," a nice little boy, or a proper boy. In *Pinocchio* you cannot have a fairy mother and the creating father at the same time: in the end the all-male family asserts itself.

The gendering of these books has often been masked by a preoccupation with the violence and threat that pervades them. Without the death jokes that surround her, Alice could even be called (as the subtitle of a 1962 Italian edition suggested) a Lolita figure *avant la lettre*: *La meravigliosa Alice, la creazione poetica di una "Lolita" vittoriana* [The Wonderful Alice, the poetic creation of a Victorian "Lolita"] (see Vagliani 109), in a way the essence of the captivating female (and of course one can hardly forget that it was Nabokov who first translated *Alice* into Russian). Similarly, if you take away the darkness that surrounds Pinocchio, you have a natural, naughty boy. Goldthwaite (1996) has suggested that the very longevity of *Pinocchio* relies on the identification of generations of boy readers with this quintessential boy:

> The secret of its wide appeal can be read in the eyes of almost any child listening to it: Pinocchio [...] is the universal boy running loose through the universal world[...]. The kid, in short, has screwed up everything, as most children do, and still come out of it a hero [181].

And Alice, it might be argued, for all her resemblance to a Victorian lady, has an essence that resonates with the female across the centuries.

And so gender is but one of the many paradoxes that contribute to the richness of parallel readings of these two books, at once so different and at once so similar: it is tempting to interpret these characters also in essentialist terms—as representatives of "everyboy" and "everygirl" who still speak to a wide readership today. Their recognizable "mythic core" (O'Sullivan 2006: 152) may well depend, in part, on their gender configuration, for all their indisputable connections to their national background and to that of their authors, as shall be discussed in the next chapter.

3. Carlo and Charles: Italy in the Age of *Pinocchio*, England in the Age of *Alice*

C* was born in the first half of the nineteenth century, into a large family. He was intended for the Church but the Church never became his profession. He made a living out of various literary and educational pursuits, although it was writing his country's most famous children's book (about the adventures of a child in a fantasy world) that made him famous for posterity and worldwide. He was involved in the political and social debates of his time, and his penchant for parody and attitudes to education are still widely discussed today. We know, however, that in his personality he combined outward respectability and gravity (he had small fixations such as wearing a hat at all times, even in the house) with a degree of unconventionality in his hobbies and a love of the theater. He was perceived by his contemporaries as an eccentric. Shortly after his death, his brother decided to destroy part of his correspondence, so his biography has been deprived of essential information (his nephew was his first biographer). Critics have detected some impropriety in the way he related to the female world (the missing biographical information may relate to this area of his life). He retired early, never married and died in his mid-sixties. [Replace C* with either Carlo or Charles]

Carlo and Charles: Two Bachelors, Both Alike in Dignity

The year 1856 was notable for pseudonyms. In Florence a civil servant and freelance journalist first wrote in the Florentine humorous magazine *La lente* under the name of "Carlo Collodi"; in Oxford, a mathematics lecturer, Charles Lutwidge Dodgson, writing verses for the *Comic Times*, first used the name "Lewis Carroll." Carlo and Charles: Carlo Lorenzini was born in 1826 in the great and historically rich city of Florence, then part of the Grand Duchy of Tuscany and in the throes of the *Risorgimento*; he was the eldest son of upwardly-mobile servants. Charles Dodgson was born in the small and undistinguished English village of Daresbury (in fact, Daresbury is now famous, insofar as it *is* famous, for Dodgson), to the middle classes and in the century of Queen Victoria. At first sight, they were very different men, in radically different social and political contexts, although they had a surprising number of things in common (see the all-purpose short bio above). Both had rural upbringings in large families (in both cases a parent died prematurely), both were intended for the church, and both were well-educated eccentrics with a taste for playing with language and participating in politics, local and national (Lawson Lucas 1996: ix). Martha Bacon observes that it is impossible to picture Carroll and Collodi as "fathers, or even babysitters":

> Lewis Carroll was an intense neurotic, obsessed with night fears, a nervous stutterer who had difficulty sustaining the most ordinary adult relationship. Carlo Collodi was a [...] knockabout journalist, hack playwright, odd-jobber on the fringes of literature, possibly the father of an illegitimate child but too scatterbrained apparently even to have been sure about this. At all events he eschewed marriage and legal heirs, finding fulfillment late in life in his dream child [Bacon 71].

In this rather ungenerous (and uninformed) description of the authors' lives and characters, what is most curious is the use of the expression *dream child* for Pinocchio, and not for Alice, for whom its use has become a critical commonplace.

Collodi wrote his masterpiece when he was 56, and at the time it was no more than another publication in a long and varied writing career (novels, reviews, plays, newspaper articles). His education had been supported by the aristocratic Ginori family for whom his mother worked, and he began his career in a publishing bookshop when he was 18. At 19 he was given permission to handle (and read) the forbidden books of the *Index Librorum Prohibitorum*—a useful privilege not accorded to every author. He came to journalism as an outsider, as most journalists and intellectuals were upper-middle class: he wrote novels that had an ironic or parodic twist, and on two occasions (in 1848 and 1859) he left a financially stable job to enroll and fight in the Wars of Independence which were attempting to free Italy from Austrian domination. From 1860 he also worked as a censor for theatrical scripts and in 1864 he became a "Segretario di II classe" in the Prefecture (the Institution that represented the central government) in Florence—a clerical but prestigious position that marked his official entrance into the bourgeois world. He died on October 24, 1890.

Charles Ludwidge Dodgson, the oldest son of an Anglican clergyman in a large family, went to Rugby School and then to Christ Church in Oxford, where he received a studentship and was appointed a lecturer in mathematics. This appointment required Carroll to remain unmarried and to take holy orders. He agreed to these requirements and was ordained *deacon* in 1861 but never became a priest like his father. He developed an interest in photography in 1856—his favorite subjects were children and famous people. He was interested in political and social issues (he wrote essays against vivisection and the electoral system, among other things), and he was an accomplished and published mathematician and logician. He wrote the first *Alice* book when he was in his thirties and lived to enjoy its success and the success of its sequel. The *Alice* books were an oddity in Carroll's *oeuvre*. His publications before 1865 included *Notes on the First Two Books of Euclid* (1860) and *A Syllabus of Plane Algebraical Geometry* (1860), and at one point Dodgson was at pains to contradict "a silly story which has been going the round of the papers, about my having presented certain books to Her Majesty the Queen" (Clark 263). The silly story (still widely repeated) was that "after reading *Alice* the Queen had asked for his next work, which turned out to be *Condensation of Determinants*" (Wilson 101). For some time he contemplated a volume of Shakespearean plays adapted for girls, that would out–Bowdler Thomas Bowdler's *The Family Shakespeare* (1807): "The method I propose to myself is to erase ruthlessly every word in the play that is in any degree profane, or coarse, or in any sense unsuited for a girl of from 10–15; and then to make the best that I can of what is left" (quoted in Ziegler 107). He continued to write compulsively: the second volume of his *Symbolic Logic* was unfinished at his death, on January 14, 1898.

In many ways, the two bachelors were the models for their own most famous characters. Lorenzini led an adventurous life: he fought the Austrians twice, as the Italian states emerged from foreign dominance, and he was made *Cavaliere del Regno d'Italia* in 1868. Dodgson seems at first sight to have led a more cloistered life, dividing his time between his Oxford college and, as head of his family, taking responsibility for his spinster sisters. But his very peculiar version of the Grand Tour took him as far as Russia in 1867, an uncommon destination at the time. In the course of this trip he visited France and Germany, but he avoided Italy and the Mediterranean countries. So Carroll never came to Florence and we do not know whether Collodi ever crossed the English Channel—we can only fantasize about a possible meeting at the Paris Universal Exhibition: we know for sure that Carroll was there on Monday 9 September 1867 (Cohen

272) and we know that Collodi applied for a passport in March of the same year. He was definitely interested in the Exhibition—as early as January he had written, in his characteristic polemical style, an article in the Florence newspaper *La Nazione* complaining that "the beautiful painting" by the Florentine painter Raffaello Bonaiuti "Cristo che trionfa dell'ultima tentazione" [Christ who triumphs over the last temptation] had not yet been chosen by the Academic Committee to be sent to the Paris Exhibition (Marcheschi 1995: c). Did Collodi ever go to Paris to see the painting? It would be nice to find some evidence that he did, and that he and Carroll met while they were looking appreciatively at the painting together, exchanging comments in French, as both had a good command of the language. But this would be another fiction, and the history of their respective biographical legacies already appears to abound in fictionality.

This is no surprise as biographies are life narratives that are the product of choice and narrativization practices: inevitably, every biography is a story that excludes other stories. In the case of both Carroll and Collodi, the first act of choice was in the violent form of burning compromising letters and defacing diaries, choices that were going to redirect future biographies into more acceptable moral destinations. Shortly after Collodi's funeral, on 28 October 1890, his brother Paolo Lorenzini burnt most of the letters that he found in his brother's house. Some were to and from living and married ladies his brother had had affairs with, and even a daughter born from one of these affairs, a very strong possibility according to Marcheschi (2016: 63), who indicates 1873 as the year in which the daughter probably died, as a teenager. Collodi's brother could not stand reading more upsetting material and the fire ended up including letters from artists, journalists, and intellectuals, innocent letters that would have thrown precious light on Collodi's literary activity. The question that Marcheschi asks, "was the private life of Lorenzini so scandalous that his brother could not even bring himself to read carefully the letters that his beloved elder brother had left?" (1995: cxxiii, my translation) is not very different from the question one may ask after learning that Carroll's brother Wilfred did exactly the same thing. Shortly after his brother's death, he destroyed precious information, for example, about the reason for the famous unexplained rift between the Liddells and Carroll. As Leach has observed, "The first real act in the creation of the myth of Lewis Carroll, was an act of destruction" (31). If she had looked at Collodi's life, she would probably have reached the same conclusion. While, as Donald Thomas notes, "there was no suggestion that this was a destruction of documents unfit for other eyes" (356), what happened to Carroll's diaries is highly intriguing. Leach points out that "some time after his death members of his family deliberately cut out and destroyed certain pages, while four of the thirteen volumes [...] went missing and have never been recovered" (23) and the history of the publication of the diaries has been one of painful family obfuscation (see Leach 93–98; 118–119; 124–125; 191–195). Whatever mysteries the missing writings of these two authors were hiding (and will hide for ever), that of having improper relations of some kind with females seems to be the most likely answer.

In both cases the family appropriation (or control) of the biographical narrative was complete when Carroll's nephew, Stuart Dodgson Collingwood, and Collodi's nephew, Paolo Lorenzini jr, wrote the first biographies of their uncles, in 1899, and 1954 respectively. In their own ways they fashioned narratives of their uncles' lives that were to be very influential. Lawson Lucas's description of Collodi as "a complex character, perpetually suspended between irreverence and formality" (1996: xvi) could apply to Carroll, although both writers' personalities were far more complex than it may appear at first glance. Collingwood downplayed the complexities, ambivalences and contradictions of Carroll into that of an almost a-sexual being, living "the life of calm contentment"(Collingwood 1899b: 271). He erased almost all references to Dodgson's numerous friendships with women and concentrated on the innocence and respectability of his relationships with his child-friends (relationships which, of course, a later generation would find more problematic).

Collodi's nephew created the myth of the rebellious "figlio del popolo," from the description of the way the young Carlo threw his cassock to the highest branches of a tree on the day he left the seminary so that he could play freely with other boys (Lorenzini 13) to his final "conversion." After a lifetime of gambling, drinking and general vice, it was said, he went back to live with his brother's family and their mother, "to be re-educated, in order to go back to that good child that he once was and that she had raised[...]. Surely in the Fairy he always saw his mother" (Lorenzini 98, my translation). The parallel between Carlo Lorenzini and his puppet is implicit but difficult to miss—dissipation and rule-breaking (see Bertacchini 1993: 43) appear to belong to both fictional character and its creator. However, there is no evidence that Collodi wrote *Pinocchio* because he needed money to pay his debts, as legend has it. If that were true he would be an ideal inhabitant of the town of *Acchiappacitrulli*, which Pinocchio visits in chapters 18–20, a dystopian place where citizens are poor because they are deceived by swindlers.

Similarly, critics have long read *Alice's Adventures* as an allegory for Carroll's own search for identity:

> If we accept the notion that the tale is an autobiographical allegory, that Alice is Charles in disguise [...] Wonderland emerges as an allegory of Charles's, not Alice's journey beset by many pitfalls, a journey in search of one's identity [...] a search for the right road, the one that will lead him to understand his impulses, to identify his sexuality and give it appropriate expression [Cohen 225–226].

As a mirror of the religious turbulence of Carroll's period in England, and as a metaphor for English cultural upheavals, the *Alice* books could scarcely be bettered. All of this is reflected in the relationship between form and fantasy in the books, and is perhaps best shown in Carroll's "guest appearances" as (among others) the Dodo and the White Knight. These characters, and the way they relate fantasy and reality neatly represent what can be argued as being an essentially British approach to life: self-effacing, eccentric, egocentric and possibly even a little autistic (see Butts and Hunt 25–30).

Paolo Lorenzini, who used the pseudonym *Collodi Nipote* [Collodi, the nephew], became a children's author himself: his *Pinocchio* sequel, *Il cuore di Pinocchio* (1917), was translated into English in 1919 as *The Heart of Pinocchio*, and his children's fantasy *Sussi e Biribissi* (1902), two boys' fantastic journey underground starting from the Florentine sewers and in the company of a speaking (although not smiling) cat, is still in print. But Lorenzini's slim and relatively late biographical sketch of Collodi did not mark the beginning of a spate of biographies; even though editions like Marcheschi's are rich in bio-bibliographical notes, and chapters on Collodi's life can be found in several monographs, nothing is comparable to the plethora of full-length biographies that have been published about Carroll, "making him one of the most biographied Victorian authors" (Siegler 2001: 229). As I have discussed earlier, Carroll has also been the object of a controversial book-length discussion of previous biographies as conflicting narratives in *In the Shadow of the Dreamchild: The Myth and Reality of Lewis Carroll* (1999) by Karoline Leach. In this almost meta-biographical work she investigates the way sources were removed, hidden, censored and intentionally neglected in later years by other members of the Dodgson family and by later biographers.

The remarkable difference in the outpouring of biographical material between Carroll and Collodi may also be attributed to the fact that *Pinocchio* was much slower than *Alice* in gaining the popularity that it has today. Traversetti (1993) reports that from its publication (1883) to the First World War *Pinocchio* was considered "nothing more than a pleasant, but negligible, book" (my translation, 129); it was far surpassed in sales by De Amicis's *Cuore* (1886) which was possibly felt to be more emphatically suited to the social and moral redefinition of the nation after the *Risorgimento* (see chapter 7). It wasn't until the 1920s that the puppet started to enter critical awareness in Italy: it was as late as the 1930s that Benedetto Croce included it in the Italian literary canon as the best children's book; and it was actually in the 1960s that criticism in Italy started to pay assiduous attention to Collodi. The success of *Alice* in Carroll's lifetime made him a much more public figure than Collodi and the *Alice* books' fame kept growing. As Douglas-Fairhurst notes, in 1898 a poll conducted in the *Pall Mall Gazette* on "What Children Liked to Read," revealed that *Alice's Adventures in Wonderland* was at the top of the list (348). Occasionally, events such as the auction sale of the manuscript of *Alice's Adventures Under Ground* in 1928, caused curiosity about the real-life Alice to resurface, in a complex interaction between interest in the ever-young fictional character, the aging real-life Alice, the difference between the two, and the relationships that both Alices had established with Carroll as their "creator."

But even in the absence of something as impressive as Morton Cohen's 570-page biography of Carroll (1995), it is possible to glimpse something of Collodi's personality through reports and surviving letters and bio-critical profiles. So, other uncanny similarities between these authors emerge, as if Carlo and Charles were displaying, at a thousand miles' distance, similar tastes and eccentricities. All this complicates any simple equation between the stereotypical characteristics of their nations/authors at a particular historical moment—the unstable, impetuous, outgoing Collodi vs. the precise, calculating, self-restrained Carroll—extrovert and introvert. Collodi has also been described as deeply pessimistic, a disappointed radical, a complex personality who "would never have resolved the individual terms of his neurosis, if it had not been for the encounter with myth and the liberating space of the fairy tale, where contradictions can co-exist" (Faeti 25, my translation). Spadolini calls his life "melancholic"—the life of a man who celebrated fatherhood but never married, whose fireplace was as cold as Geppetto's, and who had a fixation on an idealized mother who inspired him to take as a pseudonym Collodi, the village of her birth (1972a: 214). A Florentine Jaques, perhaps? In contrast, the self-contained Carroll, whose methodical routines seems to suggest a mild form of obsessive-compulsive disorder (Douglas-Fairhurst 279) which co-existed with a tendency to procrastinate (just like Collodi), was an avid theater-goer, was invited to more dinner parties than he could attend, knew lots of very important people, including members of the royal family (Wakeling 303) and used to spend lots of jolly weekends in London:

> If Dickens was correct in believing that the dandy of the Regency had become the High Churchman of mid-century, Charles Dodgson in the decade of *Alice in Wonderland* might have seemed a convenient example of the change. (Thomas 178)

Love for the theater was a passion that both authors shared—Collodi mainly as a playwright and a theater critic, Carroll as a theatergoer, and an admirer and friend of actresses (such as Ellen Terry). Not to mention the fact that they both seem to have been attracted to puppets, Carroll still playing with his marionette theater as late as 1855, when he was 23: "the idea that people could take the place of puppets, just as puppets could imitate the actions of people, continued to intrigue him" (Cohen 73). Both enjoyed opera and music in general and could play the piano—Collodi was very knowledgeable about melodrama, and wrote opera reviews regularly (Traversetti 1993).

Both authors had complicated relationships with their fathers. Archdeacon Dodgson is described as having been "a man of absolute, unqualified moral certitude [...] so alien was the concept of the open mind that for him doubt was akin to failure" (Leach 167), and "a strong-willed father" with whom Carroll probably clashed (Jenny Woolf 31). Collodi's father, a cook for the marquis Carlo Leopoldo Ginori Lisci, seems to have been hardly able to support his large family—his mother is recorded as having spent long periods with her parents in the village of Collodi, taking her (often sickly) children away from their city home in the hope that they would recover. If both Carlo and Charles were born into large families, Carroll's was middle class, and better nourished, ensuring that every one of the eleven children survived, while Collodi's early life was interspersed with the death of siblings, especially female ones, real-life versions of the *bella bambina* who in chapter 15 tells Pinocchio that she is dead and is waiting for the hearse to take her away. (The list of his sisters' deaths is a sad reminder of child mortality in Italy at that time: in 1829 Marianna died aged 20 months, in 1838 Marianna Seconda died aged 6, in 1839 Giovannina Letizia died aged 2, and in 1850 Giuseppina died aged 16. To the list we could perhaps add Collodi's teenage daughter).

Interestingly, both men at some point in their lives became friendly with an older relative who became a sort of mentor for them, providing an alternative father figure and a place to stay for a time. For Carroll, the older relative was his favorite uncle, Skeffington Lutwidge, a London-based barrister who introduced Carroll to photography, one of his greatest passions. Collodi, after his brother Paolo's marriage decided to move in with his sister Adelaide's brother-in-law, Zipoli, a priest and teacher of Latin and Greek at the local *Liceo*. Collodi Nipote writes that Collodi grew fond of the older man who was a scholar as well as an eccentric: "they got on well not just because of their characters but also because of their ideas" (my translation, 29). While living with Father Zipoli, Collodi perfected his French and learnt to play the piano well. These two men lived together for a few years, and "it was not uncommon to see them together at the bar or at the theater" (Lorenzini 31, my translation), until Collodi decided to go back to live with his married brother, who had climbed the social scale and had become a rich man, and with his mother (not an unusual arrangement at the time). Are Collodi and Carroll, in their own peculiar ways, men who did not want to grow up, men who could not see themselves in a father's role—Collodi with his alleged unrecognized daughter, and Carroll, ever fixed in his ambiguous relationships with his child-friends?

The Historical Moment: Italian Post-*Risorgimento* and British *Pax Britannica*, Politics and the Nation(s)

Pinocchio is impregnated with Italian history: it is about hunger and education at a time when the political unification of Italy had been (nearly) completed and it was still not clear what it meant for the citizens of a new nation made of different languages, dialects and customs to have to share common values. As Massimo d'Azeglio famously declared "Fatta l'Italia, ora bisogna fare gli italiani" [Italy is made, but now it is necessary to make Italians]. (Actually, the version recorded in his memoirs, *I Miei Ricordi* [1867] is slightly different if more pessimistic: "purtroppo s'è fatta l'Italia ma non si fanno gli Italiani" [unfortunately we have made Italy, but we haven't made Italians"] [7]).

The new nation was divided and poor: poverty [la miseria] is what characterizes Pinocchio's family life: when the puppet-master Mangiafoco inquires what his father's trade is, Pinocchio replies: "poor man" [fa il povero] (Collodi/Lucas 33). But in chapter 24, on the island of the Busy Bees, when Pinocchio considers begging for a mouthful of bread, the narrator introduces a moralistic tirade about the people who have the right to call themselves poor:

> The real poor of this world, who do merit help and compassion, are limited to those who, by reason of age or illness, are prevented from earning their bread by the labour of their own hands. Everyone else has a duty to work, and if they don't work and they suffer from hunger, so much the worse for them[1] [Collodi/Lucas 86–87].

It sounds like an invitation to work, to overcome poverty, which seems to have been reflected in school textbooks of the period, in which it is made very clear that only people who are incapable of working can expect compassion and charity (Bacigalupi and Fossati 65). If Alice is the dream child, real-life *Pinocchi* are nightmare children. A book which constantly and overtly alludes to a very close relationship between the destitute fictional child and real children of that age, from the very beginning *Pinocchio* alerts the reader to the specific problems for which the liberal state had tried to find solutions.

In 1873 a law was passed that forbade the employment (and the exploitation) of children as entertainers (see Ipsen 1), which is precisely what Geppetto wants to do with his newly-made puppet in the opening chapter. There was widespread concern for child vagabonds, street children (see chapter 2), orphans, and delinquent children and, of course, working children. But the united Italy did not pass its first Child Labor Law until 1886, introducing, as in the 1833 Factory Act in England, a minimum age of nine for a child to work in a factory. *Pinocchio* is about child exploitation and about the social oxymoron of the dangerous child vs. the child in danger (Ipsen 1–13), the child who is persecuted and who escapes from his family, as Pinocchio does as soon as Geppetto makes a pair of legs for him. Incisa di Camerana, in the tradition of Asor Rosa (see chapter 2), has read in Pinocchio who runs away a metaphor for the citizens of the new nation:

> As soon as he is created, the new Italian escapes[...]. The contemporary national situation is summarized in this escape. As soon as Italy is made, people cross the threshold[...]. A mass escape takes place. Almost half of the Italian population finds Italy too cramped and leaves [...] Italy looks at itself in the mirror of the united nation and sees itself hungry and desperate. Like emigration was for Italians, for Pinocchio escape is a choice of freedom, the evidence that he is born an adult, not a child who must be subjected to the adults' power [82, my translation].

All of this is a long way from the peaceful, secure world of middle-class Victorian England, with a stable currency, successful colonizing (Victoria was proclaimed Empress of India in 1876), and clear social and gender divisions. Victoria's reign is normally perceived as a period of expansion and prosperity, a period in which officers of the Empire were engaged in a mission to spread civilization across the world—proudly looking for new markets, rather than being driven by despair and hunger. Of course, this is also a world of huge social deprivation (England is also the place in which workers in cities lived in appalling conditions, working long hours and in extreme poverty) but the grim realities that had long permeated children's fiction (and characterize Collodi's book), only register in the *Alice* books in the most oblique way.

Child beggars and "street arabs" are somewhat aestheticized in Carroll's work as a photographer. In the summer of 1858, Alice Liddell was asked to pose as a beggar girl—this was one of Carroll's most famous photographs—barefoot, wearing half-torn clothes and demurely (or seductively) holding up a hand for charity. It is a very complex and ambivalent picture of "picturesque poverty," as Douglas-Fairhurst has put it, even if "ragged children had long been popular subjects for sentimental paintings" (96). The harsh realities of poverty and the thriving trade of child prostitution were the reality behind the artistic masquerade of beggar maids. "Was there, in his subconscious mind," Thomas wonders, "an attempt to find in this subject a more 'wholesome' representation of the importunate little creatures who solicited as a rule for their elders in the London streets with which he was most familiar?" (274) Unlike the real Alice Liddell, who begs as a *pose*, the fictional Pinocchio is a *real* beggar who reflects the phenomenon of children begging in the Italian streets. Concern with street kids' exploitation and child labor as well as delinquent youth had increased after the *Risorgimento* and especially in the decade following Italian unification. The mistreated and marginalized children of the Italian nation-state could not be perceived as picturesque: they had become a serious political problem.

It has become almost a critical commonplace that "Collodi remained substantially and courageously tied to the more defining and living ideals of the *Risorgimento*" (Decollanz 171, my translation). This affirmation is invariably followed by a note on the patriot Collodi's disillusionment and disappointment about the way these ideals were abandoned or betrayed by the new nation. In his journalistic writings and essays he scrutinized the ways in which the new political entity was not up to his enthusiastic juvenile expectations. For example, he complains of the architectural changes that Florence had to undergo when it became—briefly—the capital of the newly formed Regno d'Italia. The expense of building offices and other buildings for the various ministries, to be abandoned when Rome was finally available—had left the city burdened with debt (Bertacchini 1993: 158). Inevitably, the *Risorgimento* as "Foundation Story," a legendary movement with its iconic figures and heroes (von Hennenberg and Russell Ascoli 6–12), clashed with the way it had to be "institutionalized" when the new nation was formed: the unification exposed the most divisive elements—geographical, linguistic, social, political, and so on—which were subsumed into an ideal of Italianness which could mean many different and contrasting things. Collodi did his part—for example, in 1868 he was involved in the project of compiling a "Dizionario della lingua italiana secondo l'uso fiorentino" [Dictionary of the Italian language following Florentine usage]. His job was to compile lists of unusual Italian words and find the corresponding Tuscan word (Bertacchini 1993: 179).

The Northern European view of Italian political instability and late nation-building has played a substantial role in the construction of the national imageme (see chapter 1): "The creation of linear, celebratory accounts of nation-building, based most famously on the experiences of England, contributed to Italy's perceived backwardness" (Russell Ascoli and von Hennenberg 4). Poverty, late industrialization, and the North-South divide (Disraeli's English two-nation divide operated along social lines, while Italy's was mainly geographical) were chosen from the national repertoire ("the cultural shreds and patches used by nationalism are often arbitrary historical inventions" [Gellner 56]) to produce a narrative representation of a backward Italy. The connection between backwardness and lack of democracy, was possibly one of the favorite forms of self-representation for the new nation (see Russell Ascoli and von Hennenberg 27–28). According to this narrative, Italian backwardness would be explained by the lack of democracy and vice-versa, "and therefore, every progress, every opening of the socio-political structure to the 'citizens,' to the 'people,' to the 'workers' would have given Italy a push towards becoming a more modern country[...], a fairer, more efficient, more democratic nation" (Galli della Loggia 141, my translation).

The context in which *Pinocchio* was written could not be more distant, in terms of national self-confidence, from the Victorian self-representation of Britain. Collodi himself, in an article about the national character, entitled "Sangue Italiano" [Italian blood], complained about the inconsistent, grumbling, hypocritical, and individualistic nature of a middle-class Italian *Cavaliere* (Collodi in Marcheschi 1995b: 238–243). Ironically, Collodi had also been awarded the Cavaliere honor. As Camerana has perceptively remarked, "Italians disparage themselves because they won't stand being disparaged by others" (56, my translation). In contrast, as Mandler has noted, Britain felt itself to be at the center of the world, morally as well as financially and politically: "The British retained a stubborn attachment to the view that there was one moral nature and thus one ideal human morality towards which all peoples were tending, only the British more rapidly than anyone else" (76). Mandler also claims that national character was invariably denoted as English rather than British, "which caused the British to think of themselves as 'the English' with the distinctly national character of the English" (66). Henry Thomas Buckle's *History of Civilization in England* (1857–1861) was one of the most popular among many books on the national character that were published in the Victorian period: it tried to investigate, in comparative terms, why civilization had reached its peak in England, and not elsewhere. Cuthbert Spurling, in 1916, put this down to the British capacity for self-government, ancestors coming from good Teutonic stock, love for the countryside, common sense, loyalty, and the excellence of the British troops, "stubborn in warfare and persistent in the face of difficulties" (639): all these qualities combined to build a cluster of powerful discursive conventions and national representations, as the imagologists would probably put it (see chapter 1). In particular, the celebrated virtues of the British soldier appear to contrast sharply with the common perception of Italian soldiers who since time immemorial had allowed foreign powers to come and conquer the Italian peninsula—so much so that in reply to a French general affirming that "les italiens ne se battent pas," Cavour wrote in 1860 that Garibaldi "had given Italians self-confidence, and had showed Europe that Italians could fight and die in battle to re-conquer their homeland" (quoted in Belardelli, Cafagna, Galli della Loggia and Sabatucci 63, my translation). And some Italians, like Collodi, not a professional soldier, had fought in no less than *two* wars to re-conquer their homeland.

At this time, in Victorian Britain there was, as is well known, a strong fascination (or "obsession," see Goldhill) with the Roman Empire. "The British," it has been observed, "admired the Romans for their stoicism, their courage, their administration and their legal system, their concept of citizenship, their straight roads, bridges and aqueducts, their common currency and common language" (Richards 2009: 7). A fashion for Roman novels started with Bulwer-Lytton's *The Last Days of Pompeii* (1834): more that 200 novels on Roman themes were published in English between 1820 and the First World War (Goldhill 159). Elliott Mills' s *The Decline and Fall of the British Empire* (1905) projected into the future, anxieties about the decline and inertia of the young generations in pursuing the imperial mission (just as Gibbon's *The History of the Decline and Fall of the Roman Empire* (1776–1789), had reflected on the reasons for the crisis and disintegration of Rome). Imperialism was a central theme in late Victorian boys' adventure stories and references to the Roman empire in children's literature are not unusual (see Maurice): one only needs to think of

G.A. Henty's historical novel *Beric the Briton: A Story of the Roman Invasion* (1893), Edith Nesbit's time-travel novel *The Story of the Amulet* (1906), in which the child protagonists travel back to ancient Rome and beg Caesar not to invade Britain, or Kipling's *Puck of Pook's Hill* (1906) and its stories about young British Romans holding out against the invading Norsemen. As Kumar has remarked, "The pride of those who asserted *civis Romanus sum* was to be matched by those who could claim *civis Britannicus sum*[...]; the Pax Romana was to have its equivalent in the Pax Britannica" (196).

But English political observers of the newly unified Italy were not making comparisons with its glorious Roman past: they were recording the increasing disparity between North and South, and the persistence (or interference) of the Roman Catholic Church; they questioned the stability of the country's finances and the consistency of its army. They admired the hero Garibaldi (Ragionieri vii, xxv, 9). It is not by chance that in the *Wind in the Willows* (1908), Mole keeps a plaster bust of Garibaldi in the fore-court of his house: "On the walls hung wire baskets with ferns in them, alternating with brackets carrying plaster statuary—Garibaldi, and the infant Samuel, and Queen Victoria, and other heroes of modern Italy" (Grahame 54).

However, modern Italy, unlike Britain for the British, was still an unknown space for most Italians. From a secure economic position, Collodi continued to write cultural and political articles that analyzed the contradictions of the new nation and all the problems that still had to be solved, but he was not a man to separate his political concerns from his writing for children. After his translation of Perrault's fairy tales (see chapter 4), a translation that was of prime importance for his personal and professional future (Faeti 24), Collodi started writing textbooks for children. Despite very good sales, they never had the official approval needed for school adoption—a way to make sure of their quality and uniformity—despite the fact that after the unification, school manuals were introduced for the first time and school publishing became very successful. According to the Ministry for Education's report, Collodi's texts "were conceived in a novelistic way so that *dulce* superseded *utile*, and they were written in such a playful—humorous and frivolous—style, that they took away all seriousness from teaching" (quoted in Dedola 134, my translation). And yet Collodi became so engrossed in writing for children that, to some of his admirers' regret, he no longer had the time to write many articles. In his *Giannettino* (1877), the eponymous young middle-class naughty boy realizes that he knows very little about Italy, so he asks Doctor Boccadoro, who acts as a sort of enlightened preceptor, for help:

"I would like you," our Giannettino asked the Doctor one day, [...] "to help me get to know my country, that is, Italy. Because, you see, and I am ashamed to admit it, I don't know my country at all; that is, I know that Rome is its capital, I know its main cities and rivers; but if you ask me other things about my country, I don't know anything, anything at all, and it would be almost the same if they asked me about China or Japan" [Collodi 1988: 136, my translation].

Doctor Boccadoro (and Collodi of course) took up the challenge, and *Il viaggio per l'Italia di Giannettino* saw the light of day between 1880 and 1886—three volumes, devoted to Northern, Central and Southern Italy in which the doctor takes his pupil on three trips through Italy during the summer holidays. It is a version of the Grand Tour, which emphasizes the educational and formative function of the journey, a journey that helps the protagonist grow up, and the importance of keeping an open mind—advocating a form of cultural relativism. As Giannettino writes in a letter to his friend Minuzzolo, after having visited Northern Italy and about to start the second part to his journey in Central Italy:

If I were talking about somebody else, instead of myself, I would almost build up the courage to tell you that when I left home I was still a boy, and that after 40 days' spinning around the cities of Northern Italy, I have returned not quite a grown man (that would be too much to expect) but at least a little man with a good start to becoming an adult one [Collodi 1880: 10, my translation].

The journey does not just emphasize the beauties of the monuments or the cultural heritage (a testimony to a rich historical and artistic past which is clearly more important to Collodi and his patriotic agenda than natural wonders); it describes the cities and the places that were involved in the unification of Italy and explains when they became part of the kingdom.

The *Risorgimento*, evoked in crucial events and places, is the common thread of Giannettino's journey, which often turns into a pilgrimage to the symbolic places of the nation (see Squarcina and Malatesta). Unusual emphasis is placed on the different dialects encountered in the journey, at a time when the problem of linguistic cohesion in the newly established nation worried the political and educational authorities who were trying to remove dialects as barriers of communication (in favor of the Florentine "dialect" which would provide the chief basis for the Italian standard language [see Ruzza]). Places like Naples and Sicily, traditionally described by contemporary Italian and foreign travelers alike (from poet Renato Fucini to British Prime Minister Gladstone, see Camerana 12–15) as dirty, poor, and backward, are more kindly described through the lens of the picturesque and the liberal use of good-humored regional stereotypes. The peculiarities of the Italian North-South divide, and the causes of social inequalities and poverty are generally overlooked in favor of the view that these problems belong to all nations, as in this description of the Sicilian poor:

> Don't persuade yourself that the Sicilian populace has anything peculiar and characteristic. The poor in this world, as is known, more or less, are all alike: and all forms of poverty have a family resemblance, which never changes with climate or country [Collodi 1886: 171, my translation].

But poverty and illiteracy were the huge problems that the new Italian nation-state had to face, and concern with public education had increased after the unification. This must be seen in the context that in 1861, a census showed that 78 percent of the population was illiterate; consequently, a new impulse was given to children's books containing some sort of civic or moral lesson (Zago 62). Four years later, another survey showed that only 2.5 percent of the population (about 600,000 people) could speak Italian, as opposed to dialect. Despite the variety and the richness of regional dialects, Italian was, in the apt definition given by Tullio De Mauro, "a foreign language spoken in the homeland" (quoted in Boero and de Luca 11, my translation). That education could be key for social improvement is clear in *Pinocchio* when Geppetto sacrifices his jacket to buy the alphabet book.

Literacy and Education in Late Nineteenth-Century Italy and England

In Italy, laws and schoolbooks were enlisted in the fight against illiteracy. The Casati Law (1859, in the middle of the Wars of Independence) in Piedmont and the Coppino Law in the newly unified Italy (1877) had introduced compulsory education. Given the general illiteracy rate, however, the problem was not just to teach children, but adults (most school textbooks were addressed to "ai fanciulli e al popolo," [to children and the populace], as noted by Bacigalupi and Fossati [23]). Even if the Coppino Law only required pupils to attend school between six and nine years of age, poor families found it extremely difficult to deprive themselves of their children's help in the fields or in the family business. Enforcement of the law was minimal as there were more urgent issues to deal with: teachers had to be trained and better paid, schools needed to be founded or built outside the big cities, and suitable teaching materials had to be provided. As has been remarked, "The Coppino Law did not provide a solution; on the contrary, it left unresolved many issues that were destined to become more intricate and serious" (Bertoni Jovine 167). Once again Collodi could not help writing about it. In an article entitled "Pane e Libri" [Bread and Books] in the newspaper *La Vedetta* in 1884, he accused the new state of hypocritically forcing the poor people to get an education, when they could not even feed themselves:

> In my opinion, so far we have thought more about the brains than the stomachs of the suffering and the poor. Now let's worry a little more about their stomachs, and let's see whether it is more likely that the feeling of human dignity will enter their blood because bread is provided, or whether it will enter their brain through compulsory education and books [quoted in Bertacchini 2015: 85, my translation].

Collodi is not arguing against compulsory education for everybody but he does reaffirm the universal right to be fed properly and to have a place to rest after work—only when these primary needs are satisfied, "can man find himself in the condition to listen to his conscience and the ambition to better himself" (quoted in Bertacchini 2015: 85–86, my translation). And children, more than adults, need to eat properly—it is impossible not to be reminded of Pinocchio, when he is sent to school with just a "little suit of flowered paper" (Collodi/Lucas 23) and an empty stomach. It is only when Pinocchio works and earns money to support himself and his father that he learns how to read and write: Pinocchio is self-taught, not entirely unlike his creator, who completed his education when he worked for the Piatti bookshop in Florence.

Textbooks were considered essential in the literacy process (see Marciano) and Florence was, with Milan, the most important center of educational publishing in Italy. The publisher Paggi, who had commissioned from Collodi the translation of Perrault's fairy tales (see chapter 4), had started, even before the unification, a series of children's books and textbooks that could be used in the schools of the new kingdom (Bertacchini 1993: 177). Collodi's *Giannettino* (1877) is one of these books in which Collodi wears the hat of educational writer, but a writer who wants to make a radical change from the most famous educational manual of the former generation, Luigi Alessandro Parravicini's edifying and encyclopedic *Giannetto* (1837), 784 pages long, which follows the social climb of its hero, from shopkeeper's son to entrepreneur and philanthropist. Giannetto is a model hero for all readers, especially those, as is explained in the book, "who in their lives would probably not read another book" (quoted in Lombello 158).

Collodi seems to have liked the position of the pedagogue who wants to teach *differently*, using humor and trusting his pupils' intelligence—his contribution to a unified and free Italy was going to be textbooks that would teach every Italian child, with warmth and imagination. Through the adventures of naughty *Giannettino* (who, unlike Giannetto, hates school and has no manners) readers learn from experience rather than precept. Even if the book is interspersed with overtly didactic material, Giannettino's enlightened tutors take the students to the circus, and use the *lanterna magica* as a teaching tool. There is even a book within a book, "Il Libretto di Giannettino" in which the protagonist takes notes about the human body, medicine, hygiene, geography, and the products of Italy, from glass to china, to hats and gloves (and of course there is pride in the fact that Italy can produce such exquisite materials). In one example, a visit to the Museum of Natural History is an opportunity to describe animals and their lives (Dedola 144–149).

As in many textbooks of the period, there is a strong element of the cautionary tale and several episodes anticipate *Pinocchio*: Giannettino tells lies, but when the peasant Ireno, who is blamed in his place for stealing a watch, is sacked, and then falls ill, Giannettino confesses and is full of remorse. He spends the money that he should have used to buy an Atlas, in an *osteria*, where he plays cards, and loses: the boys he spends time with are thieves who make him drink too much and then have him arrested by a *Carabiniere*. The danger of bad companions (which will be developed later with the Cat and the Fox) is stated loud and clear. As in *Pinocchio*, repeated failures and adventures with an unhappy ending provide learning experiences that end in Giannettino's repentance and promises to do better next time.

The series ran to eight volumes until Collodi's death: in *La Lanterna Magica di Giannettino* (1890), the last installment, Giannettino has grown and learnt his lessons—he even replaces his schoolmaster uncle for a term. With the aid of the magic lantern he shows a class of unruly children pictures of famous Italian men as children, from Giotto to Canova, from Michelangelo to Verdi, and the difficulties they had to overcome with perseverance and passion. But in the section entitled "Buoni cittadini e buoni italiani" [Good citizens and good Italians] he reprimands the pupil who affirms with patriotic emphasis that "Italy is the first nation in the world, and Italians in war are afraid of no-one" (Collodi 1890: 163, my translation): he tells him to leave such "useless boasting" to "windbags who have breath to waste" (in contrast to Cuthbert Spurling!). The way children make their nation proud, says Giannettino, is to learn to write and speak Italian well, and study foreign languages: "A young Italian man, who, as well as his mother tongue, can speak and write French, English, and German, will not be a stranger in any country in the world, and will be able to find employment to earn a living honestly. Bear that in mind" (Collodi 1890:

163–164, my translation). It is impossible not to be reminded of the thousands of illiterate Italians who at the time were emigrating—and who often could not even speak Italian, but only their local dialect.

In England the education act of 1870 established nationally funded schools, administered by locally-elected boards, to "fill the gaps in the existing voluntary system and thereby [to ensure] that every child had a school place" (Horn 35). However, it was not until 1880 that attendance at school was made compulsory for five- to ten-year-olds (partly to discourage child-labor); older children "could be exempted to work part-time in factories, if they had reached a certain educational standard" (Chris Cook 110). Fees were abolished in 1891. Both England and Italy had experimented with student tutoring (the monitorial system) and the Bell and Lancaster schools of mutual teaching, with mixed results (see Tuman, and Bertoni Jovine 29–36). Figures for the final decades of the century indicate that illiteracy had been almost completely eliminated in England; school attendance was high, even in those country areas where new schools had been opened and "in towns it was among the most depressed areas that the effects of the 1870 and subsequent Acts were most felt" (Lawson and Silver 318). In those decades the number of boys' schools grew rapidly, and so did the ambition of tradesmen to send their children to exclusive schools, even if the subjects taught were not immediately useful to their trade:

> A boy's success in passing school examinations was recognized as a new way to get ahead in a society that prized upward mobility. Such an emphasis on schooling could have developed only in a society—like that of England in the nineteenth century—where many families could afford to dispense with the labor of their children [Burstyn 18].

This of course is in sharp contrast with the reality of many Italian children, including the fictional Pinocchio: emphasis upon the work ethic is something that runs throughout *Pinocchio* and was common in Italian textbooks of the time. Bacigalupi and Fossati have investigated the way that Samuel Smiles's *Self-Help* (1859) through its very successful Italian translation, *Chi si aiuta Dio l'aiuta* [Those who help themselves are rewarded by God's help] (1865) not only indicated to the middle classes the importance of self-reliance, but also reassured the common people that work would bring about an improvement in their economic condition. The message of many Italian schoolbooks and textbooks of the time "was more concerned with educating a whole population than stimulating the individual's initiative" (Bacigalupi and Fossati 59, my translation).

In contrast, *individual* betterment was the way the Victorians saw education (Burstyn 11) but the emphasis was mainly on boys, as education for the women of the middle and upper classes was generally just a way to prepare them to become good wives. Alice as a character as well as Alice Liddell the real girl were destined to become ladies of leisure, educated at home and taking private lessons from tutors (while in *Pinocchio* all women, with the exception of the aristocratic Fairy, work).

It is worthy of note that, despite very different educational circumstances, in both Italy and England there was ambivalence towards teaching the poor (or the lower classes). The English concern that the poor be instructed beyond their station ("It is very possible, with the best intentions, so to educate a man as to disqualify him for his position in life" [W.C. Taylor 3]) is paralleled by a similar worry in Italy on the part of the less enlightened representatives of the Church, and even by some liberals, about the danger of a classical education. They were persuaded that "popular education could not have any other goal than to promote revolutionary movements and attack the principles of religion, as well as class privileges" (Bertoni Jovine 47, my translation).

We have no evidence that Collodi ever worked as a teacher, while we know that Carroll, well placed in Oxford, the educational center of the elites, lectured undergraduates, and even, occasionally, younger pupils. He attempted to teach mathematics to children at the nearby St. Aldate's school, close to Christ Church, but lasted only a few weeks: his undergraduate students found his lectures very dull—and the feeling was mutual. Carroll noted: "I am weary of lecturing[...]. It is thankless, uphill work, goading unwilling men to learning they have no taste for, to the inevitable neglect of others who really want to get on" (quoted in Bakewell 72–73). Wakeling diplomatically claims that "although he [Carroll] may not have been a stimulating and charismatic teacher, he was proficient and diligent in his lectureship" (118). Despite this, Carroll retained an interest in education—particularly of young ladies. Between 1880 and 1885 he published a series of mathematical puzzles, "Knots" in *The Monthly Packet* (a magazine for "Younger Members of the English Church," edited by Charlotte Yonge)—ten of which were collected as *A Tangled Tale* in 1885. His next book, *The Game of Logic*, appeared in 1887 (with a board and nine counters to assist in the game) (Wilson 179). As Stuart Dodgson Collingwood noted:

> As a method of teaching the first principles of Logic to children it has proved most useful; the subject, usually considered very difficult for a beginner is made extremely easy by simplification of method, and both interesting and amusing by the quaint syllogisms that the author devised, such as—

No bald person needs a hair-brush;
No lizards have hair;
No lizard needs a hairbrush [Collingwood 1899b: 259].

The book was not a great success, but, as Morton Cohen wryly observed, it "served [Carroll] as a textbook for teaching classes of girls and mistresses in Oxford, Eastbourne, and elsewhere and for private instruction of his child friends" (446).

There is no shortage of teachers in *Alice* and *Pinocchio*. *Pinocchio* is full of educational experiences, some of which are not put to good use—as when in chapter 29 Pinocchio has to wait all night for the snail to come down the stairs, but does not appear to learn the lesson of patience. Similarly, as shall be seen in more detail in chapter 5, Alice does not learn much from her conversations with adults, such as the Red Queen, who interrupts her all the time to boast or comment on her manners, or the Duchess, with her nonsensical moralizing. But Alice can afford to make fun of school subjects and learning by rote because she *can* access education quite easily, even if her education may have relied heavily on memorization: Carroll systematically parodies nineteenth-century education—notably the catechetical method (Ostry). The Caterpillar is drawn by Tenniel with academic-gown sleeves, Humpty-Dumpty is the epitome of the arrogant academic, and the Mock Turtle provides a catalogue of nonsense school subjects, and, as we have seen, a portrait of the real Alice's drawing master, John Ruskin. Most of the rhymes in the *Alice* books are distortions of pious poems learned by Victorian children: "You are Old, Father William" is from Robert Southey's "The Old Man's Comforts" (1799), and "Twinkle, Twinkle Little Bat," from Jane Taylor's "The Star" (1806). Simonsen writes that Alice learns to think independently and creatively in the books, instead of relying on memorized facts (4), and goes so far as to argue that "one significant reason why *Alice's Adventures* has remained so popular over the years is because Carroll was ahead of his time in his ideas about children's education" (8).

It is obvious from the different educational contexts of the two books that the *Alice* books can satirize contemporary educational practices in a way that *Pinocchio* cannot. In Collodi's world, if you do not go to school, you are kidnapped, exploited by ruthless adults, and ultimately degraded to animal form, as when Pinocchio and his friends are changed into donkeys after months of school-less fun. And yet, even in *Pinocchio*, in the episode of the battle of the books by the seashore (chapter 26) which ends with Pinocchio almost killing Eugenio, Collodi can't help satirizing the schoolbooks of his time, including his own *Giannettino*, by naming the books that the children throw at each other: when in the course of the battle, some volumes fall into the sea, not even the fish can bear to taste them. In the end Pinocchio will learn from experience and by making mistakes, but not from time spent at school.

In their own peculiar ways, both authors were able to translate their educational intuitions, experiences and backgrounds into books in which didacticism is not intrusive or in any way reduces the fun of their characters' "Adventures." These books were indicating new educational directions, and designing fantasy worlds that would invite and stimulate their readers' curiosity, provide them with opportunities to change themselves, and allow them to try out different approaches to the mysterious and often dangerous world of adults. Once again, as we have seen in the previous chapters, the transnational self-identification with the main characters of the books is not incompatible with the fact that the books are so deeply rooted in their period. Unlike other contemporary children's books, they do not seem to be barely-comprehensible historical curiosities that are unable to transcend their cultures.

In the next two chapters I shall investigate how *Alice* and *Pinocchio* appear to tap into universally appreciated tropes (through folktale and fairy-tale patterns and the fantasy tradition), and how their narrative structures are sufficient to transcend their local and personal specificity, even if each text synthesizes those same narratives in its own remarkably different way.

PART TWO

Origins: Folktale, Fairy-Tale and Fantasy Traditions

4. *Pinocchio* as *fiaba*, *Alice* as Fairy Tale: Folktale and Fairy-Tale Traditions

Folktale and Fairy Tale vs. Fantasy

I have decided to discuss folktales and fairy tales in this chapter, and the fantasy tradition in the next, and the ways in which *Alice* and *Pinocchio* deal with these traditions in Carroll's and Collodi's respective countries, because I want to look at the way these books retain and challenge the most typical features of these genres/traditions. At the same time, the combination of folktale, fairy tale and fantasy in the *Alice* books and *Pinocchio* create unprecedented genre configurations which have provided "standard" patterns for late nineteenth-century and later children's literature in their respective nations.

In this chapter I adhere to basic consensus definitions of *fable, folktale*, and *fairy tale*. *Fable* is a short tale that teaches a moral lesson, often featuring talking animals which act as humans. Fables tend to be moralistic and do not always end happily even if there is a clear resolution or a moral. A *folktale* derives more or less directly from the oral tradition (although folktales are commonly modified in the process of transcription); a *fairy tale* is an authored tale, which can derive from oral tradition and may share some of the conventional traits of folktale, but is characterized by a literary and creative impulse. It originally addressed a select reading public, and it largely relies on print for its dissemination. In Italian things are slightly more complicated as *fiaba* is used for both folktales and fairy tales, and often *favola* [fable] and *fiaba* are used interchangeably.

Folktales and fairy tales have their own distinct sets of characteristics, but they also share stylistic features (such as opening or closing formulae) as well as tropes (from magical food to landscape). To complicate definitions even further, Maria Tatar has employed the term "literary folktales" for the Grimms' collection, as they represent a class of hybrid texts that blend literary and folkloric elements (Tatar 1987: 33). Length can sometimes be an issue: if the fairy tale can be described, borrowing Guillory's definition, as "a canon of the non-canonical" (26), the complex, layered, long-winded French tales produced by the French *conteuses* between 1690 and 1715 do not seem to have much in common with the shorter tales by Perrault and especially by the Grimms. The latter are generally held responsible for canonizing the more compact fairy tale, which provided the framework for national collections in England as well as in Italy. The issue of the relationship between genre and canon formation has been discussed by Wanning Harries:

> The Grimms wanted fairy tales to be simple, "naïve," economical, a reflection of their ideas about the folk, and appropriate for the social education of children; the ones they chose became canonical; and now, when we read fairy tales, we want them to be like the ones the Grimms promoted[...]. Assumptions about a good or "authentic" fairy tale created the canon of the genre, a canon that has come to include Perrault but excludes most of his female contemporaries [45].

Folktales, fairy tales and fantasy have a lot in common. Critical studies of these forms of literature now tend, however, to view them as more clearly delineated genres. As *Alice* and *Pinocchio* offer unique combinations of folktale, fairy tale and fantasy tropes, it is sometimes difficult to discriminate rigidly, and there is occasionally some overlap, as when I discuss metamorphosis or violence in the next chapter. Questions of definition, when it comes to folktale, fairy tale and fantasy, are a "thorny hedge," as Marina Warner writes in her *Once Upon a Time: A Short History of Fairy Tale* (xvi), and it becomes even thornier when we look at these texts through the lens of time, and of different national critical perspectives. The genres of folktale and fairy tale pre-date that of fantasy as a critical concept, and both *Alice* and *Pinocchio* were originally referred to by their authors and their contemporaries as fairy tales. Italian critics who deal exclusively with Italian children's literature tend to reserve the term fantasy only for "high fantasy"—fantasy with a clearly distinguished secondary world setting—and generally refer to *Alice* or *Pinocchio* as fairy tales [*fiabe*]. But even in America there are critics who consider the *Alice* books as fairy tales (Lake) and believe that prescriptive definitions of fantasy when applied to the *Alice* books are not satisfactory (different critical views on fantasy in the two countries will be discussed more extensively in chapter 5).

Fairy tales and fantasy are clearly related: both enable us to enter worlds of infinite possibility (Mathews 1), both have their roots in ancient myths, sagas and concepts of magic, and share a number of character types and motifs. However, as Sullivan has explained, "fantasy literature is a nineteenth- and twentieth-century concept and creation" (1992: 97), a genre which developed in response to realistic fiction and that owes a lot to Romanticism. Fantasy is an eclectic genre, according to Maria Nikolajeva: in an article in which she attempts to clarify and list the differences between fairy tale and fantasy (2003), she concludes that the essential difference between fairy tale and fantasy is fantasy's "anchoring in recognizable reality" (142). In fantasy, characters can be transported from the world of consensus reality into some magical realm (and vice versa), or the magic can intrude into reality.

Folktale and Fairy-Tale Traditions in Nineteenth-Century Italy and England

Where do *Alice* and *Pinocchio* fit into the history of folktale and fairy tale?

The impact of the Grimms' collection and its translation in England has been thoroughly researched (see Briggs, Blamires, Alderson, McGlathery, Thacker, and more recently Zipes 2015 among many others). Avery identifies the arrival of a new wave of tales from Germany as "a return of the fairies" (2000: 77), after a combination of Puritan disapproval and a rationalist distrust of the imagination had prevented the development of a native tradition. (This, famously, led Charles Lamb to write an indignant letter to Coleridge in 1802, complaining about what he called the "Cursed Barbauld crew," who had deprived, he believed, children of imaginative material for their emotional growth [Lamb II: 81–82]). Although this narrative, in its cruder forms, has been questioned very convincingly (Grenby 2006: 77–79), there is no denying that in nineteenth-century England, translations contributed to the creation of a national fairy-tale canon. If on the one hand national identity could be reinforced by the collection of local, regional, tales representing the spirit of the nation (as in the Grimms' enterprise), on the other hand, as Schacker has shown, in England "the new field-based tale collections from abroad were demonstrating that oral traditions still thrived elsewhere" (6). Through translations of imported collections, national fairy-tale canons became, so to speak, transnational— the motifs of the Grimms' fairy tales, and their version of the "past," were compared to existing national traditions: Edgar Taylor, who translated the Grimms' tales into English in 1823, "regarded the tales as particularly valuable evidence in a philological quest to trace social, cultural, and literary development" (Schacker 19).

The Grimms' research methods, and their efforts to make folklore available (through a rhetoric of authenticity) in a written form, to a non-specialized mass reading public, were highly influential in England. The educational and imaginative value of their enterprise was not lost on the generation of Victorian writers who were to create their own tales of magic and the imagination only a few decades later (see Tosi 2007a and 2007b). Susina (28) notes that Carroll's library was well stocked with fairy-tale collections and literary fairy tales, including the Grimms'. In the Preface to an 1868 edition of the *German Popular Stories* (an edition that was owned by Carroll [Sundmark 75]), John Ruskin writes:

> Children [...] will find in the apparently vain and fitful courses of any tradition of old time, honestly delivered to them, a teaching for which no other can be substituted, and of which the power cannot be measured; animating for them the material world with inextinguishable life, fortifying them against the glacial cold of selfish science, and preparing them submissively, and with no bitterness of astonishment, to behold, in later years, the mystery—divinely appointed to remain such to all human thought— of the fates that happen alike to the evil and the good [235–236].

Scientists sometimes co-opted the tales for educational purposes. Keene quotes a reviewer of the Grimms' tales in *The Athenaeum* in 1853: The "analytical tendency of Science, which views the Universe simply in its details, might lead us into a morbidly-exclusive perception of the mechanical anatomy of things, were it not for Imagination, which feels and enjoys results by means of the instincts of the heart" (17).

About a century later, Italo Calvino, in the Preface to his groundbreaking collection of Italian folktales, would write in a similar fashion to Ruskin about the fates of folktale characters: "Folk tales are a catalogue of the potential destinies of men and women, especially for that stage of life when destiny is formed, that is, youth" (1983: 15, my translation). The Grimms' collection "set off (unintentionally) a chain reaction that had massive repercussions for the dissemination and study of folk tales in Europe and North America" (Zipes 2012: 111). Italy came to know the Grimms' tales rather later; the first partial translation appeared only in 1875 (the same year in which Collodi published his own translation of French fairy tales, see "Collodi's translation of Perrault") and the first complete translation in 1908, by an anonymous translator (see Faustini 58). And yet, Italy is considered to be the cradle of the European literary fairy tale, with Giovan Francesco Straparola's *Le piacevoli notti* (1550–1553) and especially with Gianbattista Basile's *Cunto de li Cunti* [*The Tale of Tales*— fifty stories also known as the *Pentamerone*] (1634–36) (see Zipes 2001 and 2006, and Canepa 1999).

The first collections of Italian folktales were published in the 1860s (Boero and De Luca 34), and, possibly not by chance, this was about the time when Basile's *Pentamerone* started to attract the interest of the scholar and folklorist Vittorio Imbriani, who collected Tuscan folktales (*La Novellaja Fiorentina*, 1871) and wrote an essay on Basile. The Grimms knew and appreciated Basile and had even thought of translating the tales themselves, but the *Märchen* project proved to be too complex to leave space for other endeavors (Canepa 1999: 30).

Post-*Risorgimento* Italy needed to find a way to make a nation out of different dialects, political allegiances, traditions and customs: the study of national folklore and nation building were combined with interest in regional and local storytelling traditions. So it is certainly true that, as Zago has observed, "just as patriots were striving for the unification of the country, folklorists were seeking to demonstrate, through the study of popular traditions, the fundamental spiritual unity of the Italian people" (63). But one must take into account that a lot of these collections were regional (an obvious exception was *Novelline popolari d'Italia* (1875) by Domenico Comparetti, a senator of the newly formed Regno D'Italia), like the ones collected by Giuseppe Pitrè (1841–1916) in Sicily and in Tuscany. (Pitrè led a "double life," as Sicilian and Italian—he became a Senator of the *Regno D'Italia* in 1914). As the Italian folklorist Cocchiara has written, Pitrè's work

> demonstrates that he knew how to be both Sicilian and Italian, both Italian and Euro-pean. This had happened in other fields as well: many writers and scholars contem-porary with Pitrè had made the folk of different regions the subject of their art, thus becoming simultaneously Sicilian and Italian, Piedmontese and Italian, Tuscan and Italian, and, most importantly, Italian and European [351–352].

In contrast, the English, who "have never used folklore to assert their patriotic identity" (Simpson and Roud i), embraced folklore as a written discourse with enthusiasm, and recognized its undoubtedly commercial potential for an increasingly literate public. The 1840s and 1850s saw sub-stantial translations of French, German, and Norse tales. Characteristic was Anthony Montalba's *Fairy Tales of All Nations* (1849), which contained tales from Basile and Straparola, and from the Russian, Polish, Icelandic and many other languages. The Preface read:

> The time has been, but happily exists no longer, when it would have been necessary to offer an apology for such a book as this. In those days it was not held that Beauty is its own excuse for being; on the contrary, a spurious utilitarianism reigned supreme in literature, and fancy and imagination were told to fold their wings, and travel only in the dusty paths of every-day life. Fairy tales, and all such flights into the region of the supernatural, were then condemned as merely idle things, or as pernicious occupations for faculties that should be always directed to serious and profitable concerns. But now we have cast off that pedantic folly, let us hope for ever. We now acknowledge that innocent amusement is good for its own sake, and we do not affect to prove our advance in civilisation by our incapacity to relish those sportive creations of unrestricted fancy that have been the delight of every generation in every land from times beyond the reach of history [online ed. And see Darton 240–241].

As I have discussed in the previous chapter, nineteenth-century England was remarkable for its high literacy rate—which Italian writers could not, at that time, expect to match, and so despite their illustrious progenitors in Straparola and Basile, literary fairy tales developed more slowly. At the beginning of the century, the desire to use literary fairy tales to promote literacy and middle-class values produced a number of educational, prejudiced and badly constructed fairy tales where the wish to instruct prevailed over the wish to amuse—Lavagetto calls them "simil-fiabe" [imitation fairy tales] (2008: 50) and has collected them in a subsection of his book under the heading "La fabbrica della fiaba" [the fairy-tale factory]. (In his subsequent chapters Lavagetto devotes space to a second wave of more refined literary fairy tales by Capuana and others. See also Truglio).

Critics attribute this initial diffidence towards the Grimms to the Italian emphasis on high culture (Basile, for example, was excluded from the first *Storia della letteratura Italiana* written by De Sanctis in 1870) and in general to the "pedagogical caution" which has always been characteristic of Italian children's literature studies (Boero and De Luca 34). (It is interesting to contrast Croce, the translator of Basile's tales from the Neapolitan into Italian in 1925, who dismissed the Grimms' enterprise as fantastical and arbitrary, with Gramsci, who, when in prison, in the 1930s, enthusiastically translated a selection of the *Märchen* [Cusatelli 530]).

It is not by chance that, as has been argued, the *Kinder-und Hausmärchen* may have been introduced into Florentine circles possibly through Herman Grimm, Wilhelm's son, who spent long periods in Italy and especially in Florence. While living there, he struck up a friendship with the scholar and patriot Karl Hillebrand, and his partner Jessie Taylor, the daughter of Edgar Taylor, the first translator of the Grimms (Borghese 50). They moved in the prestigious literary circle of the *Gabinetto di lettura* [reading room] Vieusseux, founded by Pietro Vieusseux in 1819, which became a catalyst for Italian and visiting intellectuals and helped disseminate European literary trends in Italy (Florence was the capital of Italy from 1865 to 1870). It appears that in Tuscany there was considerable interest in recording folklore in its several forms (tales, songs, poems, popular theatre, etc.), especially after the *Risorgimento* (see Clemente and Festa's work on the *Archivio per lo studio delle tradizioni popolari* [the Archive for the study of Popular traditions]: "Tuscany [...] in the reality of the new united state, became a region which [...] was contributing to the formation of a national cultural identity" (105), and part of that contribution was recording folkloric traditions.

This is the context in which Collodi was writing, which may account for the presence of folktale elements in *Pinocchio*, such as its typical narrative style, replete with elements of residual orality—proverbs, colloquial expressions, Tuscanisms and so on.

As Cambon has observed, *Alice* and *Pinocchio* "draw on the reservoir of living folklore and thereby reintegrate their audience into a lost unity[...]. Oral tradition nurtured both authors, distant though they may be in so many obvious respects" (53, 57). How do these two national classics, at the crossroads between the literary fairy tale and the folktale on the one hand, and fantasy on the other, do this? How do they incorporate folktale elements and how do they reinterpret these traditions?

Even if these texts are (generally) considered ground-breaking fantasies, at first glance *Pinocchio* appears to have a lot in common with folktales (see Volpicelli, among others), while *Alice* appears to be closer in structure and theme to some Victorian fantasies and literary fairy tales, notably those by George MacDonald and Charles Kingsley. (As we shall see in the section titled "The Blue Fairy: Collodi, MacDonald, Kingsley, and Carroll," Carroll's relationship with these writers was ambiguous, and he never attempted their religious or didactic allegory [Demurova 77]— rather the reverse!). Both *Alice* and *Pinocchio* were intent on commenting on or subverting earlier traditions, especially when it came to explicit didactic content. One needs only to compare *Alice*'s anti-authoritarian discourse with other contemporary fairy tales (most notably those by Margaret Gatty) to see how disruptive and subtly anti-moralizing Carroll can be. Similarly, *Pinocchio*'s rebelliousness and its criticism of institutions and justice clash with the vapid, mawkish and self-righteous category of literary fairy tales condemned by Lavagetto (2008).

Both books use dialogue—arguably more common in folktales than in fairy tales—quite extensively, and their dialogues and soliloquies have a remarkable theatrical quality. Susina (27) has observed that *Alice* owes a lot to the pantomime tradition; Sundmark mentions "verbal duelling" in *Alice* as a form that is typical of orality and "folk fairy tales"(86); and Demurova (82) has compared some episodes of *Alice*, notably the kitchen scene, to "Punch and Judy" (which is specifically referred to when the two knights fight in *Through the Looking-Glass* [Carroll 2009: 210–11]). *Pinocchio's* theatrical quality has been often compared to the language of the *Commedia dell'arte* and of course, puppets' theatre (see Calendoli).

In *Alice* there are no fairies or magical beings—apart, perhaps, from the Cheshire-Cat—and in *Pinocchio* there is only the Blue Fairy, who, apart from her appearances in different forms, can be seen to perform "proper" magic only at the end of the book, when she turns Pinocchio into a human boy. For all other kinds of magical change, in *Pinocchio* as in *Alice*, it is impossible to find a superior agent who is responsible—for example—for Alice's growing neck or Pinocchio changing into a donkey. The protagonists, as in folktales, do not find talking animals unusual, or seem to be worried about the coexistence of ordinary and extraordinary events—although Alice does wonder (as well as wander) a lot.

There are also, in both works, tensions between realism and archetype, so that Alice is a portrait of a Victorian little girl (and was, of course, actually modeled on one) and Pinocchio is recognizable as a street child, "il ragazzo di strada," a common sight in Italian cities at the time. As mentioned in "*Alice* and *Pinocchio* as 'Gendered Books'" in chapter two, Collodi wrote an article with this title: his *ragazzo* has no name, only a nickname, and its main characteristic is transgressing rules and avoiding work. In a way, the street boy, like Pinocchio (and Peter Pan) doesn't want to grow up and take on adult responsibilities, and magical spaces like the Land of Toys (or Neverland) are also locations that create the illusion of suspended time, and possibly, even projections of adult nostalgia. These spaces are also the typical secondary worlds of fantasy and are one of the powerful structural forces that often pull *Pinocchio* and *Alice* away from the folktale or fairy-tale genre. (Others, including the "coming-of-age" motif connected to the "the archetypal birth-death-rebirth motif" (Morrissey and Wunderlich 1983: 65), and the *Bildungsroman*, are discussed in chapter 5).

Folktale and Fairy-Tale Structures

Alice and *Pinocchio* are hybrids—at once fairy tales and non–fairy tales (Berman). They are also, however, fantasies (Nikolajeva 1988), albeit in a non-conventional sense. Such hybridity is produced by the configuration of these genres on a synchronic level, but also because of the genre configurations of nineteenth-century fantasy. (Establishing boundaries between contemporary fantasy narratives and today's literary fairy tales may be easier, possibly because many fantasies are constructed as series, and many revised fairy tales have an explicit political or feminist orientation). It is the fate of these extraordinary and seminal texts to defy, fuse, complicate, or disrupt, generic boundaries.

Alice's and *Pinocchio*'s structural complexity and generic hybridity have not discouraged critics from subjecting them to the analytical method developed by Vladimir Propp (who applied it to a limited corpus of Russian folktales). This has produced detailed analyses of functions and spheres of action and very complicated explanations of how to fit these works into Proppian patterns. Both Genot (1970) with *Pinocchio* and Sundmark (1999) with *Alice*, have applied Proppian categories to the works, albeit with slightly different methodologies. Substantially following Proppian categories, they have segmented the texts into sequences and then reduced them to formulae. They have both noted repetitive patterns that are typical of the folktale, and Sundmark even argues that *Alice* conforms to a specific tale-type (based on the Aarne Antti/Stith Thompson catalogue classification), AT 480 "The Kind and Unkind Girls." Similarly, Lake writes that "the Alice books are a literary transformation of interrelated classes of tales from oral tradition, which convention describes as the Substitute Bride, the Search for the Lost Spouse, and [...] Cinderella" (10). Whatever their merits or demerits, these attempts to identify structures have at least the advantage of bringing the folkloristic aspects of these two works, which may have been occasionally overlooked, to the foreground. Both books contain, and systematically subvert, repeated patterns or characters that are quite easy to identify in the Proppian apparatus. For example, if we have donors in *Alice* and *Pinocchio*, how do they conform to Propp's spheres of action? Can madmen and eccentrics in Alice ever play the fixed role of donor unambiguously? Or rather, do not madmen and eccentrics appear to be more at home in the world of fantasy than folktale? Questions like these take us once again to the generic hybridity of these works.

Superficially, and *pace* Propp, *Alice* and *Pinocchio* appear to share a very rambling structure, the structure of the picaresque, a structure which is based on the reactions that the heroes have to the situations and characters that they encounter on their journeys; it is not by chance, for example, that Alice meets the Cheshire-Cat at a crossroads (although *Through the Looking-Glass* is less anarchic and episodic than *Alice's Adventures* [see Schanoes 2017: 4]). The structure of these classics can also be read as that of the mythical "quest," and sometimes the books even appear to operate with the simplest narrative structure of all—"and then." *Pinocchio's* publishing history and its interruptions seem to have been partly responsible for this and for the suspense at the end of several chapters—the "cliffhangers" characteristic of episodic publication. The chapter-structure of *Alice's Adventures*, similarly, clearly derives from natural breaks in a long narrative—at the end of chapter 7, literally "and then": "—and *then*—she found herself at last in the beautiful garden, among the bright flower-beds and the cool fountains" (Carroll 2009: 68). However, these blends of epic journey and fantasy are, in the case of *Pinocchio*, based on a cyclical pattern of departure and return that is repeated six times. It is as if the "predominant triad" that Lüthi (33) identifies as one of the structural characteristics of the abstract style of the folktale (often in traditional tales, things happen in threes—three sisters try the slipper, the witch tries to kill Snow White with three objects, etc.) had become more complex and central. The principle of prohibition-violation-punishment characteristic of many folktales (from "Little Red Riding Hood" to "Bluebeard") is at the root of Pinocchio's repeated transgression of adults' rules and then his having to take the consequences (see "Cautionary Tales").

Zipes (1999) argues that Collodi consciously played with the tradition of "Jack tales," which in Italy took the form of a naïve, but essentially good peasant who learns to use his wits to trick his enemies in his adventures (145). However, it can be argued that Pinocchio tends to *trust* rather than trick, his enemies—like the Cat and the Fox—almost until the end and after considerable damage has been done.

As for *Alice*, "one of the first things Alice learns in Wonderland is that punishment for transgression, a constant fear in the topside existence, is just as much a threat to her in the new environment" (Gordon 141) and Sundmark has remarked that "*Alice* can be regarded as a reward-and-punishment tale: Alice is rewarded when she says and does the right thing; she is punished when she fails to do so" (77). Pinocchio and Alice, in their respective worlds, tend to repeat the same mistakes over and over again. Alice keeps insulting animals by referring to predators or acting as one herself (Auerbach), and Pinocchio breaks his promises almost systematically, regretting his choices later in his monologues of repentance, a form of (imperfect) self-examination that is not part of the folktale hero's experience (see "Alice and Pinocchio in *Alice* and *Pinocchio*" in chapter 2). Pinocchio's actions may seem compulsive at times, as if he were a victim of his own marionette-like nature, and he does take an exceptionally long time to learn that people who love him have different plans for his life than eating, drinking and seeing the world.

Alice must come to terms with the principle of reality, and recognize that the brutality of Wonderland is just a dream. In *Alice* the dream element makes things even more complicated, although we should not forget that Pinocchio also wakes up from a dream in which the Blue Fairy forgives him:

> "Be sensible in future and you will be happy."
> At this point the dream ended, and Pinocchio opened his eyes and he was wide awake. Now you must imagine for yourselves how amazed he was when, on waking, he realized that he was no longer a wooden puppet, but that instead he had become a boy like all the others[1] [Collodi/Lucas 168].

Tolkien excluded from his classification of fairy stories "any story that uses the machinery of dream" (13), and therefore, Carroll's books. *Alice's Adventures* is, as Carroll himself observed (Collingwood 1899a: 96) an "extempore," oral, structure, with a remorseless, even desperate logic— composed, like *Pinocchio*, at need. It might be thought that *Through the Looking-Glass*—also framed as a dream—might be disqualified because of its rigid adherence to a chess-game (Carroll 2009: 114–115); rather, it is disqualified by the segues between the squares, illogical jumps and fades which are quite uncharacteristic of folktale and fairy-tale narratives. Thus in chapter 3 Alice leaps a brook into a railway carriage, and the carriage leaps a brook and she finds herself under a tree, talking to a gnat (Carroll 149–152)—the removal of causal connections and juxtaposition of incongruous elements are, of course, typical of the syntax of dreams. Nor, as we shall see, is the overall structure of either of the *Alice* books reminiscent of old tales—except in a "through the looking-glass" way: the beginnings are accidental, and the endings ambiguous. Thus, while many episodes and characters in *Pinocchio* and *Alice* show a close affiliation with the folktale and fairy-tale traditions, often it is only to baffle readers' and generic expectations, as in their very peculiar beginnings and endings.

Beginnings and Endings

The beginnings and endings of folk and fairy tales are formulaic: "fixed metrical and rhyming tags" that "serve to stabilize its form" (Lüthi 34). Both *Alice* and *Pinocchio*, on the contrary, first evoke then challenge the typical opening of a folktale by inserting direct references to storytelling and orality—they start their work with frame-breaking and self-conscious devices. *Alice's Adventures* is framed between the poetical memory of a golden afternoon in which children ask the adult to tell them a story ("Prima flashes forth her edict 'to begin it'" [Carroll 2009: 5]) and the vivid image of a grown-up Alice who tells "many a strange tale [...] even [...] the dream of Wonderland" to her children (Carroll 2009: 111). The descriptions of a past act of storytelling (in the opening) and a future act of storytelling (in the ending) replace the traditional "Once upon a time" opening which normally establishes a reassuring pact between narrator and readers. The storytelling act is projected into the past or into the future, which distances it from the formula. Also, folktale characters are not normally afflicted or motivated by boredom as Alice is—they tend to react to specific external, not internal, triggers. Curiosity (especially female) is a capital sin in folktales, but Alice, who is "burning with curiosity" (Carroll 2009: 10), is not punished like Bluebeard's wives, although the subtext of sexual curiosity has been variously explored (by Rackin 1997, for example).

Similarly, in the opening of *Pinocchio,* one of the most baffling incipits in the history of literature, the narrator mimics a typical opening of a folktale or fairy tale, and raises the child reader's expectations, only to shatter them:

> Once upon a time there was...
> "A king!" my little readers will say straight away. No, children, you are mistaken. Once upon a time there was a piece of wood.
> It was not expensive wood; but just a bit of firewood, like the ones that people use to light a fire in the stove or on the hearth to warm their rooms in winter[2] [Collodi/Lucas 1].

This opening is at the same time a celebration of orality—the direct address, the reproduction of a storytelling scene with an audience expecting a story with kings and queens—and a distancing move from orality, as the audience is very clearly reframed as little readers [piccoli lettori]—readers of a *book* that does not start the way a fairy tale is supposed to. Even if this may not have been deliberate, Collodi is here declaring that although his text will use many folktale narrative patterns, it will be and do something completely different. Instead of a king, all we get is a piece of wood—and we should also note the unusual presence of firewood in a carpenter's shop—not the kind of wood that can be carved or used to make furniture, and this is a log that will shortly talk! As Manganelli has commented,

> It is difficult to overestimate the importance of this opening fraud. With a magician's trick, the fairy-tale writer has given access to the world of fairy tale, but to a different

fairy tale, which is dramatically incompatible with the ancient regal fairyland, certified by the presence of the royal crown[...]. Will this fairy tale survive after the disappearance of its elderly and eternal golden circle? Is this an attempt to kill the fairy tale? [11, my translation].

The absence of the king, Manganelli argues, is "terrible" (12). In *Through the Looking-Glass*, the Red King is asleep and dreaming the whole book— he is, indeed, a threat to the whole of real existence:

> "He's dreaming now," said Tweedledee: "and what do you think he's dreaming about?"
>
> Alice said "Nobody can guess that."
>
> "Why, about *you!*" Tweedledee exclaimed[...]. And if he left off dreaming about you, where do you suppose you'd be?"
>
> "Where I am now, of course," said Alice.
>
> "Not you!" Tweedledee retorted contemptuously. "You'd be nowhere. Why, you're only a sort of thing in his dream!" [Carroll 2009: 167–168].

So, both *Pinocchio* and *Alice's Adventures* begin with a careful negotiation of the status of books, which turns into a rebellion against the book itself when Alice doesn't like the form of the book that her sister is reading— "what is the use of a book without pictures or conversations?" (Carroll 2009: 9).

Kings and Queens are also the object of an argument between Alice and her sister at the beginning of *Through the Looking-Glass*:

> Alice had begun with "Let's pretend we're kings and queens," and her sister, who liked being very exact, had argued that they couldn't, because there were only two of them [Carroll 2009: 126].

And of course, in *Alice's Adventures*, the King and Queen are nothing but playing cards (Carroll 2009: 109); in *Through the Looking-Glass*, they are merely chess pieces: ultimately they are only games, and not the typical, earthy, characters of a folktale.

While *Alice's Adventures* ends, after Alice's assertion of her agency, with a (too) neat explanation of the dream, *Through the Looking-Glass*, a far more emotionally-charged book, does not allow such a neat resolution. Alice addresses the kitten respectfully, yet with some severity: "You woke me out of oh! such a nice dream! And you've been along with me, Kitty— all through the Looking-Glass world" (Carroll 2009: 242). But Carroll does not subscribe to the idea that dreams are simple or innocuous. Alice continues: "Now, Kitty, let's consider who it was that dreamed it all. This is a serious question[...]. It must have been either me or the Red King. He was part of my dream, of course—but then I was part of his dream, too!" (2009: 244). And the book ends with an unanswered question: "Which do

Illustration by Roberto Innocenti in Carlo Collodi, *Pinocchio: Storia di un* *burattino*, **Milano: La Margherita, 2005, p. 190.**

you think it was?" (Carroll 2009: 244) As Gilead has noted, "in both *Alices*, the closing frames satisfy adult didactic and escapist impulses but also cast an ironic shadow on these inclinations" (283).

The ending of *Pinocchio* is equally ambiguous—displacement rather than resolution. Pinocchio's anti-heroic transformation into a real boy is unsettling—after all, he does not marry a princess, and is not showered with wealth, as in folktales. This seems to go against the usual transformations of folktale: transformations that belong to the world of the *merveilleux*, as explained in Todorov's *Introduction à la littérature fantastique* (1970), and therefore do not unsettle the reader who recognizes them as belonging to a different order of reality. But *Pinocchio* does not end with a metamorphosis, like "Beauty and the Beast" or "The Frog Prince," but with a *displacement*. Pinocchio becomes a real boy but the (dead?) puppet is still there, a wooden corpse to be contemplated as a memento of his past or possibly a reminder that we are really all puppets, and someone else pulls the strings, although Pinocchio seems to resist this idea of external manipulation for most of the book—he always rebels when someone else tries to pull *his* strings. But this is not the only interpretation of the ending: Marcheschi (2016) sees it as ironic, with the narrator ridiculing the newly transformed boy's pride.

In Innocenti's illustration of the final scene of *Pinocchio* (in the 1991 Italian edition) Geppetto and Pinocchio are posing for a portrait—but Pinocchio the boy has a sinister puppet shadow, a double for the boy, a doppelgänger. Innocenti has painted a rather disturbing family portrait.

"Disturbing" is key: in Todorov's terms, Pinocchio's (partial?) metamorphosis might be more conveniently placed in the category of the *fantastique*, in which the reader is confused and surprised and incapable of deciding to which order of reality the events belong (as in much gothic fiction—and of course *Pinocchio* has gothic undertones). A similar feeling of bemusement and surprise may also be a reaction to some of the most surreal metamorphoses in *Alice*, such as that of the screaming baby. After its rescue from the enraged Duchess and the most dangerous kitchen of children's literature, it changes into a pig—not the usual outcome of a baby rescue operation.

Cautionary Tales

A typical structural device of the folktale is that of the cautionary tale—a transgression/punishment pattern that elaborates on a character's misfortune so that moral lessons are crystal clear for the child (disobedience and curiosity, in the Grimms' tales, for example, appear to be the capital sins) and this element continues into the literary fairy tale. In the nineteenth-century context of the pedagogy of fear, Tatar has noted, "fairy tales serve as instruments of socialization and acculturation precisely because they capture and preserve disruptive moments of conflict and chart their resolution" (1992: xxvii). For the Grimms, prohibitions are often followed by tragic consequences, as in "Mother Trudy" where the protagonist's curiosity is punished when she is turned into a log and thrown into the fire (which is exactly what may have happened to Pinocchio if Mangiafoco had fulfilled his initial purpose). And we know what happens when Bluebeard's wives open the forbidden door.

Following the cautionary tale tradition, in *Pinocchio* punishments are disproportionate to the crime, and preposterous threats become real: if you do not want to go to school and remain ignorant, you literally turn into a donkey. And if you say that you would rather die than drink a bitter medicine, a coffin will be brought instantly to take you away. In both *Pinocchio* and *Alice* drinking something that may be unpleasant is connected with the cautionary tradition. Pinocchio refuses to drink his medicine, and therefore symbolically "dies"; Alice, rather more knowingly (and satirically) checks the label of the mysterious bottle first as she "had never forgotten that, if you drink much from a bottle marked 'poison,' it is almost certain to disagree with you, sooner or later" (Carroll 2009: 14).

Alice and Pinocchio, if they want to survive, need to understand what rules operate in their respective fantasy worlds: if you do not know them, you disappear, you lose your identity and you can die. So Alice needs to be able to assess what happens when you eat from different sides of a magic mushroom, or she will vanish. Given Carroll's (probably) consciously revisionist approach to these tales, it is not surprising that she is well versed in the Victorian cautionary tradition: "she had read several nice little stories about children who had got burnt, and eaten up by wild beasts, and other unpleasant things, all because they *would* not remember the simple rules their friends had taught them" (Carroll 2009: 13).

But there is an additional set of rules that Alice needs to internalize, and these are mainly social: how to be polite—even if conventions of etiquette learned above-ground are not very useful in wonderland (Susina 40–42) and the Caterpillar and Humpty-Dumpty, among others, make their own social rules; how not to insult people or animals; how to behave at a tea-party; table manners—you do not cut people you have been introduced to (Carroll 2009: 234); and how to play games—even under difficult circumstances, as when you have to play croquet with live flamingos and hedgehogs instead of mallets and balls (Carroll 2009: 73–75). In contrast, Pinocchio needs to be taught basic *civic* rules—in a world that does not seem to acknowledge the innocence of children, a world in which "children have no rights, only duties summed up by the word obedience" (Perella 8). He needs to understand that what is required of him is not to play and be idle, but go to school and look after his father; if he doesn't, he will die of fatigue, like Candle-Wick, or will be beaten to death, drowned, and exploited by adults, who are ineffectual in protecting him.

Adults in both books are of little help: although they lecture Alice and Pinocchio all the time, they do not appear to have much to teach—in *Alice* the Duchess's lessons are unreliable and useless, in *Pinocchio* Geppetto's words are never listened to and the Fairy often uses sadistic methods to make her points. Ironically, the Cricket, one of the characters who is fondest of moralizing, preaching and warning (in a book full of explicit lectures) is one of the few characters who actually dies (the others are Candle-Wick and the Serpent). (It does return at the end of the book, a shadow of its former self, only to tell Pinocchio where he can get a glass of milk for his ailing father). There is a sharp contrast here between the destructive act from an aggressive and hungry Pinocchio who kills the Cricket in the first place, and the measured response of Alice to the animals that upset her. While the lecturing in *Alice* is undermined by Alice's (and Carroll's) complicit confidence, in *Pinocchio* there is an ambivalence between satire and the necessity to listen to warnings.

It is only when the protagonists grasp the rules of their worlds (according to Susina, "Carroll shifted the context of his fairy tale from religious to social lessons" [46]) that they move more comfortably. In a way, they both become aware very soon that the world is not a country for young people. In spite of their well-deserved reputation for rebelliousness and irreverence, *Pinocchio* and *Alice* can also be interpreted as accommodating morals, only "they are of a different order and more cunningly presented" (Goldthwaite 75).

Folktale and Fairy-Tale Tropes

It would be impractical to examine all the folktale and fairy-tale tropes that infuse *Alice* and *Pinocchio*, as both authors were cavalier about their use of them. Collodi, as we shall see from an examination of three major groups of tropes—talking animals, spaces, and food—drew energetically from the folktale and fairy-tale store, using the stark emotional force of his material to emphasize his didactic points. Foxes are foxy, forests threatening, and it is a world of eat or be eaten. In contrast, the threats and menace that Alice encounters may be modulated by humor, but their ancestry is clear: Carroll makes use of the nightmare features of the tales—the unexpected monster that darkens the sky, the wood in which one gets lost (both physically and mentally), the carnivorous house, the survival tokens, the mad, violent, harridans. In the face of these, Alice and Pinocchio are as insouciant as any folktale heroes. Carroll's connections to the folktale are, because of his habitually ironic stance, suitably disguised; however, the deconstruction of Alice's dream through the thoughts of Alice's sister—"the rattling teacups would change to tinkling sheep-bells, and the Queen's shrill cries to the voice of the shepherd-boy..." (Carroll 2009: 111)—does nothing to obscure the links to much more ancient images established in the dream.

Talking Animals

Both *Alice* and *Pinocchio* feature a considerable number of talking (and non-talking) animals: Ferretti has counted 500 animal references in *Pinocchio* and more than 50 different species. Similarly, the 22 animals that speak in *Alice's Adventures* far outnumber the "humans" (and playing-cards). This is backed up by the original illustrations: both Tenniel, Carroll's illustrator, and Mazzanti, the first illustrator of *Pinocchio*, were influenced by the French caricaturist Jean Grandville, who was famous for his satiric vignettes portraying individuals with human bodies and animal faces (Despinette 19 and Hancher 32–33). He also illustrated the fables of La Fontaine—and *Les Fleurs Animées* (1867)—which may have influenced Carroll's "The Garden of Live Flowers" in *Through the Looking-Glass* (Reichertz 46, 156–157).

As in the ancient fable tradition, meetings with animal characters typically happen in such places as forests, gardens, and tracks or streets, but often, in *Alice*, they wander away after a frustrating verbal confrontation, leaving her with a sense of incompletion (Elick) and without having imparted any useful lessons. In *Pinocchio*, again as in the fable, animals have traditional associations (the sly fox, the hard-working donkey) and can provide examples for virtue and vice. Collodi was well-versed in the Aesopic tradition—he inserts highly dialogic versions of Aesop's fables into *Giannettino* and *Minuzzolo* (Bertacchini 1961: 194). However, even if some of the animals create "the choral voice of a collective superego that preaches an ethic of work, family and moderation" (Canepa 2006: 90), their wisdom and their warnings are not always taken seriously, and they become the satirized victims of their own moralizing. An interesting example is in chapter 12; when the (white) Blackbird tries to warn Pinocchio not to listen to the Fox and the Cat, he suffers the same fate as the Cricket:

> "Pinocchio, don't listen to the advice of those bad characters, otherwise you'll be sorry!"
>
> Poor Blackbird, if only he had never said it! In one great bound, the Cat struck him down, and without giving him time to say *Ah*, ate him in one gulp, feathers and all.
>
> Having finished his meal and wiped his whiskers, he closed his eyes once more and pretended to be blind as before.
>
> "Poor Blackbird!" said Pinocchio to the Cat. "Why did you treat him so badly?"
>
> "I did it to teach him a lesson. That way next time he'll know not to interrupt other people's conversations"[3] [Collodi/Lucas 35].

And of course the Cat is absolutely right in theory and as far as manners and common sense go—after all, in the natural animal world, the biggest and the strongest win and "get the last word." And the last feather. Even if the Fox and the Cat can be considered as "archetypal deceivers, like characters out of Reynard," and *Pinocchio* can be seen as a "young *Pilgrim's Progress*, with animal tempters, avengers and judges" (Blount 56–57), Collodi's satiric intent does not work in quite the same way as Aesop's or La Fontaine's. La Fontaine's fable "The Cat and the Fox" has the Cat outsmart the Fox even if they are both arch-hypocrites and downright highwaymen, while in *Pinocchio* the Cat appears to be an accomplice who repeats his companion's words. This is very self-conscious satire, which challenges and deconstructs the conventional wisdom of fable and folktale. Of all the animals in *Pinocchio*, only the mastiff Alidoro [Mercury, in Lawson Lucas's translation] who saves Pinocchio from being fried in chapter 29, and the tuna fish, who allows Pinocchio and Geppetto to ride astride him in chapter 36, play the role of the grateful animal (or helper/donor) common in folktales. Incidentally, both these animals help Pinocchio as a reward for his being kind to them, and neither of them lectures him (Canepa 2006: 88). *This* is what happens in folktales: being kind often reaps extraordinary recompense.

In *Alice* it is very difficult to label animals as helpers or donors (see Demurova; Elick; Frey and Griffin); Alice may be tested by the animals, but unlike the heroes of folktale she is not rewarded with any concrete help—not even from the Cheshire-Cat, who she calls her friend (Carroll 2009: 75) possibly because he does not take part in the Darwinian voracious struggle. (Just as Blount sees *Pinocchio* as an echo of Bunyan, so Dusinberre suggests that the Cheshire-Cat "is a prototype Evangelist, gesturing Alice along an enigmatic path towards various kinds of new acquaintances, all mad according to the tenets of the faith" [56]).

Equally, the verbal skirmishes she has with the animals do not encourage her to learn any lessons about kindness to animals (Lovell-Smith 386). Both Carroll and Collodi appear to play with this traditional element of folktale, to subvert it and refashion it in very different and very idiosyncratic ways. In *Pinocchio*, animals are not only stand-ins for humans, but like humans, they have agency (and a form of subjectivity); in *Alice*, they can be caricatures of specific humans (the Dodo) or generalized types of human (the Caterpillar), or pantomime characters (Bill the Lizard), political figures (the Lion and the Unicorn), or even a self portrait (the Gnat).

Both *Alice* and *Pinocchio* are characterized by a literalization of animal metaphors. The implicit equation between people and animals in idioms takes a very concrete visual form in their worlds. In Wonderland hares are, quite logically, mad; Cheshire-Cats grin, babies who look like pigs turn into them (as if an animal—and edible—quality was already in the child…), and butterflies warp and pun into bread-and-butter flies. In the world of *Pinocchio*, children who do not want to go to school—called *somari* [donkeys]—become actual donkeys when they are deprived of school; if you are "as fried as a fish" (the Italian idiom equivalent to the English "done for"), you end up in a pan with other fish to be fried, and if you are as slow as a snail, in this world you *are* a snail and being a helper to a fairy won't make you move any faster. Metaphors and similes generate characters and incidents—they act as idiomatic frames for the imagination (MacArthur). In *Alice* in particular, consumption is closely connected to language—her very first encounters with food and drink are framed by language imperatives (eat me/drink me). In both *Alice* and *Pinocchio* such literalization is extensive—in the *Alice* books, there are the Garden of Live Flowers and the Looking-Glass insects; *Pinocchio*'s literalization of proverbs as blueprints for narrative units has been widely investigated (see Lapucci).

Collodi's animals tend to belong to the Tuscan world of countryside and woods—*Alice* has far more hybrid as well as legendary animals, such as the unicorn. The one animal in *Pinocchio* that can belong to a literary fairy tale is the huge green Serpent, cousin to a dragon, with "his fiery eyes and the column of smoke that rose from the tip of his tail" (Collodi/ Lucas 69); he has been compared to an incarnation of evil, a devil (Geddes de Filicaia). But Pinocchio is not allowed to enter into a confrontation typical of knights and heroes, because the Serpent quite literally bursts with laughter when Pinocchio falls and lands "with his head stuck in the mud on the road and with his legs up in the air" (Collodi/Lucas 69). The giant Shark called Attila is given equally anti-heroic treatment—he was "very old and suffered from asthma and palpitations of the heart" (Collodi/Lucas 157). This is rather in the vein of Carroll, who, as was his habit, undercuts the monsters (the Jabberwock wears a waistcoat) and older traditions: "At this moment the Unicorn sauntered by them, with his hands in his pockets" (Carroll 2009: 204–205).

Both Carroll and Collodi also use animals to reflect the (un-folktale-like) humanity of their central characters. For example, at one point, and talking of serpents, Alice's neck grows so enormously long that a Pigeon takes her for a snake who could rob eggs from her nest:

> "Serpent!" screamed the Pigeon.
> "I'm not a serpent!" said Alice indignantly. "Let me alone"!
> [...] "I've tried the roots of trees, and I've tried banks, and I've tried hedges," the Pigeon went on, without attending to her; "but those serpents! There's no pleasing them!"
> Alice was more and more puzzled, but she thought there was no use in saying anything more till the Pigeon had finished.
> "As if it wasn't trouble enough hatching the eggs," said the Pigeon; "but I must be on the look-out for serpents night and day! Why, I haven't had a wink of sleep these three weeks!"
> [...] "But I'm *not* a serpent, I tell you!" said Alice. "I'm a—I'm a—
> "Well! *What* are you?" said the Pigeon. "I can see you're trying to invent something!"
> "I'm a—I'm a little girl," said Alice, rather doubtfully, as she remembered the number of changes she had gone through, that day.
> "A likely story indeed!" said the Pigeon in a tone of the deepest contempt. "I've seen a good many little girls in my time, but never *one* with such a neck as that! No, no! You're a serpent; and there's no use denying it. I suppose you'll be telling me next that you never tasted an egg!"
> "I *have* tasted eggs, certainly," said Alice, who was a very truthful child; "but little girls eat eggs quite as much as serpents do, you know."
> "I don't believe it," said the Pigeon; "but if they do, why then they're a kind of serpent: that's all I can say."
> This was such a new idea to Alice, that she was quite silent for a minute or two, which gave the Pigeon the opportunity of adding, "You're looking for eggs, I know *that* well enough; and what does it matter to me whether you're a little girl or a serpent?"
> "It matters a good deal to *me*," said Alice hastily; "but I'm not looking for eggs, as it happens; and if I was, I shouldn't want *yours*: I don't like them raw" [Carroll 2009: 47–48].

This is one of the many occasions on which Alice unwittingly intimidates other animals, as she has done earlier by mentioning her cat Dinah to the mouse. A lot has been written on Alice as a predator: for example, Knoepflmacher makes the point that in the serpent episode "the enlarged Alice has become as feral as Dinah" (1998: 172), while Auerbach argues that Dinah "seems finally to function as a personification of Alice's own subtly cannibalistic hunger" (36). In a book in which the protagonist must negotiate her identity with herself as well as other characters, the reference to not eating raw eggs may actually be key in reaffirming Alice's humanity—the culture of cooked food which distinguishes her from animals.

Pinocchio, on the other hand, is constantly being demoted to an animal state, and from his days as a watchdog and a donkey he has learned what it is like to be beaten, exploited, mistreated, and nearly drowned. One of the most painful moments in *Pinocchio* is when he recognizes Lucignolo [Candle-Wick] in the donkey that he will be replacing (once again, the puppet will take on an animal's job: that of turning a pump to draw up a hundred buckets of water, with only a single glass of milk as a payment):

> "Up to now," the market gardener said, "I have given this task of working the pump to my donkey; but now the poor animal is giving up the ghost."
> [...] As soon as Pinocchio entered the stable he saw a handsome donkey lying on the straw, worn out by hunger and too much work. When he had looked very hard, he said to himself, feeling troubled, "Don't I know this donkey? He looks familiar to me."
> And bending down towards him, he asked in donkey language, "Who are you?"
> At this question the donkey opened his dying eyes, and stammered a reply in the same language, "I am Ca... ndle... Wi... ick...."
> Then he closed his eyes again and expired.
> "Oh, poor Candle-Wick!" said Pinocchio in a whisper, and taking up a handful of straw he dried a tear that was running down his face[4] [Collodi/Lucas 164–165].

Possibly the saddest thing about this old friends' meeting is that Candle-wick in his dying scene is not allowed any residual humanity—Collodi realistically specifies that this conversation between friends is not conducted in human language. This is the only time in the book in which an animal dialect [dialetto asinino] is mentioned—in the rest of the book the narrator does not need to justify or question the plausibility of dialogues between animals and humans (or puppets). In this scene, Pinocchio does not cry to repent of his behavior or because he is hungry and afraid—he is not reacting impulsively or automatically to specific events: that single tear is the tribute from a boy who knows what it is like to work and suffer like an animal to a boy who is dying of hunger and fatigue like an animal. Pinocchio empathizes twice: as a boy and as a former animal: unlike Alice, and even if technically he is a puppet, he really knows what it is like to lose humanity for a very long time.

Folktale Spaces: Roads, Gardens and Woods

The "depthless world of folktale" (Lüthi 19) lacks a clear dimension of time and place: forests, castles, cottages and other spaces are mentioned only if the plot depends on them: "the folktale presents only pure action and foregoes any amplifying description. It provides a story line but does not let us experience its setting" (38). In folktales it is not important to describe a house or a village—we simply see the hero leaving it and setting out into the world following an external impulse (a task, an adventure, a contest, a prohibition). In *Alice* and *Pinocchio* there is a continual slippage between a folktale world of improbability or eccentricity, and reality. This is by no means unusual in folktales, and an air of reality can be found in literary fairy tales too. As Röhrich has noted,

> Although possible and impossible occurrences recklessly mingle and the laws of causality often seem forgotten, certain causal relationships do survive[...]. Magic always affects human heroes: kings, craftsmen, and farmers, the mother, the stepmother, and siblings—all people who exist in reality [3].

Even in Perrault's *Contes*, which are teeming with fairies and extraordinary beings, characters and events have a connection to a recognizable reality and moral and satirical allusions are bound to his time (Röhrich 165). In folktales familiar and quite real spaces are often transfigured by the presence of incongruous, sudden departures from normality. This alternation of familiarity and incongruity is not uncommon in the *Alice* books and *Pinocchio*. So, the rabbit's house Alice visits, in her enlarged state, becomes oppressive and terrifying, while in the depressing room that Geppetto calls a house (described in very realistic terms as "a basement room lit by a skylight under the front steps"[5] [Collodi/Lucas 6]) a chick slips out of the egg and speaks unexpectedly and ceremoniously, and a cricket lectures Pinocchio.

Pinocchio's house is not at all a comfortable "nest": it is an inhospitable place, the house of a poor man who has to sell his jacket to buy a spelling book for his son and who has had to leave the house to go to prison. This very unusual (now abandoned) male nest is in sharp contrast with the Pigeon worrying about her nest in *Alice*: in the Darwinian world of survival the mother is very active in looking after her eggs under attack by the predators (possibly a metaphor or a parody of "a domestic refuge under female religious and moral guidance" [Lovell Smith 35]), while in *Pinocchio*'s dismal and poor world the puppet is left alone, hungry, and cold. Geppetto's room is full of the metaphors of deprivation, such as the painted pot; it is a place to leave in search of food, and to go back to in repentance. This happens in the first nine chapters—afterwards Pinocchio's adventures will take him to other places, and the hut he shares with Geppetto after the adventure in the belly of the whale/shark is magically changed into a comfortable home.

For most of the book, Pinocchio, like Alice, is wandering, but he is doing so as an orphan and a vagrant, not because, like her, he is bored: he wanders away from his home, away from his family, school, and society. Bertacchini has used the expression "Toscana-Mondo" to describe the setting of *Pinocchio*—it is a landscape of roads, villages, fields and hills that is, at the same time, recognizably Tuscan, but that can easily represent any vague folktale setting (1981: 115). The space that is more characteristic of Pinocchio's wanderings is the road (see Del Beccaro 72), with all its symbolic associations with human destiny (in this context the Serpent blocking the way to the Fairy's house would represent a diabolical enemy). Pinocchio is always running, but is always being diverted and distracted from his true destination, as when he goes to the puppet play instead of school, or to the Land of Toys. His spatial digressions reflect his lack of moral direction, and parallel Alice's dream, which proceeds with typical lack of cohesion. Drawing a map of their movements would probably end up in serious topographical disorder, although it has been attempted (see Manguel and Guadalupi 213 for *Alice's Adventures*, for example). Like Alice, Pinocchio fulfills his on-the-road destiny while he detours.

Alice finds a path that is "more like a corkscrew than a path," and which "gave a sudden twist and shook itself" (Carroll 2009: 137); another has two finger posts pointing in the same direction (158). In her world, the direction is more or less immaterial (in opposition to many folktales), and the helpful stranger distinctly unhelpful:

> "Would you tell me, please, which way I ought to go from here?"
> "That depends a good deal on where you want to get to," said the Cat.
> "I don't much care where […] so long as I get *somewhere*."
> […] "Oh, you're sure to do that," said the Cat, "if you only walk long enough" [Carroll 2009: 57].

There are no civilized gardens in *Pinocchio*, and there are no flowers in the hedges [le siepi] that draw the boundaries between the road and the fields, and it might seem that the *Alices* represent a contrast to this—that Alice's most typical space is the garden, which is her goal and her destination: it is not Rapunzel's walled garden, but it is still the place of desire, "a liminal space, open but restricted, poised between nature and culture, between private domestic space and public space, and, most important, between life and death" (Jane Carroll 52). Gardens are not common in fairy tales, which, after all, use only generalized backgrounds, but where they do occur—as in "Rapunzel" or "Beauty and the Beast"—they have an ambiguity that Carroll, in his constant sub-satirical mode, exploits to some advantage. The "loveliest garden you ever saw" eludes Alice for a long time—"How she longed to get out of that dark hall, and wander about among those beds of bright flowers and those cool fountains" (Carroll 2009: 13). When she eventually gets there, of course, it is a disturbing place, full of death threats, and ruled by a mad queen.

The garden, as a cultural symbol in England, is complex, blending both folklore and biblical elements. As Carpenter noted, the metaphysical poets of the seventeenth century linked childhood to Eden, and growing up to the loss of paradise. "Does this," he wonders, "have a little to do with the Victorian and Edwardian children's writers' fondness for the symbol of a garden or Enchanted place, in which all shall be well once more?" (Carpenter 9). Carroll's use of the garden can also be seen to arise from the specific surroundings of the "real" Alice—the walled garden of Christ Church Deanery, with its small wooden door, and the Horse Chestnut tree with its horizontal branch (for the Cheshire-Cat). Also, he was writing at a period when gardening of all kinds was becoming highly fashionable: books with titles such as *Gardening for Children* by the Rev. C. A. Johns (1848), or *Garden Flowers of the Year* (1847)—both published by religious publishers, The Society for Promoting Christian Knowledge, and The Religious Tract Society, respectively—were very popular. And yet it should be remembered that the style of many English gardens derived from Italy: "the Italian influence on garden design began to spread through northern Europe [...] it was Cardinal Wolsey who influenced both Henry VII and Henry VIII with his taste for the Italian style" (Garland 1984: 27). As Walter de la Mare put it: "The *Alices* indeed have the timelessness, the placelessness, and an atmosphere resembling in their own odd fashion [...] the medieval descriptions of paradise and many of the gemlike Italian pictures of the fifteenth century" (96). In terms of national stereotypes, Alice may appear to the modern Italian reader as a typical Englishwoman obsessed by a garden in a nation of keen gardeners; on the contrary, the genteel space of the garden is alien to the everyday experience of Pinocchio and was probably alien to most of his poor nineteenth-century compatriots— what he sees as he runs from one place to another, is an alternation of roads, fields, countryside, vineyards and villages, and of course, the sea, a word and space that spells adventure in Collodi's book (Bertacchini 1964: 91).

As for the *Alice* books, it was at least partly through Carroll, it can be argued, that the garden became absorbed into English culture, and especially English children's literature as a virtual folktale motif. Equally influential was Mrs. Ewing's *Mary's Meadow* (1886) in which the children discover the early modern herbalist John Parkinson's *Paradisi in sole Paradisus terrestris*, and the idea of creating a garden:

> The idea of it took our fancy completely, the others as well as mine, and though the story was constantly interrupted, and never came to any real plot or end, there were no Queens, or dwarfs, or characters of any kind in all Bechstein's fairy tales, or even in Grimm, more popular than the Queen of the Blue Robe and her Dwarf, and the Honest Root-gatherer, and John Parkinson, King's Apothecary and Herbalist, and the Weeding Woman of the Earthly Paradise [Mrs. Ewing 29].

By the time of Frances Hodgson Burnett's *The Secret Garden* (1911), the folkloric and fairy-tale credentials of the literary garden were fully established—death, purity, safety, growth, latent sexuality, and the link between the genuine and the ersatz folk motifs seems very likely to have been the *Alice* books.

The garden is not as common as another typical folktale and fairy-tale setting: the forest or wood. In folktales the forest can be a dark and dangerous place, or a place where one escapes from danger and hopes to find a magical refuge (as in "Snow White") but also finds new unexpected forms of danger in what looks like a familiar place (such as the witch's house in "Hansel and Gretel"). It is the place where characters lose themselves, meet villains and donors, and find their vocations: there they have to face dangers, their fears and, once again, their destiny. The forest is the favorite place for a prince's quest, and for losing or finding the traveler's path or true self. The forest can work magical transformations on the people who walk through it: it can be empathetic and reassuring, or it can let the demons of our subconscious emerge.

Every good fairy tale, it has been said, must have a night moment in order to insert some drama in the story (Di Biasio 263). In *Pinocchio*, as in "Snow White" or "Hansel and Gretel," the wood is dark and dangerous, and what the puppet finds there is nearly death. This is a wood with a surplus of Gothic overtones: it does not just stand in for danger and evil, and the way to the big oak where he will be hanged is paved by fear of the dark. Immediately after he has left the Inn, Pinocchio "set off groping his way, for outside the Inn the darkness was so dark that you could not see an inch"[6] (Collodi/Lucas 40). The ghost of the Talking Cricket provides temporarily a glimmer of light but "the moment he had spoken [...] the Talking Cricket was suddenly extinguished, the way a candle is extinguished, when you blow on it, and the path became darker than ever"[7] (Collodi/Lucas 41). In the darkness Pinocchio is terrified of the murderers he meets, who are dark and hooded. The night in *Pinocchio* is a place in itself (Tommasi 56), from the wintry scary night of chapter 6 to the darkness surrounding the puppet in the belly of the whale. And of course it is at Midnight (a word that is repeated throughout the episode, and that recalls folktale prohibitions) that the Omino, the Little Man, will come with his carriage to take the boys who don't want to go school to the Land of Toys. It is a journey made in darkness. Marx has noted (6) that in *Pinocchio* the typical folktale polarization between dark colors (denoting fear and terror), and white/light colors (denoting virtue and safety) is very noticeable. Once again, a staple of folklore is emphasized to produce a highly dramatic effect.

The forests in *Alice* are, naturally enough, far less terrifying: in fact, when she escapes from the White Rabbit's house, Alice "soon found herself safe in a thick wood" (Carroll 2009: 37). In *Through the Looking-Glass*, the second wood that she comes to "looked much darker than the last wood, and Alice felt a *little* timid about going into it" (2009: 155). It is the wood "where things have no names," and it is pleasantly cool and shady (2009: 156), and the terror, if any, that it contains, is purely philosophical. Similarly, Carroll's use of colors is much more inward-looking and cerebral in *Through the Looking-Glass*: it can scarcely be an accident that the word "white" occurs 68 times, and the word "red" 68 times; or that there are 68 chess-board squares accessible for three knight's moves—if the board were big enough (Hunt 2016).

Of all the spaces and places that Pinocchio visits in his life journey, it is the moment before entering a town, that of the Busy Bees, that Pinocchio feels the most lonely: "The thought of being all, all alone in the middle of that great uninhabited country filled him with such melancholy that he was on the point of crying then and there"[8] (Collodi/Lucas 84). This is strange—Pinocchio never feels lonely in the countryside or when he walks across the fields—walking in solitude is what he normally does. De Rienzo notes that the feeling that he experiences the moment he enters this society based on hard work and business transactions, a place that has no time for gratuitous actions or gifts, is very modern (322). Alice feels lonely in chapter 2, when she is growing in the Hall, an enclosed space, and no-one takes any notice of her: "I do wish they *would* put their heads down! I am so *very* tired of being all alone here!" (Carroll 2009: 19). Physical enclosure or emotional detachment changes these spaces into places of loneliness for the child characters.

Food

Hunger, and plentiful (often magical food) are a common feature of children's literature, folktale, fairy tale and fantasy in general—sometimes standing in symbolically for other basic human needs. "If you take out sex and violence, as writers of children's books often wish to, or are required to […] then you must still have some element which, in fashionable critical terms, gratifies desire. No sex, no violence: what are you left with? Food" (Hunt 1996: 9). Alice and Pinocchio may be food deprived, but violence has not been taken out of their respective books, as will be seen in the next chapter. Encounters with food in children's literature are most usually satisfying experiences—from Badger's huge suppers and breakfasts in *The Wind in the Willows* to the hot meal to which Max returns in Maurice Sendak's *Where the Wild Things Are*. This is not the case in *Pinocchio* or *Alice*.

In folktales and fairy tales, images of endless provision of food abound: magic tables set themselves with "roasted and stewed meat" when one pronounces the simple words "table, be covered" (in the Grimms' "The Magic Table, the Golden Donkey, and the Club in the Sack" [Zipes 1987: 137]); a girl puts an end to her hunger and poverty when she is given a magic pot that produces endless quantities of sweet porridge to the extent that, having forgotten the words to make it stop, the porridge fills "the kitchen, the whole house, then the next house and the street, as if it wanted to feed the entire world" (in Grimms' "The Sweet Porridge" [Zipes 1987: 376]). In Charles Perrault's "The Ridiculous Wishes" the poor woodcutter wastes the wishes granted him by Jupiter with his desire for sausages (79–82). Social historians and literary critics alike have provided the evidence that these tale-types were representative of the food shortages and general destitution that afflicted sections of the populations of the nations that produced these stories. Not unlike other fairy tales, "Hansel and Gretel" appears indeed to waver between the two extremes of hard fact and a symbolic dimension; between the parents' hunger, whose concern for daily bread dehumanizes them, and the excessive hunger of the witch, who has crossed the taboo boundary between what is considered edible food and what is clearly not.

As in folktales and fairy tales, in *Pinocchio* realistic concerns interact with magic solutions. Like the Grimms' "Hansel and Gretel," the roots of which are in a starving populace, *Pinocchio* is set in times of scarcity and famine which are described in realistic terms: in poverty-ridden Italy, food was an elemental matter. However, the night that the disconsolate siblings spend in the wood, lost and hungry but supporting each other and looking hopefully at the moon, is much less dramatic and "Gothic" than Pinocchio's "nottataccia" of chapter 6. Here the starving, terrified puppet tries to find some food in a nearby village, dark and deserted, "looking like the land of the dead" (Collodi/Lucas 16), where he gets drenched instead of fed. Pinocchio is obsessed with food, in the typical obsessive way of the starving peasant who can never fill his stomach. Food is also connected with the names of some characters, Mastro Ciliegia [Master Cherry], Geppetto's nickname is Polendina [polenta], and the ogre is called Mangiafoco. Pinocchio is constantly worried about getting food—the paradox is that this wooden marionette clearly has a human, empty stomach and badly needs his food—he has "a ravenous hunger" [una fame da lupi] (Collodi/ Lucas 13). The whole of chapter 5 is devoted to the puppet's hunger, as he looks for "a bit of bread, even a bit of dry bread, a little crust, a bone left by the dog, a spot of mouldy pasta ["polenta" in the original Italian], a fish bone, a cherry stone" (Collodi/Lucas 14). "Oh, what a terrible disease hunger is,"[9] he cries, weeping and in despair. (Incidentally, and quite mysteriously, his nose grows "another four inches" after the disappointment of seeing that the pot on the boil in Geppetto's house is only painted and not real).

In chapter 23, as Pinocchio looks at the tombstone of the dead Bambina, one of the manifestations of the Blue Fairy, he worries about who is going to look after him when it comes to food. "Now I've lost both you and my papa, who is going to give me something to eat? [...] It would be better, a hundred times better, if I were to die too!"[10] (Collodi/ Lucas 79). He is right to be worried. Unfortunately Geppetto is not always capable of providing the food that he needs: the three pears in chapter 7 are hardly adequate, and often food is supplied in the form of mocking replicas, like the *trompe-l'oeil* painting of the boiling pot or the cruelty of the fake food given by the Fairy, who uses food withdrawal as a pedagogical strategy. As for the world around Pinocchio, one needs to think only of the meanness of the people on the island of the Busy Bees in chapter 24 who are not willing to give a crust of bread for free to those who can work to earn it, and the harsh punishment for stealing a bunch of grapes in chapter 22. No-one gives food freely and generously in the world of *Pinocchio*: the word "fame" [hunger] is repeated 37 times in the book. In *Commedia dell'Arte* many puppet characters, like Arlecchino or Pulcinella, suffer from hunger—there is even a character called Famiola, whose name derives from the Piedmontese "I l'hai fam" [I am hungry] (Marcheschi 1990: 122).

In contrast, in the *Alice* books, "hunger" is not mentioned, but "hungry" appears twice in *Alice's Adventures* and three times in *Through the Looking-Glass*. Some critics, like Talairach-Vielmas, see Alice as a *greedy* girl rather than a hungry one, with an unrestrained appetite. Others, such as Garland, argue that in the first book Alice consumes food without any explicit hunger while in the second book "the presence of hunger and the absence of eating became important, both in themselves and in their stark contrast to the depiction of hunger and eating in Wonderland" (Garland 2008: 32–33). Alice's hunger is not unique: in canonical Victorian literature women's hunger occupies an important place, from *Jane Eyre* to *Tess of the d'Urbervilles*, and Victorian novels "are filled with examples of men taking in starving women" (Michie 22). Unlike the heroines of Victorian novels, Alice takes full responsibility for her own hunger and acknowledges it—while escaping the fate of Laura after she has devoured the goblins' fruit in Christina Rossetti's *Goblin Market* (1862) (which, incidentally, ends with Laura and her sister Lizzie recounting their adventures as mothers—the same future projection that we find in *Alice*).

Whether she is greedy or really hungry, Alice's desire for food is as urgent as Pinocchio's (but for different reasons). As the narrator observes, "she always took a great interest in questions of eating and drinking" (Carroll 2009: 65) but, like Pinocchio, her attempts to actually secure food are constantly frustrated. As in *Pinocchio*, consumption is based on withholding (Mavor 97). At the caucus-race prize giving Alice is the only person not to get something to eat, at the Mad Hatter's tea table, she never gets to a place where there is an un-used teacup; and the rule in the Looking-Glass world is "jam to-morrow and jam yesterday—but never jam *to-day*" (Carroll 2009: 174). All this reaches a climax of food frustration at her coronation banquet, a true "revolt of food things" (Parrish Lee 494) in which she cannot eat food she has been introduced to: this is speaking and living food, like the chick that comes out of Pinocchio's egg (see chapter 5: "the scrambled egg [*frittata* in the original Italian] flies away through the window" [Collodi/Lucas 13]). The banquet ends in a shambles of inversion between food/objects and people (bottles turn into birds, the leg of mutton is sitting in the Queen's chair while the Queen disappears into the soup).

While it may seem implausible to argue that Alice's diet (in rich, middle-class Oxford) was in any way comparable to that of the starving Italian street boy, it should be pointed out that her diet might have been quite restricted. As Avery notes, "children would have been given bread and milk—ham and eggs being thought too indigestible, butter and cream too rich [...]" (Avery 1994: 158). With regard to Alice's encounter, mutton was a staple of the monotonous middle-class child diet in Victorian times: "until the age of about 17, [...] they were fed exclusively on milk, oatmeal, bread (ideally, 8 days old), potatoes[...], mutton, and suet or rice pudding" (Freeman 213). Perhaps mutton appeared to children as a very intrusive, constant and *real* presence in their meals, even if joints did not introduce themselves. Allen suggests that the food imagery in Carroll is there because of the "Victorian fascination with food[...]. Half-forbidden as a subject of polite conversation, and much used in rewarding and punishing children, it was conveniently regarded as the main, or indeed only, object of a child's appetites, and was often referred to with a certain coyness by adults" (381).

In both books the places where food is prepared are dangerous or inadequate—there is no food at all in Geppetto's one-room house and Alice's kitchen is a turbulent and surreal place, from which Alice rescues a baby—"if I don't take this child away with me [...] they're sure to kill it in a day or two" (Carroll 2009: 55). Both are typically unsafe places for children, parodies of the warm nourishing atmosphere that the kitchen has, in children's books especially, become a symbol of—in contrast to its ambivalent status in fairy tales such as "Cinderella."

As in "Hansel and Gretel" in which the siblings leave the house of starvation, reach the house of plenty, and are ready to become food themselves, the destiny of Pinocchio is that of avoiding being eaten not just once but several times, as fried fish, or in the belly of the shark. "I don't want to be digested" he screams to the philosophical tuna-fish who finds it more dignified "to die in sea-water than to be preserved in olive oil"[11] (Collodi/Lucas 152). Alice experiences something of the same danger that is part of animal life when she meets the puppy in the garden—but, because of the size changes, Alice alternates, as we have seen, between the role of predator and that of prey. In *Alice*, Darwinian competition constantly reminds us that in the animal world one eats and/or is eaten: "she was terribly frightened all the time at the thought that it might be hungry, in which case it would be very likely to eat her up in spite of all her coaxing" (Carroll 2009: 38–39).

In the upside-world of *Alice* and the violent world of *Pinocchio*, no one is really safe from predatory instincts and general voraciousness. When Pinocchio arrives at the island of the Busy Bees, the first thing that he asks the Dolphin is "Would you be so kind as to tell me whether there are any villages on this island where one may eat, without running the risk of being eaten?"[12] (Collodi/Lucas 85). Here Pinocchio makes the connection between two basic human needs: that of feeding and feeling safe (Gasparini 72). In contrast, when food abounds, Pinocchio does not seem in the mood to enjoy it, as on the occasion of the succulent meal at the Red Lobster Inn, eaten with relish by the Cat and the Fox (Collodi/Lucas 38):

> Inside the Inn, they all three sat down to table; but none of them had any appetite.
>
> The poor Cat, who was feeling seriously indisposed with stomach trouble, could only manage thirty-five mullet with tomato sauce and four portions of tripe and onions, and, because he thought the tripe insufficiently seasoned, he treated himself three times over to more butter and grated cheese!
>
> The Fox would have gladly nibbled at a little something too, but as the doctor had prescribed an extremely strict diet, he had to make do with a simple jugged hare with a very light garnish of plump pullets and tender poussins. As an appetizer after the hare he ordered a little hotchpotch of game-birds, partridge, rabbit, frog, lizard and green grapes; then he wanted nothing more[...].
>
> The one who ate least of all was Pinocchio. He asked for a lobe of walnut and the heel of a loaf, and left it all on his plate untouched. Poor boy, his thoughts were so concentrated upon the Field of Miracles that he had succumbed already to indigestion from an expected surfeit of gold coins[13] [Collodi/Lucas 38].

The fantasy of a place with enormous amounts of food available to be eaten to the exhaustion of one's appetite recalls the medieval and utopian land of Cockaigne, where delicacies of food and drink are plentiful, and restrictions and aestheticism are reversed and parodied. The Land of Cockaigne is also a folktale type and its appeal seems to have depended on the permanent and endless supply of food rather than gastronomic delicacies: "culinary cockaigne is largely lacking in the typical dishes gracing the tables of the aristocracy[...]. With regard to content, the dietetic dreams of Cockaigne [...] fulfil the fantasies of luxury food entertained by the great majority of both country folk and townspeople (Pleij 98)." In *Pinocchio's* world this fantasy of the availability of food takes the form of a list of dishes, some of which (the Cat's choices) are quite ordinary, like the red mullets or tripe, but they are served in extremely abundant portions. It is the poor peasant's dream, of taking full advantage of the chance—for once—to feel fit to burst.

Nicholson has observed that even in *Alice* there is a hint of Cockaigne, when a bottle and a cake literally ask to be consumed:

> Metaphorically these images belong to a genuine Wonderland—a paradise or place where the food supply is always greater than any demand made on it, or where food is miraculously provided, like the fabulous Land of Cockaigne. This is surely one of the profoundest and most universal of all human wishes: the place of unlimited food [53].

Foods and dishes that are mentioned in *Alice* and *Pinocchio* can be analyzed along class lines. Jylkka has noted that in *Alice in Wonderland*, bread is associated with lower-class characters and sweeter foods with the upper class: for example, the Unicorn would not eat brown bread, an item in the diet of the lower classes in Italy and in England alike, although English peasants and laborers were much better nourished than Italian ones (see Sorcinelli). In Wonderland, "The type of food they eat or the food available to them," Jylkka argues, "classifies them to their fellow characters and to the reader as upper- or lower-class figures" (3). Avery concurs: "To the English mind, if children were indulged over their food it was a sign of an ill-bred family" (Avery 1994: 158–159).

Sugar was expensive and used sparingly among the working classes in England—in Italy it was even less common—the Blue Fairy uses a "pallina di zucchero" [sugar ball] as something very special, a reward after drinking a bitter medicine—clearly not an everyday food. The fact that Pinocchio misses the event at the Fairy's house, where two hundred cups of coffee with milk and four hundred rolls buttered inside and outside will be served, to go to the Land of Toys, tells us a lot about his motivation: white bread and *caffelatte* were the staple breakfast of the middle classes and food not to be missed by the poor. When in chapter 24 the good lady offers Pinocchio "a lovely dish of cauliflower seasoned with oil and vinegar" (Collodi/Lucas 88) if he helps her carry a pitcher, Pinocchio is not terribly enthusiastic until the lady offers "a lovely sweetmeat filled with cordial as well" [un bel confetto pieno di rosolio (Collodi 1993: 171)]. As for the tea/coffee dichotomy that still divides England and Italy as regards favorite hot drinks, it is interesting to notice that a few years before Carroll was writing, the social status of coffee had started to decline as it was still associated with working-class consumption. By mid-century tea came to be associated with Victorian upper-class society, and *Alice* reflects this trend (Susina 114).

Similarly, in *Pinocchio* we see a realistic depiction of eating habits which can be divided between "poor food" and "rich food," or "food for the poor" and "food for the rich" (Fresta). While the Cat seems to favor simple foods, the Fox has more refined taste—meat being still a rare occurrence on Italian tables in the nineteenth century. His "lepre dolce e forte" (Lucas translates this Tuscan dish, literally "sweet and strong hare," as "jugged hare," but that is far from equivalent: the Tuscan sauce includes pine nuts, dark chocolate, and white wine vinegar [Vivarelli 93]) is one of the dishes that were collected in Pellegrino Artusi's *Scienza in Cucina e l'Arte di Mangiar Bene*, published only ten years after *Pinocchio*, and a text which helped shape the self-perception of Italy as a nation, in a similar way that *Pinocchio* has done. Many Italian cookery books for centuries emphasized regional differences, but the integration of Italian cuisine for the new nation came in 1891 with Artusi, who collected regional variations of recipes and offered them to the middle classes of united Italy as *Italian* cooking. His book became *the* Italian cookery book (the book given to newly married women, for example) for many decades and it is believed that it did more to instill a notion of Italian identity than many political strategies. Its secret lay in the fact that it did not attempt to erase regional variations—food diversity was accepted as an inescapable fact of Italian identity. This can be seen, for example, when Artusi discusses frying and specifies that people should use the fat that is the best produce of that area for frying: at the time when he was writing, in Tuscany they preferred oil, in Lombardy, butter, and in Emilia they used lard—all were quite acceptable to Artusi (Montanari 56–62). In *Pinocchio* there are several references to dishes whose recipes were collected later in Artusi's book and in particular, precise references to regional dishes which were going to become the most typical examples of Italian cooking only a few years later: *risotto alla Milanese, maccheroni alla Napoletana* (both mentioned in chapter 33; Lucas translates them as "shepherd's pie" and "steak and kidney pudding" in an attempt at cultural translation [138]) and *tortellino di Bologna* (chapter 35, translated as "a bit of spaghetti," [156]). It is as if the idea of a nation's cooking was born a few years before the actual nation was formed: "the patriot Collodi was the witness of that mix of culinary traditions that saw the lovers of risotto go South with Garibaldi's Thousand and come back home in love with the maccheroni" (Garbarino 57, my translation).

Pinocchio, Alice **and the Fairies**

The use of folktale and fairy-tale structures and tropes by Collodi and Carroll is complex, as a result of their literary and cultural contexts, as well as the personal interest they took in traditional tales. Two circumstances are particularly revealing of their attitudes: the first is the fact that Collodi translated Perrault's tales and the second was that Carroll disapproved of the use made by his contemporaries, especially George Mac-Donald and Charles Kingsley, of folktale materials.

Collodi's Translation of Perrault

After the unification of Italy there was a strong movement to bring to the people the best works of European culture, including folklore and fairy-tale studies, especially in Florence. In 1875 Collodi was commissioned by the publishing bookshop Paggi to translate Perrault's *Contes* and *Histoires* and some of Mme D'Aulnoy's and Mme Leprince de Beaumont's fairy tales. His volume, illustrated by Mazzanti (who was later to illustrate the first edition of *Pinocchio*) was called *I racconti delle fate* [*Tales of the Fairies*]—and, although it was not the first translation of the French tales into Italian, it was the first which used names that are still current today for these tales and characters, such as "Cappuccetto rosso" and "Barbablù" for "Little Red Riding Hood" and "Bluebeard," which replaced the names "Berrettina Rossa" and "Barba Turchina" used in Cesare Donati's 1867 translation (Dedola 112).

Collodi seems to have taken this translation very seriously—in the short "Avvertenza" [Warning] that introduces the collection, he writes that not being faithful to the originals would have been "sacrilegious" and apologizes for the very small liberties that he has taken with the text, ending on a light note: "a sin confessed is half forgiven, and so be it" (Collodi 1875/2002, my translation). The language Collodi chose for his collection was an idiomatic Italian "dressed in Tuscan colours" (Zago 66), and many critics have pointed out that Collodi transformed Perrault's fairy tales back into folktales, turning their characteristic courtly atmosphere into a rustic Italian setting and using "hyperfiorentinisms" typical of the spoken language (Paolini 458). However, this is not the case with stories by Mme D'Aulnoy and Mme Leprince de Beaumont. In translating these more complex tales, Collodi avoided "folklorization"—although the Tuscan world of fairs and markets transmigrates here too. In "L'Oiseau Bleu" [L'Uccello Turchino] by Mme D'Aulnoy, the four "marionnettes plus fringantes et plus spirituelles que toutes celles qui paraissent aux foires Saint-Germain et Saint-Laurent" (online ed.) are translated by Collodi as "four marionettes, and they were livelier and prettier than those you see in the theatres *at the great fairs of Padua and Senigaglia*"[14] (my emphasis).

All this work had clearly prepared the way for his writing of *Pinocchio*—much as Angela Carter—an unexpected connection across time, space and language—translated Perrault's tales and then was inspired to write her own versions in *The Bloody Chamber* (1979) (see chapter 6). So, how does Collodi accommodate elements of the classic French tales in his text? Clemente has noted a similarity between Mme Leprince de Beaumont's "Le Prince Chéri" and *Pinocchio* in the way the Fairy Candide (who first appears as a white rabbit) controls and punishes Chéri with animal transformations until he repents and is transformed back into a human being. "The Fairy Candide is at the same time the Talking Cricket and the Blue Fairy, educationalists who go unheard" (Clemente 213, my translation).

Collodi's reworking of Perrault in *Pinocchio* is often ironic and/or parodic, possibly with the exception of the atmospheric scene in which the Blue-haired Fairy is transported by a carriage drawn by mice, and complete with poodle coachman, which is strongly reminiscent of the scene in Perrault's "Cinderella" in which the Fairy Godmother turns a pumpkin and some mice into a carriage drawn by horses. The Blue Fairy is, of course, a fairy-tale trope that comes straight from *Les Contes de Fées*.

A good example of parodic debasement of fairy-tale elements is the puppet master Mangiafoco. He is quite clearly an ogre in the Perrault tradition, but while his counterpart in "Le Petit Poucet" is very fond of eating rare mutton (the blood in his meat makes him even more ravenous for raw human meat), the Fire-eater makes a fuss about having enough wood for his spit as he likes his mutton well cooked. Like Alice in the pigeon scene, eating cooked food establishes a degree of superiority over animals or beasts or monsters: it is the mark of the civilized human. Mangiafoco is so human that he is even moved to tears by Pinocchio's sad story of not having a mother, a poor father and of his wish to sacrifice himself for "his brother" Arlecchino as wood for the spit. The comical scene at the theatre ends with the ogre giving Pinocchio five gold pieces (chapters 11–12).

The Blue Fairy: Collodi, MacDonald, Kingsley and Carroll

Among all the staples of fairy lore the *Fata dai capelli turchini* [The Fairy with indigo hair] stands in *Pinocchio* as an original interpretation of a typical agent of transformation and magic. Her very nature is shapeless—she undergoes death and metamorphoses and Pinocchio encounters her in all her transformations: a dead *bella bambina* [beautiful girl] a sister, a peasant woman, a goat, an elegant lady, and a mother. The Blue-haired Fairy is an elusive and eccentric character—she transforms herself more than she transforms the world around her. Frey and Griffith have explored her religious connotations ("the Fairy is a version of the Madonna and Pinocchio the supplicant sinner begging to be taken out of a dangerous and sinful world" [103]); Citati has called her the Lady of the Animals (she does not wave a magic wand, but relies on animal helpers), the Queen of Metamorphosis, and the Weaver of Destinies (216). Feminist perspectives have read her as the female other of Pinocchio, "Pinocchio's only model of change as growth" (Mazzoni 83). In *Pinocchio* she may represent the highest possible moral standard in the book, and is therefore superior to all the other characters.

It is interesting to compare her with the view of woman that can be found in "L'azione morale della donna nella civile società" ["Woman's moral action in society"] a speech that Collodi delivered in 1882 at a school prize-giving. Would woman, who is fragile physically as well as intellectually, Collodi wonders, endowed with a "shy and sensitive nature [...] ever be able to fight the social conflicts that challenge the strongest characters?" (quoted in Mirmina 408, my translation). In his social comedies and in his newspaper articles he appears to be more optimistic about the possibility of a woman having the same rights as a man (see Marcheschi 2016: 66–67). Marcheschi also makes the point that Collodi inverts the usual polarity that connects the mother with "the heart," and the father with reason:

> the Blue-haired Fairy [...] embodies the possibility that a woman could educate her offspring in a rational as well as emotional way [...] Geppetto makes sacrifices for Pinocchio like a mother, while the Blue-haired Fairy, as strict as a father, gives out punishments and rewards, taking care of Pinocchio's moral and rational education [Marcheschi 2016: 75, my translation].

Through all the Fairy's transformations, the only thing that remains the same (even as a goat) is her impossible blue hair, which has elicited the most diverse interpretations, from a vision of the Virgin Mary to an inverted Bluebeard (Abbadie Clerc 104). The Fairy appears only in the second part of *Pinocchio*—the first 15 chapters, the cautionary tale that ends with Pinocchio's death, has no fairy, but only a

> beautiful Little Girl with indigo hair and a face as white as a wax image. Her eyes were closed and her hands were crossed over her breast and, without moving her lips, she said in a faint voice that seemed to come from the other world: "There is no one here. They are all dead."
> "Please open the door yourself!" implored Pinocchio, weeping.
> "I am dead too."
> "Dead? So what are you doing up there at the window?"
> "I'm waiting for the bier to come and take me away"[15] [Collodi/Lucas 46].

It is possibly easier to explain the presence of this dead girl with eyes and mouth closed and her arms folded (in the way corpses are positioned in a coffin) in a story that ends with the death of the main character: she could be an omen, a ghost who cannot help Pinocchio, or the inversion of a donor who points at the puppet's own helplessness when the murderers attack him. She is the fitting, albeit terrifying character straight out of a Gothic cautionary tale. When Collodi resumed the tale, after Pinocchio's hanging, the narrator needed to explain that the Girl with Blue (or Indigo) Hair "was none other than a very good fairy, who had lived beside that wood for more than a thousand years" (Collodi/Lucas 49).[16]

The Fairy has a magical relationship with the world of the dead, because she dies, again, in chapter 23, no doubt to elicit a sympathetic response and repentance in Pinocchio, but also, perhaps, to show Pinocchio that in order to grow up and to change, you need to lose a little of yourself, a little innocence, or even the joys of childhood. When Pinocchio meets her again, she is a woman: "I'm a woman: so much so that I could almost be your mother" (Collodi/Lucas 90). Pinocchio, unlike Peter Pan, is very happy to have his playfellow change into the mother that he never had: "I shall call you my mama. I've been longing to have a mother like all the other boys for such a long time" (Collodi Lucas 90).[17] But the Fairy will never change into Pinocchio's mother permanently to compose a fantasy of family (Geppetto and the Fairy never meet)—she will appear in Pinocchio's dream for the last time, change him into a boy, and then disappear, never to return (as the Fairy is only seen by Pinocchio, Mascialino argues that it may be a projection of Pinocchio's desire).

The Fairy's punitive pedagogy (to the point of psychological torture as when she leads Pinocchio to believe that she is dead) and her general coldness (she gives Pinocchio only one single kiss in his dream) associates her more with fairy-tale stepmothers than with generous fairies (Perella 20). Perhaps she is a bit of both, a magical creature travelling in a carriage pulled by mice in true Perraultian fashion and at the same time a parent using emotional blackmail and moral lessons to get her "son" to mend his ways. To further her purpose she does not mind lying and performing practical jokes as in the very theatrical scene when Pinocchio has a fever. One also gets the impression that the author may not always believe the Fairy's teachings, but she does represent a moral guide, and a moral spur to Pinocchio. In a novel that shows very little faith in institutionalized justice (only innocent people end up in prison), as Stewart-Steinberg has observed, "Pinocchio's movement is a figure for the essential paradox of modern pedagogy, the desire, that is, to have heteronomously imposed behavior transformed into obedience as an act of free will" (51–52).

The powerful female figures in the folktale and fairy tale (although there are surprisingly few Godmothers, mostly originating from Perrault [Elizabeth Cook 43]) have complex implications: they are by turns deadly, attractive, sensual, devious, cruel, comforting, punishing, and transforming—and the mystic Mother (see Rowe 330). Thus the Blue Fairy in *Pinocchio* can be read as substitute mother for Pinocchio—while Alice has no need of such a figure.

This shape-changing guide and moralist who is so dominant in *Pinocchio* seems to have been naturally associated in the English mind with the didactic, Christian tradition from Bunyan through Mrs. Barbauld and countless others (Dusinberre 56–57). George MacDonald provided some powerful examples, reminiscent of the Blue Fairy: Carpenter points out that the godmother in *Phantastes* (1858) (another book featuring a White Rabbit), is the first of a long line of such beings in MacDonald's stories, such as Irene, the great-great-grandmother in the Curdie books (*The Princess and the Goblin* [1872], *The Princess and Curdie* [1883]) and the North Wind in *At the Back of the North Wind* (1871). "Each is aged, indeed timeless; each can shrink to child-size, and the next moment stand giant-like and terrible" (Carpenter 75). William Raeper, MacDonald's biographer, suggests that at their best they "constitute the obverse of the harsh Calvinist male God whom MacDonald repudiated" (151).

It is in Charles Kingsley's *The Water Babies* (1863) that the closest English equivalent to Collodi's Blue Fairy appears (as noted by Jaques 216). The career of the abused chimney-sweep, Tom, is aided and controlled by a female spirit (described by Goldthwaite as one of the Blue Fairy's "sisters" [195]) which, or who, appears variously as an old Irish Woman, Mother Carey, and the twin teachers, the savage Mrs. Bedonebyasyoudid, and the distinctly erotic Mrs. Doasyouwouldbedoneby (Nelson 153) before being revealed, or not revealed, as something unfathomably mystic:

> "My name is written in my eyes, if you have eyes to see it there"[...].
> And her eyes flashed for one moment, clear, white, blazing light; but the children could not read her name; for they were dazzled, and hid their faces in their hands [Kingsley 181].

Perhaps needless to say, there has been a good deal of critical uncertainty—as we have seen with *Pinocchio*—as to what these figures mean: Goldthwaite, for example, reads Mrs. Doasyouwouldbedoneby as "'the fairy spirit of the Old Testament,' Mrs. Bedonebyasyoudid as "the fairy spirit of the New Testament" and the combined spirit as the Virgin Mary (67–68). Alderson sees them as Retribution and Consolation, while "Tom and Ellie's blinding by the light of the Ineffable at the end of the story has less to do with Christian revelation than with Goethe's 'chorus mysticus'" (xxv). However, quite what Kingsley meant by each aspect of the Fairy character is unimportant—as a friend of his observed: "His reverence for what is called 'consistency' was very limited" (Alderson xxiii).

Yet there is no question but that he meant *something*—that he was manipulating the folktale and fairy-tale elements for his own didactic agenda—and so it is not difficult to see that Carroll, who in his *Alice* books was irreverently "on the child's side," was likely to react against him. Carroll's cast of mind, logical and obsessive, was in great contrast to Kingsley's butterfly brain: not only did Carroll not attempt any moralizing but, as an inveterate parodist, he subverted Kingsley's attempts at it. Thus the fact that any equivalent of the Irish Woman or the Blue Fairy is not found (overtly) in *Alice*, demonstrates the contrasting, but fundamentally similar attitudes of Collodi and Carroll to the folktale "roots" of their stories.

It has been suggested that Carroll was not drawing on traditional tales, despite the fact that he referred to *Alice* several times in his diaries and correspondence as a fairy tale (Susina 25–28)—as "a desperate attempt to strike out some new line of fairy-lore" for the three little girls "hungry for news of fairy-land" (Collingwood 1899b: 165, 168). Of course, Carroll was not making the same nice distinctions that I am between fairy tale and fantasy, and as Goldthwaite observed, "Whatever Dodgson may have construed 'fairy-tale' to mean, he did not write one" (154). What he *was* doing, it may be plausibly argued, was gently satirizing the attempts at writing new fairy tales, based on old lore; this is not unlikely, as *Alice* grew from its personal beginnings to an intricate texture of parody and satire, and Carroll was nothing if not combative.

Thus the mythic female forces manipulated by MacDonald and Kingsley are reduced to strident but ineffectual figures—the mad Queen of Hearts, the bullying Duchess and the didactic Red Queen; instead of wisdom or morality, they all lecture nonsense at Alice. The Red and White Queens may well be parodies of Mrs. Doasyouwouldbedoneby and Mrs. Bedonebyasyoudid, while the shape-changer of *The Water Babies* becomes the Cheshire-Cat, grinning at Kingsley (and MacDonald). Carroll not only takes any effective magical power from the Cat but also, as we have seen, makes him positively *un*helpful. The other, at least potential shape-changer, the Caterpillar, is equally unhelpful, and—perhaps not incidentally—is blue (Carroll 2009: 39).

Knoepflmacher (1998) sees this period in English literary fairy tales as a conversation (MacDonald, Kingsley and Carroll knew each other or each other's work). He notes of *At the Back of the North Wind* that "Given MacDonald's close personal and literary relations with both Ruskin and Lewis Carroll, it hardly seems unwarranted to read [the first scene in which North Wind appears] as a friendly corrective to their fearful ambivalence about female power" (231). Equally, he sees Jean Ingelow's *Mopsa the Fairy* (1869), with its female figures—the powerful Albatross, the soft-hearted apple-woman, the Fairy Queen, the malicious Gypsy woman, and Mopsa herself—as a commentary on Carroll: "Ingelow prefers to insist on the irrevocability of loss and change" (292).

As we have seen, the literary status of *Alice* and *Pinocchio* is ambiguous: they are both of the folktale and the fairy tale and in opposition to them. They use and subvert their sources, and yet have become, in world culture, folktales and fairy tales themselves. Herbert Read observed that "*Alice* has a suppressed background of culture which a true fairy tale never has. *Alice* will always delight our particular civilisation; it will hardly become part of our traditional folklore, like 'The Three Bears'" (quoted in Goldthwaite 94). And yet it is the very singularity of the backgrounds of both *Alice* and *Pinocchio*—cultural, historical, and personal—that has proved the catalyst for their universal recognition. Similarly, Philip Pullman has noted that "There is no psychology in a fairy tale. The characters have little interior life[...]. One might almost say that the characters in a fairy tale are not actually conscious" (quoted in Warner 116). Both *Alice* and *Pinocchio* break this "rule," developing their protagonists' characters into sympathetic beings within the constraints of the folktale and fairy-tale traditions. The tropes of tradition are seen through the lenses of different national contexts, and illuminate many aspects of social and literary history.

But *Alice* and *Pinocchio* are also fantasies, tapping into psychological and cultural areas that move beyond the traditional boundaries of the folktale and the fairy tale. Reading the books in that broader context leads us into equally rewarding areas of investigation, as shall be seen in the next chapter.

5. Fantasy and Form in *Alice* and *Pinocchio*

Concepts of Fantasy in England and Italy

Even more noticeably than when one attempts to define the fairy tale (or *fiaba*), looking for a literary consensus on a one-dimensional definition of fantasy appears a formidable, if not impossible, task. Fantasy is a genre (or a mode) that can overlap with several other genres, such as fairy tale, fable, horror, science fiction, Gothic, and so on (actually, the fact that it overlaps with so many genres is one of the few characteristics that all definitions agree upon). In the previous chapter, I argued that the *Alice* books and *Pinocchio* are hybrid books that inherited many folktale and fairy-tale tropes precisely when both nations were producing a stream of literary fairy tales. At the same time, these classics helped create a tradition of fantasy fiction (even if at the time of their publication, this term was not used in the sense that we use it today). The fantasy tradition that they inaugurated was, as will be explained later, a tradition that incorporated elements of the *Bildung* in that it allowed its characters a degree of agency and development, and explored questions of identity that the fairy tale is not capable of exploring.

To make things even more complicated, Anglophone and Italian critics do not share a common critical language when it comes to defining fantasy, and so, inevitably, there is no critical agreement as to which books belong to the fantasy genre (most Italian critics would not hesitate to classify both *Alice* and *Pinocchio* as fairy tales—*fiabe*). The comparison between these different critical positions has been explained very effectively by Lindsay Myers in her book on Italian fantasy (*Making the Italians. Poetics and Politics of Italian Children's Fantasy*, 2012) and more recently in the revised and expanded Italian edition (2017). At the core of this difference is the fact that *Italian* critics of *Italian* literature based in Italy tend to use the term "fantasy" exclusively for works set in secondary worlds, such as the novels by Tolkien, Lewis or even Rowling (and their imitators), which contain elements of medieval romance and which draw heavily on the past for their context, content, and style (Sullivan 2005: 445). However, as an *Italian* scholar working on *English* Literature from an Anglophone critical perspective, I use the term fantasy 1) to describe Anglophone texts which would be probably described as fairy-tales [*fiabe*] in the Italian tradition but as fantasy in the Anglophone tradition (such as *Alice*) as well as to describe 2) Italian texts, such as *Pinocchio*, which are generally considered as belonging to the fairy-tale genre from the Italian perspective, but which in the UK are almost always classified as fantasy (even if, as I argue in this chapter, *Pinocchio* and the *Alice* books, cannot ultimately be satisfactorily classified exclusively in terms of *one* genre).

Interestingly, Ermanno Detti, in his Introduction to volume 26 of *The Lion and Unicorn* (2002), an issue dedicated to Italian children's literature, insists that in Italian children's literature "modern literary genres" do not exist (144). He sees most works as falling within the categories of fairy tale, short story, or nursery rhyme:

> However, *although Italian authors do not write detective fiction, horror stories, fantasy tales*, or romantic fiction, we can detect upon close examination that certain literary tendencies have been consolidating themselves in Italy that begin to resemble modern literary genres [my italics] [145].

Although the Italian literary market is still dominated by translations of fantasy books from English, there has always been a native tradition of fantasy. Myers has charted the evolution of Italian children's fantasy from the unification to the present day by applying a traditional Anglophone approach to fantasy for children that had been labeled, variously, as belonging to the fairy tale or adventure genre; by doing this, she has, quite simply, recovered a whole tradition from obscurity. By analyzing and classifying these texts into coherent narrative groups, she has opened the door to their inclusion into an international fantasy canon, a canon from which they had hitherto been excluded by virtue of the fact that some Italian critics had insisted (and still insist) that they are not fantasies. She has shown, among other things, that Italy has a long-standing tradition of fantasy which Anglophone critics would probably label "domestic" (see

Smith). It is obvious that any comparative study of children's fantasy needs to take into account these cultural differences, but at the same time it needs to move beyond these critical barriers to find a common ground at least in terms of the terminology that it employs.

Neither *Alice* nor *Pinocchio* fit comfortably into the broad categories of high and low (or domestic) fantasy—but there has been no shortage of critical subcategories into which they might be slotted. Tolkien, of course, regarded fantasy as a *characteristic* of the fairy tale (Tolkien 43); Anne Swinfen (1984) distinguishes between animal, time, dual world, visionary, secondary world and primary world fantasy; Farah Mendlesohn (2008) lists portal-quest, intrusion, immersive, and liminal fantasy; Brian Attebery argues that fantasy is a "fuzzy set" (Levy and Mendlesohn 3)—although what constitutes the "core" of fantasy is naturally located in a specific time and place; the editors of *The Ultimate Encyclopedia of Fantasy* suggest nine categories of fantasy in terms of when they first emerged: fairy tales, animal, Arthurian, Arabian nights, Chinoiserie, lost-race, humorous, sword and sorcery, and heroic, or high (Pringles 19–37).

These strategies of definition are reflected in Myers's sub-categorization of types of Italian fantasy, which follows a strict chronological order, linking the subcategories to the historical and political contexts of specific decades. As mentioned in chapter 2, *Pinocchio*, "catalyst and model" (Myers 2012: 50) started the "Monello fantasy," a subgenre characterized by social satire (about institutions such as the school and judiciary systems), fairy-tale and fable elements, "picking and choosing aspects from these traditions and blending them with the popular plot" (Myers 2012: 50) to articulate moral lessons. The Monello fantasies of the first decade of the twentieth century "subtly overturn established, hierarchical structures, exposing the weaknesses of the contemporary Italian state and wilfully undermining its authority" (Myers 2012: 64). So, once again, the "international" formal elements of fantasy (such as dystopian spaces, or bodily metamorphosis) interact with the historical context in which *Pinocchio* was written, and the difficulties and general inadequacy of post-unification Italy in taking care of its children. Similarly, the instability of forms that we find in the *Alice* books (variously defined as "domestic fantasy" or "portal-quest fantasy" [Mendlesohn 42–43]) and the topsy-turvyness of Alice's world may be better understood if we bear in mind the impact of Darwinism on English society and colonial explorations—which Carroll may have satirized in *The Hunting of the Snark*. *Alice* and *Pinocchio* are very good examples of the way transnational fantasy forms and tropes can combine with different national self-representations to produce works that incorporate ideas of the nation in a way that is no different from, and often is even more powerful than, realistic fiction: Alice and her Wonderland are as representative of England and Englishness as is any novel by Dickens, and Pinocchio is as Italian as are any of the protagonists of Manzoni's *I promessi Sposi* [The Betrothed], a nineteenth-century novel set in seventeenth-century Lombardy and still firmly established in the school curriculum in Italy (unlike *Pinocchio*). But that, of course, is another story.

International Fantasy Tropes

A lot has been written on the attempted suppression of the folk and fairy tale by the religious and evangelical tradition of the late eighteenth century in England (see chapter 4). Of course, the giants and ogres and banshees and, more especially, their associated aura of fear and violence had never gone away. The children of Mrs. Trimmer and the tractarians wanted their readers to live in a world where deprivation and punishment, and the tropes of distortion and death, were ever present. As Maria Tatar noted, folktales were "ever adaptable":

> They could easily be harnessed into service as stories for children so long as a few key changes were made—changes that divested the tales of their earthy humor, burlesque twists, and bawdy turns of phrase to make room for moral instruction and spiritual guidance [1992: 8].

Therefore it should not be a surprise that in fantasy, elements of the old tales, mediated by their national and local contexts—complexly cautious satire (*Alice*) or free-wheeling politics (*Pinocchio*)—resurface too. Much work has been done on the symbols and structures and genres connecting folktales and fairy tales with fantasy (some of which has been discussed in chapter 4). Fantasies across the world—and fantasies for children—share a remarkable number of characteristics and a case can be made for the derivation of modern fantasy from ur-narratives of myth and folklore. Here I would like to look at the most common, darker, psychological elements and the tropes that carry them.

The tropes that I have chosen to look at in this chapter are the most universal, and may well be at odds with general expectations of what constitutes appropriate material for contemporary, or ideal, childhood. Certainly they were unexceptional to the English and Italians of the nineteenth century: death and violence are central, sometimes literal, sometimes threatening, often pervasive; threats to the integrity of the self or the body—metamorphosis, distortion, displacement, and loss of identity—can be radical or subtle; and all of these, at different cultural moments, have manifested themselves in upside-down worlds (inversions, mirrors) ranging from the satiric to the horrific—and dystopian spaces (the mode of choice of much contemporary young adult fiction).

Alice and *Pinocchio* obviously share much of this ancestry: all of these elements are present in both texts, although they manifest themselves in remarkably contrasting ways. Overall, a lot of things happen *to* Pinocchio, while a lot of things happen *around* Alice—which may be a metaphor for the whole issue of cultural differences between them. Both books are suffused with questions, which are related to the specific historical context in which the works were produced and some of which are universal: the question of adult-child relationships, the power and suppression of the most violent aspects of children's fantasy, and the extent to which children's fantasy fiction can be covert therapy for its authors. As Attebery has pointed out of myth itself: "The idea of myth as something timeless and universal [has given way] to an understanding of particular myths as dynamic and culturally specific" (20–21).

This analysis may seem to dwell on the negative, but both *Alice* and *Pinocchio* are, essentially, positive texts, which take up cudgels, as it were, for childhood and liberty of thought. Their shared journey towards body normalization is resolved (as in many, but by no means all, folktales and fairy tales) in a stabilized, if not necessarily happy, ending.

Death and Violence

Death and violence are pervasive in folktales and fairy tales as well as in fantasy fiction: there is a strong cautionary element in folktales that I have discussed earlier in relation to *Pinocchio* and *Alice*. As Tatar has observed about the Grimms, "in fairy tales, nearly every character, from the most hardened criminal to the Virgin Mary, is capable of cruel behavior" (1992: 5). In these narratives, child abuse and dysfunctional families are the norm rather than the exception, and curiosity and disobedience are evils that deserve very harsh punishments. Folktales are the receptacles of the wisdom of another age, and use fear to acculturate children into social roles and desirable behaviors. Death and violence can be used to trigger the action, such as the death of Cinderella's mother or the abandonment of Hansel and Gretel in the woods, but actual acts of violence tend to be mechanical, and described unemotionally—as is the norm for the folktale—from the outside. No description of actual pain is given and the victims of the violence rarely show any psychological reaction to their suffering: the girl in the Grimms' "The Maiden without hands" who has her hands chopped off by her father, for example, just continues her part in the story with stumps. Death can be reversed in the same mechanical way, as in Snow White and the way she "resurrects" after the fragment of poisoned apple is dislodged from her throat, or the Grimms' "Fitcher's Bird" (a version of the Bluebeard type AT 312) which ends with the last wife assembling her sisters' chopped pieces (head, legs, arms) and bringing them to life again.

Not so in the world of fantasy, where death and violence are more complex phenomena, most notably in contemporary fantasy fiction in which the central hero often takes over the formidable task of saving the world, and casualties in the war between good and evil are inevitable, but suitably mourned (as in Tolkien, Rowling, or Pullman). The protagonists of *Alice* and *Pinocchio* do not have to save the world, but the cautionary element of death and violence is accompanied by instances of physical abuse and death which resonate more deeply than in simple folktale "mechanics." Violence, which comes from those adults that children should be protected by, is often gratuitous, and its effects on the main characters are generally described in detail, as happens in *Pinocchio*.

In *Alice* there is a degree of eccentricity in the way violence and death are ubiquitous: nonsense and humor tend to deflate horrific acts that are often announced but not carried through. It is not just the Red Queen who would like to behead everybody—we should not forget that during the trial, in chapter 11, the king himself intimidates the Hatter with death threats: "'Give your evidence,' said the King; 'and don't be nervous, or I'll have you executed on the spot'" (Carroll 2009: 99). And, a few lines later: "'Give your evidence,' the King repeated angrily, 'or I'll have you executed, whether you are nervous or not'" (Carroll 2009: 99).

The Knave faces execution for having stolen the Queen's tarts, but what appears to be a disproportionate punishment may be better understood if we take into account its historical context, and the large number of crimes that were punishable by death in Victorian times. Abate has illustrated the way in which capital punishment was a controversial and heated subject for debate at the time Carroll was writing: "British citizens were doing more than simply reconsidering the broad issue of which offences ought to be punishable by death during the Victorian era: they were also reexamining their specific practice of public execution" (37). She then goes on to argue that in *Alice* empty threats lose their power, but I would be more inclined to think that, on the contrary, they build an atmosphere of insecurity, of continuous danger, a sense that something bad and violent *may* happen, and that some of the threats could be more real than empty.

This sense of vague, impending and unpredictable danger and vulnerability surrounds Alice and worries her constantly: when she is afraid of being eaten, when she feels lonely and cries, or when she shrinks so rapidly that she is afraid that she may disappear: "She felt a little nervous about this; 'for it might end, you know,' said Alice to herself, 'in my going out altogether, like a candle'" (Carroll 2009: 14). After she realizes that the fan she is holding in chapter 2 has the effect of making her smaller, she tells herself that it was a narrow escape, "a good deal frightened at the sudden change, but very glad to find herself still in existence" (Carroll 2009: 20). After all, she is lucky to have survived, as in the course of only the first few chapters she falls down an apparently endless hole, shrinks, grows huge, shrinks again, falls into a pool, grows, gets trapped in a house, is threatened with burning, shrinks, encounters an enormous puppy and is afraid of being eaten, grows again, is attacked by a pigeon, encounters a violent kitchen, and so on. Her hostile environment produces mysterious changes in her body, the adult figures she talks to are useless and aggressive, and the stories and poems scattered in the books that she is unable to reproduce correctly are replete with death and violence. I have already mentioned the relevance of the Darwinian struggle for survival; there appears to have been an awareness, on the part of the Victorians, that violence was ingrained in primitive societies and that this substratum was still, in a way, lurking in supposedly civilized society: "The tendency to perceive violence as underlying the foundations of all civilized society was implicit in Victorian anthropological and ethnological studies of primitive cultures" (Feldmann 112).

The *Alice* books are full of death jokes and black humor. For example, in the chapter "Looking-Glass Insects" the Gnat relates the sad fate of the Bread-and-butter-fly, who lives on weak tea with cream, and, not being able to find any, inevitably, dies: "'But that must happen very often,' Alice remarked thoughtfully. 'It always happens,' said the Gnat" (Carroll 2009: 154). When Alice talks to the flowers, they note that she is "beginning to fade" (Carroll 2009: 141). Alice is seven years and six months old, and when she says to Humpty Dumpty, the academic philosopher, that one can't help growing older, he replies, "*One* can't, perhaps, but *two* can. With proper assistance you might have left off at seven" (Carroll 2009: 188). The fact that brutality is *comic*, surreal, and nonsensical, is what keeps the highly emotional side of violence at bay (and this may well be a characteristic of the English national character even now—burying emotion under humor [See Fox]).

As Kincaid has observed, "much of this aggression [...] it is true, surfaces in laughter and therefore need not be admitted consciously" (93). And, after all, even the gryphon seems to believe that the Queen's menaces are *fun*: "they never execute anybody, you know" (Carroll 2009: 83). And yet, violence and brutality are not things that many adult readers might want to confront in a children's book. It is interesting that Virginia Woolf, of all people, chose to underline the joyous element of *Alice*: "Only Lewis Carroll has shown us the world upside down as a child sees it, and has made us laugh as children laugh, irresponsibly" (79). Similarly, *Pinocchio*'s dark side has been occasionally neglected: according to Margery Fisher, for example "Few doses of moral medicine have ever been administered with such a richly flavoured spoonful of jam" (Fisher 12). And yet, the flavored spoonful of jam can be bitter and even poisonous: *Pinocchio*'s violence is dark and realistic. Unlike Alice, Pinocchio is led astray and is the victim of deceit and even sadism, even if he is never really evil. The Fairy's behavior, especially when she pretends to be dead and drives Pinocchio almost to despair, is tantamount to psychological abuse. "The story of Pinocchio," Manganelli has written, "is a story of abuse and love[...]. Everyone tries to kill Pinocchio, but only Geppetto and the Fairy can transmit the childish horror of desperation" (102, my translation).

When it comes to physical abuse, one is really spoilt for choice in Collodi's book. The Cat and the Fox are Pinocchio's assassins: first they hit him with "two horrible great long knives as sharp as razors" (Collodi/ Lucas 46), and then they hang him. After waiting three hours for him to die, they leave him to his agony:

> In the meantime a strong north wind had blown up and, howling and roaring violently, it buffeted the poor hanging puppet hither and thither, making him swing about furiously like the clapper of a celebratory bell. The swinging caused him severe pain and the noose, growing tighter around his neck all the time, was choking him.
> Little by little his eyes grew dim, and although he could feel death approaching, he kept hoping that at any moment some good soul would happen by to help him. He waited and waited, and when he realized that no one, but no one, was coming, his thoughts at last turned to his poor father ... and half-dead, he murmured, "Oh, my dear pa! If only you were here...."
> He had no breath left to say anything else. He closed his eyes, opened his mouth, straightened his legs and, giving a great shudder, hung there as if frozen stiff [Collodi/ Lucas 47–48].

Violence, in *Pinocchio*, is often connected to greed for money, and it is this lust for money that lies at the heart of the child-trafficking being carried out by the book's most hateful child torturer—the Omino—a figure whom the narrator observes "had made a mint of money and had become a millionaire" (Collodi/Lucas 137). It is this round-faced man who lures the children towards the Land of Toys, and then sells them after they have transformed into donkeys. His violence is of the most disturbing kind (he has been compared to Fagin in Oliver Twist [Perella 14]), as when he bites the ear off a rebellious donkey twice—on the second occasion we are told that "he took the top half of the other ear clean off" (Collodi/Lucas 126). The extreme poverty of the peasant who can't afford to feed his child is contrasted here with the greed of the child abuser.

And yet, even in the middle of the tragedy of animal debasement, there is a moment in which Pinocchio and Lucignolo look at each other sporting donkey's ears, and can't help laughing, as children are known to be able to do, when they are together, even in the middle of tragedy:

> And then a scene unfolded which might seem incredible if it wasn't true. That's to say that when Pinocchio and Candle-Wick saw each other afflicted with the same disaster, instead of being ashamed and grieved, they began to make faces at each other's enormously overgrown ears and, after a good deal of rudeness, they broke into a hearty laugh.
>
> They laughed and laughed and laughed so much that they had to hold their sides [Collodi/Lucas 134].[2]

Sharing the grotesque and hilarious side of an unsettling experience with a companion is one of the ways in which children can resist tragedy. Later in the book, however, when Pinocchio is whipped, lamed and left alone in an exploitative world of adults it becomes impossible for him (or the narrator) to reframe disgrace as fun.

Danger of death (and this means not so much death jokes but *real* near-death experiences) is omnipresent in *Pinocchio*, a figure who risks death by fire, air, and water (Gasparini 96). In Collodi's world, even a boys' fight by the sea can turn into tragedy. Eugenio is hit by a treatise on Arithmetic: "he turned as white as a sheet, and uttered only these words: 'Oh dear, help me ... I'm dying!...'" (Collodi/Lucas 99).[3] Collodi in the next sentence uses the highly expressive word "morticino" to refer to him: it means "little corpse" or "little dead boy." But Eugenio will not die, nor will Arlecchino, the dog Alidoro, the tuna fish, Geppetto, and the Fairy. At the end of the day, not many die in *Pinocchio*: even the Cricket comes back as a ghostlike character. The only human who dies tragically is Lucignolo. In this book of dangers and last-minute rescues, it is painfully clear that from such a harsh experience of abuse and trauma, one cannot come back whole: not even fantasy can allow that.

Resilience and resistance are Alice's and Pinocchio's most remarkable qualities. The English girl, in this power struggle between adults and children, in which children are not protected, learns to say no to the unacceptable (Gubar argues that Carroll conceives identity formation in terms of denial—she sees it as a tool for the shaping of self [120]). Her rebelliousness is that of the confident, well-fed, and well-educated middle-class girl, while Pinocchio's is that of the Italian street boy, but their attitudes towards these violent and dangerous worlds are very similar. As Gillian Beer has noted, "growing is the universal experience undergone and forgotten by us all" (2016: 6)—Pinocchio and Alice, in an amplified and fictionalized way, share the resilience that comes, quite simply, from being *children.*

The ability of these books to transcend their very precise geographical areas of origin and become universal and popular patterns of childhood, may well lie in the dark side of fantasy, which they so thoroughly explore, and in the way these characters devise strategies to keep darkness and violence, ultimately, at a safe distance: humor, laughter, and seeing the grotesque side of adult madness or cruelty. The darkness in *Pinocchio* and *Alice* differs in form but not in essence. Both characters resist the threats of violent fantasy worlds and violent adult figures, but the books do not hide the violence, although protective adult readers, or adults in denial, may not acknowledge it.

The power and the appeal of the global fantasy of *Alice* and *Pinocchio*, then, may not lie in their vague "timelessness"—could there be such a thing. Rather the reverse: the dark side, the ambiguous side really holds the power. I would argue that it is this powerful darkness—rather than any comfortable closure, that both overrides and feeds off local and national characteristics.

Metamorphosis, Bodily Distortion, Displacement and Loss of Identity

Metamorphosis, body displacement, and grotesque distortion are the bedrock of fantasy, and fantasy has a tendency to dissolve structures, and to lean towards a state of entropy (Jackson 72–73). Fantasy is one of the textual spaces where "the morphological normativity that works in the established ideas of normality as anthropocentric [...] best exemplified by Leonardo's figure of the naked [...] body which allegedly constitutes the measure of all things" (Braidotti 123) is constantly challenged and interrogated. Although metamorphosis can enact an adventure that takes the protagonists out of their bodies rather than out of their worlds, mutations and alterations of children's bodies can often be found in dystopian spaces within fantasy locations. In the nineteenth century, examples range from Alice shrinking, elongating and almost disappearing in Wonderland (a land with a distinctly dystopic flavor), to Flora's deformed and object-shaped guests at her birthday party in the Land of Nowhere in Christina Rossetti's *Speaking Likenesses* (1874), to the grimy chimney sweep Tom becoming a water baby in the clear stream as agent of spiritual cleansing in Kingsley's *The Water Babies* (1863), to Pinocchio changing into a donkey in the land of Toys.

There are spaces in nineteenth-century children's fantasy that appear to "trigger" change in the characters' bodies. Even if the White Knight in *Through the Looking-Glass* appears to insist on the mutual independence of mind and body ("What does it matter where my body happens to be?[...] My mind goes on working all the same" [Carroll 2009: 216]), in fantasy it does matter where bodies happen to be. Especially when they are unstable, displaced, scarred, dismembered, or duplicated, they appear to defeat the mind-body dualism and end up dictating their own agenda to the intellectual self (which is an experience that humans know only too well). The very concept of transformation, or metamorphosis, refuses the idea of separation between the self and other selves: as Ted Hughes has put it, in his translation of Ovid's *Metamorphoses*, in the beginning "nature wore only one mask, since called Chaos. A huge agglomeration of upset [...] the total arsenal of entropy already at war within it" (Hughes 3).

The *Alice* books and *Pinocchio*, in different contexts and literary traditions, refashion the tropes of bodily distortion and metamorphosis and produce vulnerable bodies. The body *in itself* can be said to be a trope as we cannot escape thinking about the body in terms of representation—as Moira Gatens observed, "my experience of the body, for me, is just as socially constructed as my experience of the body of the other" (Gatens 35). And of course, when we talk about characters' bodies and their transformations, as Hillman and Maude observe:

> there are no bodies in literature. Not only there is no obvious way for the concrete materiality of the body to be fully present in or on the written page; even more profoundly, there would seem on the face of it to be an apparent mutual exclusivity of the body and language [3].

As characters as well as bodies (the little girl, the puppet) Alice and Pinocchio are in constant flux as culture refashions their bodies all the time in illustrations, adaptations, and different media. Wonderland is populated by grotesque eccentrics—who also abound in Collodi's book, although there is nothing in Carroll to match one of the most hateful child exploiters in all literature, the slimy and sinister Omino who can bite off the ear of one of the boys-turned-donkeys and then smile, "as soft and unctuous as a pat of butter, with a little red-apple face"[4] (Collodi/Lucas 123). Eccentricities are, of course, distortions from the norm, and Alice and Pinocchio suffer from both distortions of themselves and distortions of the worlds around them. Sizes change, and things morph into other things. Unlike Alice, Pinocchio changes his corporeal identity quite dramatically—Alice changes too, but for all her distortions, she is still recognizable (at least to the reader in Tenniel's drawings) and to herself (perhaps the Pigeon would not agree).

As we have seen, *Alice* and *Pinocchio* are generic hybrids and hybridity is a major feature of fantasy, as magical transformations are the substance of dreams, myth, fairy tale and fantasy. However, unlike the characters in Ovidian myths, the victims of transformations in nineteenth-century fairy tale are rooted in magic, and are usually restored to their original forms at the end of the tale (like the Frog Prince, or the Beast) after a curse, a punishment, or a transgression. As Italo Calvino has put it, fairy tale characters "must follow the common fate of submitting to enchantments, that is, of being subjected to complex and unknown forces, of making the effort to free oneself from them as a basic duty, together with the duty to free others" (1983: 16, my translation).

In fantasy fiction, transformations can be permanent, as in *Pinocchio*, or the baby turned into a pig in *Alice*, and/or they may be accompanied by an inner transformation—fantasy makes a different use of the cautionary element which brings about psychological change—or can be triggered by a psychological change. In the case of Pinocchio, he needs to overcome his gullibility, to establish where his loyalties lie and to "develop an ethical system of his own" (Kuznets 72)—for it is only when he achieves this, that he can be turned into a human boy. But the cautionary element is still present, as it is present in Ovid's *Metamorphoses*, as a punishment that is appropriate to the transgression, or a passion or a human failing that brings about the rage (or the compassion) of the Gods operating the change. In the same way as Lycaon is turned into a wolf for his wolfish behavior, Pinocchio is turned into a donkey for his inability to submit to the learning process. As Daphne is turned by the gods mercifully into a laurel to escape rape, so Pinocchio is changed back from donkey to puppet to avoid drowning.

When the Lion asks Alice whether she is animal, a vegetable, or a mineral, as in the Victorian parlor game (Carroll 2009: 206), he seems to believe in a rigid taxonomy of species that Ovid, as well as Darwin, did not conceive of as definitive. Alice is constantly looking for a guiding principle in Wonderland, only to be disappointed. She lives in a metamorphic world of flux where babies turn into pigs, and queens into kittens or sheep. As Jaques has noted, Alice stumbles "upon creatures that seem to exist solely to sever species boundaries and problematize the unthinking human use of the animal kingdom" (47). In the book, every attempt to define categories, or a hierarchy of species, is doomed to failure: Alice is classified as a monster, or serpent, or a wilting flower. Everything is mutable in her world, and the animate can turn into the inanimate in an Ovidian as well as Darwinian crossing of the boundaries between species. Change and mutability are part of life, and the substance of her dream.

What could Pinocchio reply to the Lion's attempt at classification? He shifts between the vegetable, the animal, and the human—vegetable (wood) and human being (boy) being the most extreme polarizations. What is Pinocchio made up of? In a century replete with mutants and hybrids (one needs only to think of the creature in *Frankenstein* [1818] or Olympia in Hoffmann's "The Sandman" [1816]) Pinocchio is constantly wavering between puppet and human status—and this hybrid nature is what characterizes him from the very beginning when he is given a human creator and a "father." He has to skip all stages of development as he passes from being a log of wood to being a "son," and yet, "while Pinocchio does not come into the human world trailing clouds of glory, he is not an example of Locke's tabula rasa either" (Kuznets 70). The text builds the illusion of a past of bonding experiences between father and son. The paradox is that Geppetto is disappointed at the failure of his educational project only minutes after he has finished carving: "wretched child! Just think of all the trouble I've taken to make him into a good puppet"[5] (Collodi/Lucas 11). Interestingly, he has also conveniently forgotten that his original plan was to use the puppet to make money and see the world—it is as if Pinocchio had been attributed an "extratextual past." When he meets the puppets (again, shortly after having been "created"), they immediately recognize him as a brother:

> "Divine Providence! Do I dream or do I wake? Yet over yonder that is surely Pinocchio!..."
> "Yes, it's really Pinocchio!" shouted Punchinello.
> "Yes, it's him all right!" screamed Signora Rosalba, peeping out from behind the scenery[...].
> "It's our brother Pinocchio!" [...]
> "Pinocchio, come up here with me!" called Harlequin, "Come and embrace your wooden brothers and sisters!"[6] [Collodi/Lucas 27].

Pinocchio, unlike Harlequin or Pulcinella, is not a staple character of the puppet theater (although, strictly speaking, we are talking about wooden marionettes with strings), so this recognition scene presupposes a previous knowledge that is not supplied in the text. And yet Pinocchio appears less human, and smaller in size, when he is welcomed in the puppets' theater. In late nineteenth-century Tuscany, as in most areas of Italy, there was a well-established puppets' and marionettes' tradition for adults as well as children, both as a popular street theater in city squares and fairs, and as a more sophisticated entertainment in the houses of the upper classes, as testified by travelers and contemporary scholars. The first *Storia dei burattini* was published in Florence in 1884 (by Pietro Ferrigni, one of Collodi's best friends, whose *nom de plume* was Yorick), only one year after *Pinocchio* was published in volume form (Rak 83). We also know that in Piazza della Signoria in Florence (then called "Piazza del Granduca") there was a permanent puppet theatre, which Collodi would no doubt have found it difficult to miss in his daily rambles. In Collodi's *Giannettino*, the schoolbook that preceded *Pinocchio*, several pages are devoted to this form of entertainment (see Marcheschi 1993).

There are all sorts of physical transformations in fantasy, from total transformation into a completely different being to a partial one, from lower forms to higher forms or the reverse. Characters can have different levels of awareness of the change, as they experiment on their own bodies the instability of forms in reality: "metamorphosis is the most drastic and most completely objective of the changes that can produce fantasy" (Irwin 104). The difference between *Alice* and *Pinocchio* is that in Wonderland the metamorphic principle seems to be operating at random: food and drink can cause changes in shape and size, but also metaphors can become real and the inanimate turn into the animate for no reason at all (such as the pack of cards turning into courtiers and servants), or to make a point, such as the pudding that talks. In *Pinocchio* metamorphosis is connected to moral rules. As has been noted, "in traditional children's stories authors frequently employ unpleasurable metamorphoses in a rather heavy-handed coercive manner as disempowering punishments imposed on the fictive child in order to enhance the child's moral development" (Lassén-Seger 2006: 62). So, in Collodi's world, if you do not want to go to school and learn, you turn into a donkey (as the marmot tells Pinocchio. "It's long written in the Decrees of Wisdom that all those unwilling children who take a dislike to books, schools and teachers and spend their days in amusements, games and entertainments must sooner or later turn into little asses"[7] Collodi/Lucas 131); if you steal, your punishment is to work as a guard dog, but if you are hard-working and generous, you are rewarded with a human body, as has been discussed in the previous chapter. In this

Pinocchio resembles literary fairy tales and fantasies of the Victorian age (such as Kingsley's *The Water Babies*) in which the educational value of punishment is reasserted, and there is a "marked insistence upon the efficacy of punishment as therapy" (Gordon 143).

However, this is not the instant, conventional and unsurprising transformation of folk or fairy tale with no questions asked. It is a process of which Pinocchio is painfully aware—a slow process. It starts with the slow but steady growth of donkey's ears, then the impossibility of standing upright, accompanied by "weeping and swaying," as in this scene with Lucignolo:

> They both doubled up, their hands and feet on the ground and, going on all fours, they began to walk and run about the room. And while they ran their arms turned into legs with hooves, their faces lengthened and became muzzles, and their backs grew a covering of light grey fur brindled with black[...]. The worst and most humiliating moment was when they felt a tail growing behind. Then, overcome by their shame and misery, they tried to weep and lament their fate.
> If only they had not tried! Instead of moans and groans, they emitted an ass's braying and, braying resoundingly, they chorused together: "*Hee-haw, hee-haw, hee-haw*"[8] [Collodi/Lucas 135].

Later, even as a donkey eating his hay, Pinocchio thinks with longing about human food, and the pain that he experiences when he is whipped "so hard that his fur came off"[9] (Collodi/Lucas 139) and lamed, is real. His body is vulnerable to his human master's whims—the last of which is to turn the donkey into skin for his drum. The narrator is very straightforward about Pinocchio's fate: "I do know that right from the start Pinocchio had a very hard and cruel life"[10] (Collodi/Lucas 137).

In *Pinocchio* the mirror is the means by which the puppet can witness his own transformations, but only when his puppet status is altered, as when he changes into a donkey:

> He went searching for a mirror at once to see what he looked like, but, not finding a mirror, he filled the washbasin with water and looking into it he saw something he would never have wished to see: what he saw was his image adorned with a magnificent pair of ass's ears[11] [Collodi/Lucas 130].

Or when he is transformed from puppet into a boy:

> Afterwards he went to look at himself in the mirror, and he looked like someone else. He no longer saw reflected there the usual image of a wooden marionette, but he saw the handsome reflection of an intelligent and lively young boy with dark brown hair, blue eyes and a festive expression of happiness and merriment[12] [Collodi/Lucas 168].

It appears that Pinocchio only needs a mirror when he loses his puppet shape. At the precise moment he feels that he is losing his "primary" identity and substance (Gabriele 45), he needs to "double check" with a mirror. In *Pinocchio* mirror surfaces offer a reflection of the body, which signals that the perceived change is real, while in *Alice* it is more of a distorting agent—it produces a world of reversibility and inversions, a world of mirror-images which can disfigure the originals.

Carroll's use of the mirror in *Through the Looking-Glass* is complex and paradoxical. On the one hand, it is a straightforward portal into another world; as Lori Campbell notes, "From ancient Egyptian and Greek mythology to medieval romance and Shakespearean drama [...] the notion of accessing a space beyond the everyday has captured the imagination" (5) and the device is "a stock convention" seen in such books as Morris's *The Wood Beyond the World* (a cleft in the wall), Barrie's *Peter and Wendy* (nursery window), Lewis's *The Lion, the Witch and the Wardrobe*, and beyond. More importantly, "By drawing our gaze to the exact places where consciousness and un-consciousness meet, the portal spotlights the intricate human processes by which we navigate the world, ourselves, and the relationship between the two" (Campbell 2).

Thus the mirror itself is far from innocent, and humankind has had a long and uncomfortable relationship with it. As Sabine Melchior-Bonnet has observed in *The Mirror. A History*:

> Our relationship with the mirror may reveal itself to be empty and fatal, but it is initially seductive because it draws its brilliance from elsewhere in the Platonic paradise—the world of symmetry and connections[...]. Another logic, a logic of dreams and desires, free of mimetic rivalry, dictates this "other" side. But the crossover is also a transgression, a novel adventure in which the child and the poet believe, a route that is no longer marked by the boundaries of the real [262].

Initially, it might seem that the looking-glass is merely a device to exploit the surreal and comic possibilities of the opposite—the clock on the looking-glass-world mantelpiece has a smile—or the logical results of inversion—living backwards, running to stay in the same place, walking away from the place to which you wish to go. This interpretation is particularly inviting given Carroll's obsession with balance: red and white are contrasted in the chess pieces—as when the Red and White Knights fight over Alice (Carroll 2009: 209–211), or the point at which Alice has the White Queen and the Red Queen asleep on her lap (Carroll 2009: 230).

Even contrasts that might have appeared to be threatening are defused: the Knights' battle ends with them shaking hands; the Red and White Queens, although temperamentally opposite, share the same world view, and are curiously sympathetic: "'Your Majesty must excuse her,' the Red Queen said to Alice, taking one of the White Queen's hands in her own, and gently stroking it: 'she means well, but she can't help saying foolish things, as a general rule'" (Carroll 2009: 229).

However, Carroll is far from immune to the long literary and folktale history of the mirror, and much of that involves distortion and sinister overtones. Mirrors famously talk, or talk back ("Snow White"), are part of curses (Tennyson's "The Lady of Shalott"), provide a distorted evil perspective (Andersen's "The Snow Queen"), and commonly contain or constrain malevolence or malevolent worlds. Thus, for all its logical balance, the looking-glass world (inevitably) reflects these folkloristic uncertainties, and becomes increasingly sinister. Alice is far from secure; as Melchior-Bonnet puts it:

> Alice gets lost in this maze and lives in a mode of discontinuity and instability[...]. On this side of the mirror, identity is most inconsistent, and it takes very little more for slight madness to degenerate into delirium[...]. A master of symbols, the mirror is also the labyrinthine space that rejects communication and threatens the ability to distinguish fantasy from reality [263, 264].

After all, the encounter with the looking-glass world starts with a threat:

> The kitten wouldn't fold its arms properly. So to punish it, she held it up to the Looking-glass, that it might see how sulky it was, "—and if you're not good directly," she added, "I'll put you through into Looking-glass House. How would you like *that*?" [Carroll 2009: 127].

The mirror-within-the-mirror writing of "Jabberwocky" is the stuff of nightmare (shortly before publication Carroll moved Tenniel's frontispiece picture of the monster to a less-challenging position in the text)—and the ultimate question of reflection is existential—what if the Red King wakes? Who is dreaming who? (It should be noted that Carroll took dreams seriously. As Brian Attebery has noted, "The now outmoded convention of a dream framework for fantasy, as in [...] Carroll's *Alice* books, was probably intended not to undercut the credibility of the stories, but to reinforce their ties to the powerful experience of dreaming" [7]). And the sinister question of existence as a dream is posed by the sinister (in all senses) Tweedle-twins, characters curiously, if vaguely, reminiscent of the loathsome Omino in *Pinocchio*.

At every turn, although those turns are more or less strictly dictated by the chess-board, violence and madness are only just held at bay: Alice is terrified by the drums in the Lion and the Unicorn scene (Carroll 2009: 207); frightened by a jumping train (2009: 152); threatened by the monstrous crow that disturbs Tweedledum and Tweedledee's battle (2009: 172). Death is everywhere—from, as we have seen, the Bread-and-butterfly (2009: 154) to the fate of the innocent oysters (2009: 166), to Humpty-

Dumpty's dark jokes (2009: 188): danger is commonplace. When the White Queen comes running out of the wood, "'There's some enemy after her, no doubt,' the King said, without even looking round. 'That wood's full of them'" (2009: 204). In both a practical and metaphorical sense, the mirror-world both distorts the normal world, and reflects the inherent distortions of that world. Veronica L. Schanoes, in *Fairy Tales, Myth, and Psychoanalytic Theory*, suggests that

> The mirror not only reflects Alice's physical environment, but also reflects and responds to her inner landscape, the fantasies, experiences, and desires in her mind[...]. This segment of *Looking-Glass* is a fine precursor of the roles mirrors play in fairy-tale revisions; the mirror reflects girls' and women's fantasies, experiences, and desires under conditions often hostile to it [Schanoes 2014: 100, and see also La Belle].

Thus, although the very structure of *Through the Looking-Glass* may seem to be in direct contradiction to the free-wheeling action-and-reaction of *Pinocchio*, the contrast between the ordered and the anarchic—represented by Alice (clinging on to the conventions of the world she knows) and the madness that swirls and swoops around her—is perhaps even more threatening and distorting.

We tend to forget when we read that Pinocchio is a puppet as most of his interactions are with humans and he experiences the whole spectrum of sensory experience: he can feel hunger, weariness and pain. Despite his lightness, endless energy and his wild running, he can shed tears and he can die. Is, then, Pinocchio perceived as "un ragazzo" (boy) or "un burattino" (puppet)? In Collodi's book, Pinocchio refers to himself as a puppet or as a child depending on circumstances. This ambivalence is reinforced by other characters and the narrator. For example, his schoolmates tease him because he is a puppet, but they also admire him for his very efficient kicking and elbowing in a fight. In chapter 17, after Pinocchio has been persuaded to take the medicine, the Blue Fairy's comment that "children should learn that a good medicine taken in good time can save them from a serious illness or even death"[13] (Collodi/Lucas 56) contrasts with the narrator reassuring the reader that wooden puppets rarely get ill and recover quickly. Pinocchio's humanoid, hybrid nature oscillates between the two states, and the time between the oscillations and the final change at the end is filled with continual body changes. His wooden body allows him to go through ordeals that a human would not be able to survive, so his adventures are the result of the interaction between his substance and the surrounding world: he must avoid fire, but he can hurt his schoolmates quite severely, and he can float easily on water, so it will be easier for him to take his father ashore (body endurance is something that Alice and Pinocchio have in common). As has been observed, his metamorphoses depend on his physicality, "a physicality that conditions experience but is also conditioned by experience" (Gagliano 102, my translation).

If Alice's fall down the rabbit hole can be interpreted as a symbolic birth, Pinocchio's "birth" appears to be happening in installments (it is "programmatiquement un corps morcelé," as Genot has remarked [1976: 301]), as the body is fabricated from the top to the bottom: hair, eyes, nose, chin, hands, legs and feet, in this order (the ears are temporarily forgotten, as Geppetto realizes in chapter 3 when he can't pull them to draw Pinocchio back home after his first attempt to run away). His voice and characteristic energy and movement, however, pre-exist the construction of the body—it is as if the essence of Pinocchio were already there, in the wood, and struggling to free itself. Geppetto is the agent that carves it from the wood in its various stages of completion, as Michelangelo had done more famously with the series of unfinished statues of the *Prigioni* (prisoners or slaves). Collodi could have seen the statues in Florence (where they can still be seen at the Museum of the Accademia) trying to catch the moment in which they try to free themselves from the bonds and physical weight of the marble (see Tosi 2016: 357). Pinocchio is getting out of the wood, out of the original tree of metamorphosis (Tadini 57), in the opposite direction from Daphne who turns into a tree, her thighs embraced by climbing bark, her arms turned into branches, and the green leaves intertwining with and then replacing her hair. Pinocchio's metamorphosis from the original wood sometimes appears incomplete, as when he can't tear his hair in desperation after he has seen the tomb of the *bella bambina* in chapter 23: "While he was grieving like this, he made as if to tear his hair; but as his hair was all of wood, he could not even have the satisfaction of thrusting his fingers into it"[14] (Collodi/Lucas 79).

The initial vegetable state is reaffirmed when Pinocchio is given clothes to wear. Even at this crucial moment which marks his entrance into the human community, Geppetto makes him clothes that belong to the natural world: "a little suit of flowered paper, a pair of shoes of tree-bark and a cap fashioned out of bread dough"[15] (Collodi/Lucas 23). We can follow a progression between vegetable to animal to human through the sequence puppet—donkey—boy. His transformation into a donkey is not represented as an improvement over wood: on the contrary, it is regressive and frightening: "a punishment that enhances the child character's moral development" (Lassén-Seger 2004: 36) and takes him to a subhuman state that is worse than that of a puppet—as Pinocchio becomes, practically, a slave. It is a learning experience which makes him lose his imperfect but still humanoid state and takes him to near death.

Even if the puppet is born vegetable, he is clearly gendered at birth. As such, he represents the paradox of a male-puppet with no primary or secondary sexual characteristics, a body *in fieri*: very close to the concept of "body as situation," the embodiment of what de Beauvoir suggested as an alternative to the dualism between constructions of sex and gender. In Judith Butler's reading of de Beauvoir, the body becomes a set of interpretive and cultural possibilities that defies the constrictions of anatomy: "To be a gender [...] is to be engaged in an ongoing cultural interpretation of bodies and hence, to be dynamically positioned within a field of cultural possibilities. Gender must be understood as a modality of taking on or realizing possibilities" (Judith Butler 36). And Jaques has noted that toys, when they imitate humans, tend to be hyper-gendered—these toys "embody their gender identity in a manner which highlights their artificiality through paradoxical similarity" (214).

Issues of identity are at the center of *Alice* and *Pinocchio*, and this is not surprising as these characters are subjected to continuous physical transformations, sometimes actual, and sometimes only apparent, as when Alice is perceived as a serpent, and Pinocchio is seen as a fish. This produces a form of fracturing of identity. As has been noted, "Alice loses her sense of self and the objective of both Alice books is to help her relocate her identity, if it can be found" (Torpey 118). She is very often puzzled, "is very fond of pretending to be two people" (Carroll 2009: 15), and tells the Mock Turtle that the day before she was a different person (Carroll 2009: 92). Her conversation with the Caterpillar resonates throughout the book:

> "Who are *you?*" said the Caterpillar.
> This was not an encouraging opening for a conversation. Alice replied, rather shyly, "I—I hardly know, Sir, just at present—at least I know who I *was* when I got up this morning, but I think I must have been changed several times since then."
> "What do you mean by that?" said the Caterpillar, sternly. "Explain yourself!"
> "I can't explain *myself*, I'm afraid, Sir," said Alice, "because I'm not myself, you see."
> "I don't see," said the Caterpillar.
> "I'm afraid I can't put it more clearly," Alice replied, very politely, "for I can't understand it myself, to begin with; and being so many different sizes in a day is very confusing" [Carroll 2009: 40–41].

As in the wood where things have no names: "'And now, who am I? I *will* remember, if I can! I'm determined to do it!' But being determined didn't help her much" (Carroll 156). Nina Auerbach has commented on Alice's inward focus:

Other little girls travelling through fantastic countries, such as George MacDonald's Princess Irene and L. Frank Baum's Dorothy Gale, ask repeatedly *"where* am I?" rather than *"who* am I?" Only Alice turns her eyes inward from the beginning, sensing that the mystery of her surroundings is the mystery of her identity [33].

As far as social identity is concerned, after his creation, Pinocchio's naming by Geppetto establishes him as belonging to the category of the poor—the humble pinenut reminds Geppetto of a Pinocchio family, who "all did well for themselves. The richest was a beggar"[16] (Collodi/Lucas 7). Bodily dispositions are "ways of talking, walking, eating and conducting oneself [...] that are judged, legitimated, and recognized through hierarchical distinctions made between the superior and the inferior" (Blackman 62). Pinocchio inhabits the bodily disposition of the poor—his clothing is so cheap that he can't even sell it to buy the spelling book, but at least he seems to inhabit his double puppet-human body with a degree of confidence. Alice, on the contrary, needs to resist the possible identification with other female bodies (Ada, with her ringlets; Mabel, who doesn't know as many things as she does; or the maid Mary Ann) and being in an inferior social position than that of animals: "'It was much pleasanter at home,' thought poor Alice, 'when one wasn't always growing larger and smaller, and being ordered about by mice and rabbits'" (Carroll 33). Childhood is conceptualized as a state of growing—even if we change and age as adults gradually (if we are lucky—and it has been established that our nose keeps growing in adulthood, even if we don't tell lies), the child body is characterized as a body that undergoes cognitive and physical change in the space of few years, in a comparatively fast trajectory from immaturity to full maturity. As Massey has written about Alice: "the child is half-way to the metamorphic state: she can never become an adult without relinquishing that state" (91).

Nevertheless, Alice also takes responsibility for her actions:

"I know *something* interesting is sure to happen," she said to herself, "whenever I eat or drink anything: so I'll just see what this bottle does. I do hope it'll make me grow large again, for really I'm quite tired of being such a tiny little thing!"

It did so indeed[...]. She went on growing, and growing, and very soon had to kneel down on the floor: in another minute there was not even room for this, and she tried the effect of lying down with one elbow against the door, and the other arm curled round her head. Still she went on growing, and, as a last resource, she put one arm out of the window, and one foot up the chimney, and said to herself: "Now I can do no more, whatever happens. What *will* become of me?" [Carroll 2009: 32]

The experience of growing implies a spatial change and corporeal mutability which becomes even more noticeable and sudden during puberty. Alice and Pinocchio are represented as prepubertal, but their growing experiences appear to be equally sudden, identity-related, and connected with shifting power relations with the adult world. The alterations in Alice's size determine her position of power, as when she meets the enormous puppy in chapter 4, or as she confronts the court in the final chapter of *Alice's Adventures.* During the trial, Alice grows—and grows in power:

> Just at this moment Alice felt a very curious sensation, which puzzled her a good deal until she made out what it was: she was beginning to grow larger again [Carroll 2009: 99].

> "Here!" cried Alice, quite forgetting in the flurry of the moment how large she had grown in the last few minutes, and she jumped up in such a hurry that she tipped over the jury box with the edge of her skirt [Carroll 2009: 103].

> She had grown so large in the last few minutes that she wasn't a bit afraid of interrupting him [the king] [Carroll 2009: 107].

And finally rebels altogether: "'Who cares for *you?*' said Alice (she had grown to her full size by this time). 'You're nothing but a pack of cards!'" (Carroll 2009: 109). Similarly, Pinocchio appears to shrink when he meets bigger humans in positions of authority, such as the Carabinieri in chapter 27, or the Green Fisherman in chapter 28: they "hold ascendancy over Pinocchio only because of their greater size" (Klopp 69).

Alice's experiences of elongation and shrinkage produce a body that becomes alien to herself, a body that has become *other*, as when she grows suddenly tall:

> "Oh, my poor little feet, I wonder who will put on your shoes and stockings for you now, dears? I'm sure *I* shan't be able! I shall be a great deal too far off to trouble myself about you: you must manage the best way you can—but I must be kind to them," thought Alice, "or perhaps they won't walk the way I want to go! Let me see. I'll give them a new pair of boots every Christmas."

> And she went on planning to herself how she would manage it. "They must go by the carrier," she thought; "and how funny it'll seem, sending presents to one's own feet! And how odd the directions will look!
> > *Alice's Right Foot, Esq.*
> > *Hearthrug,*
> > *Near the Fender,*
> > *(with Alice's love)*" [Carroll 2009: 16–17].

In 1955 a British psychiatrist gave the name "Alice in Wonderland Syndrome" to a psychiatric disorder: its sufferers perceive their body parts to be larger and smaller and/or perceive objects around them as much larger or smaller than they are. Apparently, it is not an optical problem or a hallucination, but a problem in the brain, which processes the environment in a different way than is normal (Stapinsky).

Thus Pinocchio's growing nose is similarly perceived as a body part with a will of its own and not necessarily connected to lying—Pinocchio's nose grows twice before he even tells a lie and there are circumstances in which he lies and his nose does not grow, as in chapter 22.

Both Alice and Pinocchio experience very similar feelings of alienation from their own body parts—both characters are subject to mutability as well as vulnerability. Alice's metamorphic world may be connected to some extent to the impact of Darwinism on Victorian culture, and the idea that species are not fixed or stable: "This consciousness of the fluent, of the physical world as endless onwards process, extended to an often pained awareness of human beings as slight elements within unstoppable motion and transformation" (Beer 1983: 127). Pinocchio's transformations belong more to the world of myth and archetype, although the choice of wood as the primary substance may be a deliberate choice on the part of Collodi to make a point that this fantastic story of metamorphosis is in fact closer to the reality of Italian poverty than one might imagine:

> For Collodi deliberately to subvert the expectation of wealth and class status in favor of such an unenchanted and everyday material as wood is to announce that this story is going to be about unextraordinary proletarian Italian lives, from carpenters to school boys to farmers to thieves [Latimer 116]

The final transformation from the puppet who, in Geppetto's original plan, was going to be exploited (like those poor Italian children who were sold to ruthless *Omini* who would then employ them as beggars), to a rescuer of his parent, has been compared to the body of the national hero Garibaldi, self-fashioning himself as the new man with a free conscience, a citizen of the newly-formed Italian state. As Mengozzi has noted: "Garibaldi was the example of a man who had earned his body through a thousand difficult trials, and had become the model of a new man" (265, my translation). (In Mengozzi's book, about the way bodies of patriots and heroes of the *Risorgimento* are represented and conceptualized in various types of written documents, he argues that *Pinocchio*'s fictional *Capretta* [goat] island is an allusion to the island of *Caprera*, the place where Garibaldi retired after his contribution to the process of Italian nation-making).

Critical views—at the extremes—are divided between those who think that Alice's bodily changes allow her to rule Wonderland (such as Auerbach 152) and those who believe that they are a metaphor of entering womanhood, and that "Alice's body changing is no evidence of her gaining empowerment" (for example, Talairach-Vielmas 11), and there are several positions in between. For example, references to eating or being eaten which derive from, or are frequently found in the folktale (see chapter 4) can also be interpreted as veiled metaphors of sexual growing (equating appetite with monstrosity), or evoking mythical associations with Eve's fatal eating of the apple in the Garden of Eden: "Eating in Alice, then, is not merely sexual, but fatal. The 'charmed circle of childhood' is the circle of a woman's life; it is both womb and tomb" (Michie 28). Rackin notes the text's failure to contain an embodied Alice, "one of the bravest, most physical, and quickest moving of all the loving heroines and heroes in Victorian fiction" (1997: 171) while Labbé reads the *Alice* books as "a representation of Carroll's conflicting desires that his golden child become the perfect woman" (19). Carroll's passion for photography could be interpreted as a desire to freeze the mutability of the female body into permanence (Knoepflmacher 1986: 301). Hyland (1982) sees Alice containing the adult and the child within the same body: as she has no mentor in Wonderland, she needs to masquerade as an adult "ordering her life according to rules" (106), but at the same time, on occasion, she can be "the anarchic child once again, rejecting any form of organization" (110).

A similar shift from child to adult happens to Pinocchio at the end of his adventures: before the final transformation takes place, he has already changed into a responsible and adult version of himself. He no longer plays or runs or even goes to school—he works to support his father and even supports the Fairy, when he is led to believe that she needs his financial help as she is sick in hospital. Pinocchio behaves like a human adult long before he is physically transformed into a human. When in chapter 25 he asks the Fairy, who precedes him in her own metamorphosis from little girl to grown woman (and then lady and goat), to teach him the secret of growing up, she replies that "puppets don't ever grow. They are born puppets, live as puppets, and die puppets"[17] (Collodi/Lucas 90). A long tirade about what it takes to become a man (do what you are told, learn to be a good boy, tell the truth, etc.) then follows, but Pinocchio is already beyond all this when he takes on the adult role of provider for his "family." His final metamorphosis, as has been noted in chapter 4, is really a doubling, in which a part of himself, a sort of wooden skeleton or carapace, is left behind, to remind us, possibly, that every change is a loss and a rebirth and that the journey towards humanization and/or adulthood entails a degree of mourning, resisting, and often adjusting.

Both Alice's *Adventures* and Pinocchio's *Avventure* place vulnerable child bodies in surreal, dangerous, and often quite violent adult worlds. Both undergo forms of devolution into inferior species that challenge their already unstable identities. For Alice, growing in size is not as natural as growing up, while Pinocchio for most of his adventures feels and behaves like a human being, but is denied the possibility of growing up. In their journey towards body normalization they witness all sorts of grotesque and painful transformations: we can only imagine the fate of the other boys-turned-donkeys, and the way they die of fatigue, like Lucignolo. In *Alice*, from the Dodo to the Gnat to the Fawn, creatures reflect the same degree of vulnerability and mutability that she has discovered in herself. In the cautionary adult-controlled world of *Pinocchio* and the metamorphic anxiety-ridden world of *Alice*, human pain and animal pain are not so distant after all. In both *Alice's Adventures* and *Pinocchio*, the child's journey towards identity and stability is not at all linear (in *Through the Looking-Glass* Alice appears more capable of maintaining her physical self—see Schanoes 2017: 1). Its trajectory is undermined and distorted by trials, pitfalls, dilemmas, but especially, by the constant mutability of forms. As Alice says to the Caterpillar, "I am not particular as to size [...] only, one doesn't like changing so often, you know" (Carroll 2009: 45).

Worlds Upside Down

The topos of *mundus inversus* has been a topic of popular culture, theater, and literature since classical times: engravings and illustrations of the world-upside-down over the centuries have depicted most typically a man standing on his head, but also many reversals in normal relationships between people (such as servants ruling over their masters, women beating up their husbands, adults obeying children), or people and animals, such as horses riding their riders, and so on (Donaldson 22–23). The Roman Saturnalia, as well as the Medieval and Renaissance Carnival celebrations, as Bakhtin has famously argued, typically depict a world in which political, social and gender hierarchies are inverted, albeit temporarily. We find in both *Alice* and *Pinocchio* a similar hierarchical inversion to that of folklore (Demurova has pointed out "the possibility of some connection of Carroll's fairy tales with this old tradition" [83] while Perrot connects the baroque motif of surprise in *Pinocchio* with the "carnivalesque dimension" [45]).

The figure of the world-upside-down has a rich tradition in English theater, ballad, and satire: one only needs to think of the fate of Justice Overdo, who is put in the stocks in Ben Jonson's *Bartholomew Fair* (1614) or the eccentric comedy *The Antipodes* (1640) by Richard Brome. In this, the central character is led to believe that he has travelled to the other side of the earth, to a place called Nodnol (London spelt backwards) in Taerg Natrib (Great Britain) where women rule over men, judges run before criminals, and criminals beg to be arrested. From the Greek "opposite feet," the concept of the antipodes plays on the paradox of symmetry and identification. As has been noted, "The notion upon which *The Antipodes* is based—that upon the Southern side of the globe manners and morals are exactly contrary to those upon the Northern side—has generally been taken to be Brome's own" (Donaldson 81). It follows that the notion of geographical opposites coincides with moral opposites, so that the rhetoric of inversion becomes the matter of satire of madness and eccentricity.

The satiric implications of inversion and topsy-turvyness in fantasy worlds are pervasive in both *Alice* and *Pinocchio*. When Alice falls into the rabbit hole she expects to land on "The Antipathies [...] among the people that walk with their head downwards" (Carroll 2009: 11). She encounters, instead, many linguistic inversions (in Wonderland, *cats eat bats* is the same as *bats eat cats*) and parody is the typical genre of reversal and satiric recognition: throughout the *Alice* books didactic verse turns not just into nonsense, but into an anti-educational agenda. For example, lullabies are normally sung to sooth a baby, not to suggest beating it; crocodiles are not as effective role models as busy bees (aggression replaces industry); and bats that twinkle in the sky may not be quite as evocative as little stars doing the same. Carroll actively challenges, through comic distortion, the didacticism of the original poems. The typical trope of age inversion is employed in "Father William," who in the eponymous poem behaves more like an unruly youth than a wise aged man:

> "You are old," said the youth, "as I mentioned before,
> And have grown most uncommonly fat;
> Yet you turned a back-somersault in at the door—
> Pray, what is the reason of that?
> [...]
> "You are old," said the youth, "one would hardly suppose
> That your eye was as steady as ever;
> Yet you balanced an eel on the end of your nose—
> What made you so awfully clever?" [Carroll 2009: 43–44].

Similarly, in *Pinocchio*, boys are the only rulers of the Land of Toys—a similar device was used by F. Anstey who centered his fantasy *Vice Versa* (1882) precisely on the body-swapping, comic inversion of father and son. In *Through the Looking-Glass*, the world-upside-down trope is explored as mirror inversion: the Jabberwocky poem is printed in mirror writing; you need to run if you want to remain in the same place; the normal cause-and-effect sequence is reversed; Hatta is the mirror version of the Mad Hatter and Haigha is the mirror version of the Hare. The antagonistic Tweedledum and Tweedledee are twins as well as doubles, embodying "a paradoxical structure reflected in their equal fondness of the words 'ditto' and 'contrariwise'" (Meier 117). Reicherz has investigated the way the world-upside-down trope entered children's literature in the nineteenth century and the way Carroll has drawn on this tradition: "his satiric fantasy is consistently presented in terms of the then ongoing convention of the world-upside-down" (51).

Of course fantasy worlds are often built on inversion and reversal—reality must be distorted but still recognizable and the pattern of reversal provides a good *consistent* framework to represent spaces and characters. It is the satirist's job to point at distortion in contemporary society by showing an exaggerated version of that (social, political) distorted society: the world-upside-down can also be interpreted as a mad version of our own. Rackin believes that the *Alice* books show the anxiety about the possible upheaval of an ordered class system and fixed gender roles, as well as a crisis of faith:

> Soon, it seemed, England would be merely a free-floating political aggregate held together by nothing more glorious than money or (enlightened) self-interest, devoid of its once-cherished cultural and spiritual landmarks—a godless place not unlike the chaotic underground into which poor Alice falls in her first adventure, or the "backwards" world she discovers just behind the comforting bourgeois looking-glass [1991: 11].

If Wonderland is, among other things, a distorted vision of England, *Pinocchio* starts by depicting a situation in which two elderly men (Geppetto and Mastro Ciliegia) are fighting mechanically, just like puppets, while the real puppet behaves like a human being and, as soon as he is created, runs away instead of letting himself be controlled by his puppeteer. Collodi continues this exploration of the upside-down-world; when Pinocchio runs away from Geppetto, and is caught by the Carabiniere (it is interesting that Pinocchio's first opponent in his story is a representative of justice), everyone in the street readily believes that he has been abused and beaten by the old man, who ends up in prison. It is a cynical, brutal world in which decency is punished and deceit thrives. As Barberi Squarotti has observed, "There is no adventure or fairy-tale atmosphere after the puppet has left his home: there is the immediate revelation that things, in the outside world, go exactly the opposite way of what you might expect" (90, my translation). The poor, in this unfair world, do not feel safe and have no protection from the crowd and from the judicial system alike. This brings us to the treatment of justice in the two texts, which is remarkably similar, as has been noted by Lawson Lucas in her article "Nations on Trial: the Cases of Pinocchio and Alice." Courtroom scenes are the climaxes of both *Alice* and *Pinocchio*: "Both episodes show high, and normally respected, authority exercising its official function as an expression of the ordinary conduct of the State, and they illustrate the arbitrary and irrational miscarriage of justice which appears to be the norm" (Lawson Lucas 1997: 54–55). In both books wigs and spectacles suggest antiquated and incompetent behavior, especially in *Pinocchio*, where the judge is an ape wearing glasses with no lenses.

But there is more. Both episodes are well-established in the world-upside-down tradition: in *Alice* sentence comes first, and verdict afterwards, important evidence is the same as *un*important evidence, not signing one's name is considered a proof of guilt, and the whole trial is interrupted by the Queen ordering the witnesses' heads to be cut off. It is clearly a demented justice system, but of course not significantly more demented than the Victorian judicial system itself, which made the child subject to the workhouse and the prison: as Gordon reports, "there are records of children in their teens being hung for petty crimes in the 1850s" (136).

In Collodi's *Paese of Acchiappacitrulli* ["Sillibilly trap," in Lucas's translation (61)] Pinocchio is robbed of his gold coins by the Cat and the Fox:

> In the presence of the judge, he recounted in every particular the iniquitous fraud of which he had been the victim; he gave the forename and surname and a detailed description of the robbers, and he ended by demanding justice.
> The judge heard him out with much kindliness; he took a lively part in the narration: he was moved to pity, he grew upset, and when the puppet had nothing further to say, he stretched out a hand and rang a bell[...].
> Indicating Pinocchio, the judge then said to the constables, "This poor fellow has been robbed of four gold coins; seize him, therefore, and cast him into prison at once"[18] [Collodi/Lucas 65–66].

After four months in jail, the prisoners are pardoned and released in celebration of a great military victory. As only "malandrini" [miscreants] are released, Pinocchio needs to reassure the gaoler that he is indeed a miscreant (a typical instance in which he lies, and his nose does not grow): "'In that case you have every reason,' said the gaoler, lifting his cap in respect and, giving him a good-day, he opened the gates of the prison and let him escape"[19] (Collodi/Lucas 67).

Even if *Pinocchio* is not set in an other-world such as Wonderland, its treatment of justice resembles the Victorian topsy-turvy world of Samuel Butler's *Erewhon* (1872) far more than *Alice's Adventures in Wonderland* (with which *Erewhon* has been superficially compared, see Alexander Taylor 96). In *The Victorian Colonial Romance with the Antipodes*, Blythe analyzes settlers' narratives and romances about the Antipodes:

"as a metaphorical return to an England free from metropolitan inequities and social constraints [...] the Antipodes offered a distinctive narrative path for writers [...] while signifying equally a distant land both familiar and strange, the opposite and yet distorted or idealized mirror of home" (4). The Justice in *Erewhon*, one of these antipodean fantasies, as in *Pinocchio*, is much more lenient with the criminals than with the victims (crime is treated like an illness), who are punished on top of the fact that they have been robbed or deceived, as in the following Erewhonian trial:

> The next case was that of a youth barely arrived at man's estate, who was charged with having been swindled out of large property during his minority by his guardian[...]. His father had been long dead[...]. The lad, who was undefended, pleaded that he was young, inexperienced, greatly in awe of his guardian, and without independent professional advice. "Young man," said the judge sternly, "do not talk nonsense. People have no right to be young, inexperienced, greatly in awe of their guardians, and without independent professional advice." [...] He then ordered the prisoner to apologize to his guardian, and to receive twelve strokes with a cat-of-nine tales [Samuel Butler 113].

The plight of this naïve young man is remarkably similar to that of Pinocchio: justice stands on the side of the exploitative adult.

Like Alice, the main character of *Erewhon*, Higgs, enters a new world and in the encounter with its topsy-turvyness, his subjectivity "dissolves until he enters a liminal in-between state [...] though he physically masters the range, he psychologically and emotionally disintegrates" (Blythe 139). The journey into the reversible, eccentric and symmetrically opposite world of the Antipodes is a journey into alterity. Although fantasy worlds never lose their internal coherence, they can produce substantial and unsettling changes in whoever visits them. The upside-down worlds of fantasy in *Alice* and *Pinocchio* baffle and interrogate the characters by offering them radical changes of perspective about the unity of the subject and basic moral standards. These worlds, somewhat like the institutions of the newly formed Italian nation, and England, do not always operate on the basis of common sense, cause and effect, and reward and punishment. On the contrary, they offer the estrangement typical of the traveller of dystopia, in order to let readers appreciate their satirical intention. This is fantasy at its most pointed, and in many senses, at its closest to "realism"—showing the other side of the coin.

Dystopian Spaces

The recent explosion of dystopian fiction for Young Adults has focused attention on an area of children's literature studies that centers on the role of the individual (generally a teenager) in totalitarian media-controlled future societies: "utopian and dystopian writing for children and young adults has been produced for a variety of reasons, and it has had a range of effects, from play and escape to sustained political reflection" (Hintz and Ostry 1). However, it is a fact that the settings of many children's books, not just contemporary YA dystopian novels, appear to have utopian as well as dystopian qualities, whether or nor such settings happen to resemble actual places. Obviously, all renderings of landscape in all texts are the result of the work of imagination so that even "real landscapes" inevitably become countries of the mind (see Meinig, and Watkins)—one only needs to think of the Edwardian London of J. M. Barrie's *Peter and Wendy* (1911), where dogs act as nurses and respectable fathers decide to live in dog kennels.

The protagonist traveler of classic utopian or dystopian fiction for adults generally leaves his familiar world in order to discover a new place through various adventures and meetings with the native inhabitants of the unfamiliar world: displaced and estranged, the wanderer tries to grasp the rules of the new society. This is typically the case of Alice, who, out of boredom and a sense of curiosity (a state of mind shared by many travelers of classic utopian fiction) sets off on a journey to Wonderland, a site of puzzling experiences, which provides an alternation of utopian and dystopian visions. Wonderland is indeed a baffling place—a world of wonders that often turn into nasty surprises—not to mention the fact that it could all be a dream of the Red King (the dream was a classic device of adult utopian fiction, such as William Morris's *News from Nowhere* [1890]). The complex dialectic coexistence of nightmare and dream seems to be a feature of classic utopian/dystopian fiction: from Gulliver's rational utopia which turns into barbarism, to the Savages' reservation in the "perfect" society of Huxley's *Brave New World* (1932), to Winston Smith's dream of a Golden Country (an interval of color and warmth in the drab world of Orwell's *1984*), utopia and its reversal have come to establish a relation of ambiguity and instability of meaning (Tosi 2006a: 37). And of course the river bank in Oxford, and Wonderland itself, have been idealized over the centuries as quintessentially English landscapes, sites of utopia, reinforcing the strongly nostalgic national myth of a real England as rural. As Hunt has noted, "English fantasy [...] derives some of its power and individuality from its melding of basic forms of narrative coherence— journeys—with landscapes of profound national symbolism" (1987: 13). Jane Carroll has called Alice's golden afternoon on a riverbank, "a true incarnation of the pleasance" (72), the typical *locus amoenus* of medieval literature, with all its association of drowsing and dreaming. But Alice's dream itself is highly ambivalent—if we associate utopia with an impossible dreamlike state, and dystopias with nightmarish pictures of society, Carroll's pastoral dream is a frame for a much more unsettling dream experience. Or, as McGillis has observed, "Carroll refuses to decide whether the dream in all its subversive glory or the dream as filtered through a nostalgic recollection is what matters" (20).

The coexistence of utopian and dystopian is also a characteristic of *Pinocchio*'s embedded secondary worlds. I have already discussed the Town called Sillybillytrap as a typical world-upside-down space where justice and common morality is inverted (as are rewards and punishments). As a result of injustice and unfairness, it is the naïve inhabitants of, or visitors to this place that are heavily punished—they are fleeced (often quite literally) by swindlers:

> On entering, Pinocchio observed that all the streets were populated by bald dogs yawning with hunger, fleeced lambs trembling with cold, poultry relieved of both comb and wattles, and begging in the street for one grain of maize, big flightless butterflies, who had sold their lovely colourful wings, tail-less peacocks, ashamed to be seen like that, and pheasants strutting in silence, mourning the loss of their shining gold and silver feathers, now gone for ever[20] [Collodi/Lucas 61–62].

It is a place of damage, dispossession, mourning for past happiness, and loss of identity.

On the Island of the Busy Bees (*Il Paese delle Api Industriose*, chapter 24), "the streets, full of people scurrying here and there, seeing to their tasks, were a hive of activity: everyone was working, everyone had something to do. You might hunt high and low, but you could not find a lazybones or a good-for-nothing anywhere"[21] (Collodi/Lucas 86). Obviously Pinocchio does not appreciate all this activity: through his eyes we see just how harsh the town's work ethic is; no one who is able to work has the right to beg and the inhabitants are so mean that they will not even part with a crust of bread and share it with the hungry. He also has to listen to lectures from all the people who refuse to give him food, as well as from the narrator. (The only person who gives Pinocchio food and drink in exchange for a little help carrying a pitcher, and who does not deliver any lecture at this stage, is the woman who turns out to be the Blue Fairy). As Marchianò has commented, the Island is "a separate place, a beehive of orthodoxy in which Pinocchio, controlled by the Fairy, tastes the modest joys of a virtue that has been forced on him" (153, my translation). Bees and the beehive are ancient symbols of order and industry—the bees' commonwealth as a model for human organizations and societies can be found in the classics, such as Virgil and Pliny, and in Renaissance emblems and texts (most notably, in Shakespeare's *Henry V*: "For so work the honey-bees / Creatures that by a rule in nature teach / The act of order to a peopled kingdom" [1.2.190]).

The stigma of idleness had a Puritan streak in England and a moral imperative in Italy—Pinocchio is the example of the peasant boy who succeeds in climbing the social scale at the end of the story, through hard work and self-education. Industriousness is also a typically nineteenth-century bourgeois virtue, which is celebrated both in folktales, literary fairy tales, and fantasies. Margaret Gatty's rewriting of "Sleeping Beauty," for example, opens with a discussion among fairy godmothers about which is the best virtue they should donate to their princesses at the time of Christening. After the gifts have been bestowed, the fairies agree that Love of Employment is the best, and the true path to happiness. If Collodi's depiction of the place of the Busy Bees is ambivalent (its inhabitants are not very sympathetic to Pinocchio's hunger, but he needs to overcome his laziness), Carroll's parody of Watts's "Against Idleness and Mischief" (1715) turns the busy bee of the original poem (which employs every "shining hour" to gather honey, build cells, "and labours hard") into a far less active crocodile, who appears to spend his time improving "his shining tail" while he pours waters on his scales, and waiting for little fishes to enter his claws: not even bothering to attack them (Carroll 2009: 19). It appears that both authors use the symbolic associations of the bees as a model for zeal and fruitful activity for children, to challenge and problematize it. Collodi imparts a definite dystopian flavor to a community of people who, perhaps, should be more sympathetic towards a hungry puppet/child (Pinocchio asks more than twenty people, and they all reply "Aren't you ashamed? Instead of idling around the street, why don't you go and look for a bit of work instead, and learn to earn your bread!"[22] (Collodi/Lucas 87), while Carroll, quite openly ridicules the didactic use of the bee and replaces it with the image of an idle crocodile, which appears to be able to satiate its hunger, not by keeping active, but by keeping absolutely still.

The Land of Toys (chapters 30–32) is a land of perpetual amusement ("you spend it playing games and having fun from morning to night"[23] [Collodi/Lucas 119]) with a very peculiar time-scheme, as Candle-Wick explains: "There's no school on Thursdays, and every week is composed of six Thursdays and one Sunday. Just think: the summer holidays begin on the first day of January and end on the last day of December"[24] (Collodi/Lucas 119). The Land of Toys is the illusion that drags Pinocchio away from his destiny to become a boy—he leaves on the night before the day he will be transformed into a human being ("tomorrow I shan't be a puppet any more; I am going to be a boy like you and all the others"[25] [Collodi/Lucas 118]), only literally hours away from the fulfillment of his dream. It is as if the puppet were not yet ready to submit to the reality principle and his destiny, but needed to enter, at the last minute, another secondary fantasy world which would prolong his carefree rebellious childhood, with disastrous consequences. Collodi is very precise when he tells the reader how long Pinocchio spends in his dystopic locations: four months in prison, and five months in the Land of Toys. This is not the indefinite and vague chronotope of fairy tale but the detailed time frame of fantasy (or even realism)—the long and tedious period in an enclosed space (especially if the inmate is innocent) versus the exact time it takes for the children to change from human beings into donkeys: it takes exactly "five months in this lovely life of playing games and enjoying themselves the whole day long, without ever having looked a book or school in the face"[26] (Collodi/Lucas 129).

The Land of Toys is also a gendered utopia/dystopia: a community or a microcosm of members of the same sex who live together, and as such it is the exact opposite of the boarding school story genre. Il Paese dei Balocchi is a school-less utopia: "there are no schools there; there are no teachers there, there are no books there"[27] (Collodi/Lucas 119). One is reminded of *The Wind in the Willows* (1908), a typical example of "a boy-hood fantasy of eternal school holiday with chums" (Marshall 39), an all-male community of similarly minded gentlemen having fun together. But possibly the English all-male gendered utopia which most resembles the Land of Toys, is Evelyn Sharp's "The Boy Who Looked Like a Girl" (1897). This tale is built on the contrast between two opposed gendered worlds, The Land of Good Weather, a place "where they are all girls [...] and they've nothing to do all day long" (81), and the "Land of Bad Weather," in which "there are nothing but boys [...] and you can't hear yourself speak" (Sharp 74):

> There were boys everywhere, as far as he could see; short boys, tall boys, ugly boys, pretty boys, fat boys, thin boys, every kind of boy imaginable—except quiet boys. For they were all as noisy as they could be; instead of talking, they shouted; instead of smiling, they roared with laughter; and instead of either, they knocked one another down [78].

Noise is what characterizes Collodi's gendered utopia:

> The oldest were 14; the youngest were just 8. In the streets there was such rejoicing, such a din, such a screaming as to numb the brain [...] some of them were laughing, others shouted, others called out, other clapped their hands, others whistled, others

imitated hens cackling after laying eggs. In fact there was such a pandemonium, such a chirruping, such a devilish uproar, that if you didn't stuff your ears with cotton-wool, you'd go deaf[28] [Collodi/Lucas 127].

The general euphoria of this place seems to hide (or lie in) the fact that this is not just a school-less utopia, but also a parent-less one. There are neither adults, nor mentors: it is a world of happy *male* orphans who appear to live alone, each in their separate rooms. The readers do not get to know any of the other inhabitants—if Pinocchio and Candle-wick make new friends, they are not mentioned.

It has been suggested that *Alice's Adventures in Wonderland* "is about enclosed spaces reflecting an enclosed life [...] the action is all in Alice's head" (Hunt 2015: 35), and in *Through the Looking-Glass* the chessboard does not exactly encourage freedom of movement or free will. As we have seen, framing his books with reality-fantasy portals (the rabbit-hole, the looking-glass) links Carroll to a venerable tradition; within *Alice's Adventures* he manipulates portals—specifically doors—to reflect both Alice's frustrations and her pragmatism in overcoming them. Thus in chapter 1, when she finds herself in a hall: "There were doors all around the hall, but they were all locked" (Carroll 2009: 12) and it is not until the end of chapter 7, after an epic of size-changing, that she finally matches her size with the key and the door into the garden. Among the doors she comes across is the one guarded by the Frog Footman, and this is where an exasperating conversation takes place, which ends with Alice taking the matter into her own hands: "'Oh, there's no use in talking to him,' said Alice desperately: 'he's perfectly idiotic!' And she opened the door and went in" (Carroll 2009: 52). She encounters another obstructive frog and another door in *Through the Looking-Glass*, and she takes even more decisive—and regal—action.

Doorways and windows, then, are "portals" in both the *Alice* books and *Pinocchio*: the puppet's first action is to run away from Geppetto's house. As has been observed, "the house represents the space of obligation, of submission [...] outdoors is the space of choice, the place in which the subject is king and can affirm his will" (Vagnoni 45, my translation). Pinocchio's desire to escape from enclosed domestic spaces is the visual equivalent of his psychological rebellion and resistance to adult rules. The street is indeed the place where Pinocchio seems to feel more comfortable, but it is also the place where he meets his opponents and where he is "tempted." Pinocchio's world is more "realistic" than Alice's: "Pinocchio never really loses his bearings, no matter how strange and menacing the situation he encounters; Alice does, and this is her dreamlike privilege, for, unlike

Pinocchio, she discovers and inhabits an utterly unreliable world" (Cambon 56). Alice and Pinocchio continually need to adjust their perceptions of the fantasy worlds they inhabit so that they can exert some control over them. Even apparently "happy" and carefree spaces (such as the Land of Toys or Alice's garden) can turn into nightmares in which the child's life and identity are constantly under threat. Adjusting and resisting strategies are what both characters need to learn in their fictional life journeys.

Narrative Structures at the Crossroads: Fairy Tale, Fantasy and *Bildungsroman*

I have often used the word "hybrid" to describe the structure of *Alice* and *Pinocchio*, and the way they refashion folktale traditions and tropes, as well as fantasy traditions and tropes. At this point, in the analysis of the narrative structure of these books, I would like to look closely at a third narrative tradition in this generic triangulation, that of the *Bildungsroman*, and the way this perspective, that of the well-established realistic narrative tradition of the novel of development, is evoked, resisted and refashioned in *Alice* and *Pinocchio*, and the way it interacts with fantasy.

The term has been applied, most famously, to Goethe's *Wilhelm Meister* (1796) and is originally based on an eighteenth-century concept of *Bildung*. Apart from fine distinctions which could be made, especially in German literature (see, for example Hirsch 293), the term can be employed in its more general sense, as a "symbolic form of modernity" (Moretti 5), the narrative result of "a revolutionary period in which traditional societies were giving way to the vicissitudes of modern industrial development" (Tally 37). A *Bildungsroman* is a novel about the maturation process of an individual and her/his interaction with society, and although it is a genre that addresses an adult audience, some of its more typical characteristics can appear to fit, albeit in slightly different ways, both *Alice* and *Pinocchio*.

These are, for example, the conflict between self-determination and the demands of socialization, or mobility vs. interiority (Moretti 15, 4), the didacticism ("the novel of formation is conceived as a didactic novel, one which educates the reader by portraying the education of the protagonist" [Hirsch 298]), and a narrative voice "characterized by irony towards the inexperienced protagonist" (Hirsch 298), as well as the heroes' ideas and ideals that are modified by "the sobering forces of reality" (Hirsch 301).

The *Bildungsroman* is "an epistemological genre, a form through which the reader may gain knowledge while also following the learning process of one or more key characters" (Tally 45). In particular, the English version of the *Bildungsroman*, because of its happy ending and the value placed on childhood perceptions that are confirmed when the characters become adults, and its paradigmatic opposition between good and bad characters, has been compared to a fairy tale:

> Can you picture a child reading *Wilhelm Meister, The Red and the Black, Lost Illusions*? Impossible. But *Waverley* and *Jane Eyre, David Copperfield* and *Great Expectations*: here we have the "great tradition" of children's literature[...]. Yet, how could this change in the age of readership have taken place? Could it be that the "novelistic" appearance of these works is upheld in each of its parts by an older sort of framework, one more suited to, and easily recognized by childhood? Could it in fact be that, deep down, these novels are fairy tales? [Moretti 185].

The English *Bildungsroman*, Moretti argues, is also uncommonly full of eccentrics: a dense array of peculiar, maniacal characters inhabiting an "anthropological garden" of caricatures (192–193). In "these masterpieces of heteroglossia" (here Moretti is referring to Scott, Fielding, Sterne and Dickens) "the dominant exchange [...] is *misunderstanding*, which is the opposite of communication and the collapse of all dialogue" (194). These are words that could describe quite easily most exchanges in *Alice*, while Moretti's chapter on the centrality of the law in the symbolic universe of the English *Bildungsroman*, could apply to both *Alice* and *Pinocchio*, especially when he remarks that the incredibly high frequency of interrogative sentences of these novels "reveals that these are not dialogues, but rather *interrogations*" (209).

 The term *Bildungsroman* is frequently used, independently of its specific historical and literary context, to describe the theme of coming of age in children's or YA literature. In Watson's words, "Maturation is a theme, not a genre. It saturates children's stories and colors narratives of every kind" (1). In a sense, as Falconer has noted, "the *bildungsroman* is a natural crossover genre, because it typically represents a protagonist developing from child to adulthood" (74). While the *Bildungsroman* is generally associated with realism, Falconer does not see fantasy as incompatible with the genre in its more standard configuration. In her analysis of Pullman's *Dark Materials* trilogy, for example, she argues that this genre can be used for a form of moral education within the textual space of fantasy (she calls it, appropriately, *fantasy Bildungsroman*)—as the self (and our consciousness of personal identity) is a work in progress that is constructed as a fantastic other (79). Trites, who has analyzed the influence of the classic

Bildungsroman on adolescent literature and has related it to cognitive theory, contends that "we write novels about growth because our embodied brain knows growth" (13); her study of the metaphors of growing or time passing that authors supply in their texts indicates that we cannot think about the passing of time other than in metaphors, "And because we have so internalized embodied metaphors as part of our cognitive structure, most authors for young people cannot help but employ images of embodiment to describe maturation metaphorically" (Trites 21). One of the most widely used metaphors is that of the journey—in time and space—for the central character, which brings us to the problem of time in the *Bildungsroman.*

In this genre the journey is generally scaled down to the average human life span, as linearity is the way we experience history (Attebery 61). In fantasy, of course, such expectations can be baffled—natural and consensus reality can be violated at every turn, and this includes concepts of linear life spans (for example, Tolkien's conception of Elvish time is not the same as the time of his Hobbit heroes, and this produces sensibly different attitudes, personalities and behaviors). While the classic realistic *Bildungsroman* is always linear, the *fantasy Bildungsroman* can rely, quite paradoxically, on a circular chronotope, as happens to Alice at the end of her dream and to Pinocchio, who is reunited with his father (and it can also relate to Harry Potter, according to Tally 42): the young age of the protagonists requires a re-entry into the original family unit.

But the metaphors of the journey in time and metaphors of growth are complicated in both Carroll and Collodi. In *Alice in Wonderland*, time is personified and revengeful, so that it is always teatime at six o'clock, and in *Through the Looking-Glass*, cause and effect are inverted. However, as the time of narration continues in a standard progression, the illusion of linearity is safe. As for physical maturation, Alice grows physically, but does not grow *up* (except metaphorically and ironically), while Pinocchio's very substance prevents him from growing up.

If growing is a linear journey, again, there is an element of the picaresque in both texts which distracts and diverts them from what their protagonists want to achieve (or say they want to achieve). If "structurally, the picaresque novel is composed of a number of episodes loosely strung together; the novel of formation represents a progression of connected events leading up to a definite denouement" (Hirsch 299). In a way, both *Alice* and *Pinocchio* combine an apparently picaresque structure (see "Folktale and Fairy-Tale Structures" in chapter 4) with a less than casual closure. As has been noted, Alice has legitimized and popularized "the figure of the female adolescent wanderer and adventurer[...]. She stands out as the first female Odysseus" (Dedebas 57–58). It is as if these texts tried to resist the linearity of the *Bildungsroman* with the impediments provided by fantasy (transformations, magical encounters, and so on). After all, Pinocchio does not grow up but, rather, transforms himself, and both Alice and Pinocchio attain a form of maturation without external help: when characters advise and stimulate him, Pinocchio just does not listen (Summerfield 75), while *Alice's* eccentrics depict a warped society whose views and judgments systematically clash with the needs and progress of Alice herself. And yet the *Bildung* element is very clearly there, in the way in which both characters take responsibility for their actions, and the way that they must, ultimately, adhere to the reality principle, although they come from different places: Alice from a dream world, and Pinocchio from, possibly, the pleasure principle of immediate gratification (West).

One needs only to contrast the books' structure with the folktale, from which, as we have seen, they borrow so many tropes. In folktales, coming of age is the result of a rite of initiation, or the need to pass one single and very difficult test, which can cause a sudden transformation and social improvement. So, Beauty must overcome her revulsion for the Beast, Cinderella must dazzle the Prince at the ball, Sleeping Beauty does not age for a hundred years (characters do not age in fairy tales—they are already divided between young and old) and numberless Princes must fight the monster to marry the Princess. There is no psychological change, no development of the self. Fairy-tale teenagers act and react, and become adults immediately after their actions and reactions have rewarded them.

In contrast, in the *Bildungsroman*, as well as the *fantasy Bildungsroman*, the hero wonders and wanders: what does this world want/expect from me? What are the rules of this world? How do I want to behave in this specific situation and how am I expected to behave? The novel of development tells the story of the difference between, as Moretti would put it, the tendency towards *individuality* and the opposing tendency towards *normality* (16).

Thus the classic *Bildungsroman* traces "the progress of a young person towards self-knowledge and a sense of social responsibility" (Summerfield 65) in the progress from child to adult (in a way, *Pinocchio*, like *David Copperfield*, starts with describing how the hero is born). While in realist fiction, this generally happens in one book, in contemporary fantasy characters have the advantage of developing and growing in series fiction—in the course of several books the reader, layer after layer, uncovers the increasing complexity of the central characters, but also of the minor, or bad ones. In the *Harry Potter* saga, for example, we learn about the motivations and the unhappy childhood (the back story) of the arch-villain Voldemort in the course of seven books. And, in fantasy series that "grow" (in length) together with their characters, but also with their readers, it becomes increasingly difficult to distinguish between good and bad characters as in the fairy tale, as even good characters in fantasy have temptations, or make mistakes that become part of their experience and of ultimately what they are.

To argue that *Alice* and *Pinocchio* are series books because *Alice* has a "sequel," and *Pinocchio* is in two parts, may appear somewhat implausible and of course Alice and Pinocchio do not become adults at the end of their respective stories (although Pinocchio does say that he wants to become a *man*, and not a boy: "sarebbe ora che diventassi anch'io un uomo" [Collodi 1993: 174]). However, they do develop a form of interiority, as well as strategies to cope with the exterior world, as soon as they learn to read the signs and the rules that they represent.

There is an established critical tradition that sees *Pinocchio* as a *Bildungsroman*, from Kuznets ("Collodi thus fashions [...] a bildungsroman with fairy tale elements" [68]) to Morrissey and Wunderlich ("Pinocchio, the hero of the fantasy bildungsroman" [71]) to Panszczyk ("This particular tale [*Pinocchio*] is a bildungsroman of sorts, but not a human one" [207]). Zipes reads *Pinocchio* "as a type of *Bildungsroman*, or fairy-tale novel of development" (1999: 146), but also qualifies this statement by underlining the realism of the representation of the difficulties experienced by peasant boys at the time in which Collodi was writing (and also notes that Collodi, in the first version of his book, never intended Pinocchio to develop or be educated or become human). Richter calls *Pinocchio* "a novel of progression" (94), and interestingly, contrasts it with *Alice*, which he defines as a novel of regression to a dream childhood, and typical of British children's literature of the second half of the nineteenth century. *Alice*, according to Richter, starts when *Pinocchio* finishes, with the literate child who reads silently, and gets bored. I am not sure that these two definitions really work for either *Pinocchio* or *Alice*. One can easily read a degree of nostalgia in *Pinocchio* too—the dream world of a lost rebellious and carefree puppet childhood, and of course Alice starts a journey precisely because she is bored. Both need to negotiate the desire to belong, and their autonomy—between the passive alignment to what society wants, and their spontaneity. Alice learns along the way that not all adult rules make sense, while Pinocchio does not learn to read and write *at school*, as his father and the

Fairy want, but when he is on his own, after work—when he is *ready to learn*. But their resistance does not mean that they refuse to experience the world as a learning process. At the beginning, Pinocchio is "surprised, confused, and unable to read the signs put before him in his world" (Stewart-Steinberg 41). He falls for the lies of the Cat and the Fox, he lets his friends lead him astray, he is lost in a world that wants to eat or kill him. In the end he is much wiser, and distinguishes more easily between friends and enemies—he even treats his former assassins with irony and uses proverbs to comment ironically on their situation, "another sure sign of the puppet-child's reformation in consonance with an adult society of law-and-order and general middle-class values" (Perella 16).

Pinocchio's initial incapability to read and interpret his world makes him very similar to Alice. In the strangeness of her situation (fantasy provides far more bizarre situations than realism) she gradually comes to understand that she may not learn much from adults, but at least she can learn how to handle them:

> She learns to deal with new situations by acquiring new weapons—not only defensive weapons, but at times aggressive ones, as well. She learns to be independent, resourceful, daring, adventurous, and even [...] assertive. By the story's end, she has imbibed these lessons so well that she can turn and face the whole court of her aggressors [Honig 77].

Alice changes and grows because, like Pinocchio, she goes back to reality with more knowledge and awareness than she was endowed with at the beginning of her adventures. These fantasies of development "structure their growth on the capacity to learn" (Avanzini 94, my translation): the process is from curiosity (*Alice*) and immediate gratification (*Pinocchio*, and in some ways, *Alice*), to knowledge, and from difficulty in reading/negotiating rules (both), to survival, mastering of their surroundings, and self-education.

These fantasy novels of development do not simply depict "the triumph of the little guy" (Cech 175) (or the little girl, for that matter), but depict archetypal child heroes who look and also sound quite *real* in their naiveté and childish reactions. The fantasy genre conflates with the *Bildungsroman*: the central characters are given heroic proportions in the way they interact with dangerous destabilizing worlds that defy the rules of consensus reality, but at the same time they are universal because they submit themselves to transformation and maturation. A central aspect of many fantasy novels is that characters mature psychologically so, paraphrasing Honig, one could say that the fantasy *Bildungsroman*, in order to be successful, demands a hero or heroine who is equal to the rigors of the fantastic plot but who is also equal to the rigors of the learning process that they have to go through (71).

Moretti identifies in the "rationalization of the accomplished journey" the ideal finale of the *Bildungsroman*, the "retracing of one's steps to reconsider what belongs to the past" (69). This could describe the endings of both *Alice* and *Pinocchio* if we look at the way the protagonists define their experiences. The *Alice* books end with the protagonist rationalizing her adventures as dreams, while *Pinocchio* ends with the realization that the boy has outgrown the puppet, and that the puppet, now empty of life, looks "buffo" [funny] to him (as Manganelli has noted, only Pinocchio could kill Pinocchio [203]). For both Pinocchio and Alice, this is the final moment in which they simply look back, both physically and psychologically, to their past experiences and label them with a name (the curious dream, the funny puppet): closure happens after an interior as well as external mapping has been completed.

PART THREE

New Journeys:
Postmodernist Experiments
with *Alice* and *Pinocchio* and
Parallel Genre Readings
in Empire Fictions

6. The Postmodernist Journeys of *Alice* and *Pinocchio*: Adventures in Transnational and Transtextual Identities

Alice, Pinocchio and **Postmodernism**

Quite recently, Stefano Benni's "illustrated novel" *La Bottiglia Magica* (2016) has managed to have Alice and Pinocchio meet—at last—in the same book. In such textual exchange operations, the reader is alerted to possible collisions between different storyworlds. This may produce a form of intertextual surprise (or an "ontological scandal," in the words of McHale 1989: 85) that derives from the quite unexpected discovery of a breach in the seams that divide one self-contained fictional world from another. In the world of *La Bottiglia Magica* the fictional worlds of the *Alice* books and *Pinocchio* are perceived simultaneously, and this is a typical postmodernist "surprise joke." The "portability" of Alice and Pinocchio, which is one of the attributes of literary characters, is probably their most outstanding feature—they are typically transtextual characters in the sense that they exhibit a certain sameness and recognizability over time (some standards of consistency must be observed) but at the same time they lend themselves to "unauthorized possible continuations or variations of the original figure" (Richardson 531). One can argue that "portability has become something of a mania in contemporary fiction" (Vermeule 49), and Postmodernism has deconstructed and re-assembled not just plots, but character configurations in canonical works with great enthusiasm, from the portrayal of Bertha in Jean Rhys's *Wide Sargasso Sea* (1966) to Friday in J.M. Coetzee's *Foe* (1986), from King Lear's daughters in Jane Smiley's *A Thousand Acres* (1991) to, most recently, Hamlet as a foetus in Ian McEwan's *Nutshell* (2016), to name just a few.

In Benni's text, Alina, the Alice character, is a contemporary girl who escapes, in the company of the genetically modified cybercat "mouse," from a boarding school in which the teachers try to brainwash the girls into a fixed gender identity, while Pin[occhio] is a migrant who leaves his father Jep to try his fortune over the sea. They go through similar experiences as in the original novels, so Pin needs to run from cyber–Carabinieri, and Alina has to tell the Jabberwocky the scariest nursery rhyme she knows if she wants to be allowed to sit at the tea party, hosted by a replica of herself. In this psychedelic highly intertextual pastiche of texts and characters (which include David Bowie, Donald Duck, and White Fang, among others) the boy and the girl meet only briefly, through a message in a bottle, but they are both going through a journey in which they are trying to find their way and fight fear—a journey towards their most authentic identity and towards a better future. (See the Appendix for another version of the meeting of these characters, Peter Hunt's story "Strange Meeting in Wonder-Tuscany".)

Alice's Adventures in Wonderland and *Pinocchio's Adventures* began as local texts, and having transcended their origins, have become international classics. In chapters 1 and 2 I discussed the way in which world culture recognizes *Pinocchio* as "quintessentially" Italian, and *Alice* as "quintessentially" English, while simultaneously acknowledging their international appeal. In order to explore and develop this paradox, in this chapter I look at the way in which these texts have been considered postmodernist *avant la lettre* and in particular the way postmodern novelists Angela Carter and Robert Coover have refashioned these classics. In their transtextual journeys, Alice and Pinocchio have lost their original national connotations, in order to become symbols of a transnational, postmodern fractured self.

Even if Walt Disney's interpretations have provided the most recognizable image of Pinocchio and Alice for much of the Western world, the texts enjoyed great success and inspired a spate of imitations as soon as they were published. The *Pinocchiate* (see chapter 2), for example, have episodic structures and characters who are very similar to those found in *Pinocchio* (Myers 2012) and the *Alice* books were widely imitated in the Victorian and Edwardian eras (see Sigler 1997). *Alice* and *Pinocchio* have continued to be widely disseminated, in the original as well as revised

forms, in different media. Postmodernism in particular has been attracted
to fairy tale and fantasy, and has produced self-reflexive, de-mythologized
and dis-enchanted versions, where fairy tales are critically and ironically
revisited, updated, and disrupted. Parodic hyperrealism and comic dis-
missal of the magic and romantic elements coexist with the exposure of
make-believe or illusionist conventions. In particular, feminist revisions
"hold mirrors to the magic mirror of fairy tale" as "gender is almost
inevitably the privileged place for articulating [...] de-naturalizing strategies" (Bacchilega 23–24). Together with a corpus of feminist critical writing, these retellings have been very influential in all cultural fields (see
Zipes 2009: 121).

Both Alice and Pinocchio, as characters and books, have been mas-
sively suggestive for postmodern re-visioning. The de-centering of the
human, the desire to challenge traditional narratives, the interest in blur-
ring, fragmented or fluid identities, self-referentiality, the reflections on
"nomadic subjectivities" (Braidotti 6), and pastiche and black humor are
only some of the critical stances that we connect with Postmodernism
and which may appear immediately relevant to *Alice* and *Pinocchio*. There
is much in these "didactic books" to inspire a textual metamorphosis based
on techniques and themes characteristic of Postmodernism.

Even if, as I argued in chapter 4 and 5, neither *Alice* nor *Pinocchio*
can be satisfactorily labeled simply as fairy tales (although they were perceived as such by their respective authors), they have been subjected to
some of the textual metamorphic devices typical of postmodernist fairy
tales. One of the distinguishing features of both *Alice* and *Pinocchio* (and
one that contributes to their national and international appeal) is that
although they are derived from fantasy and folktale traditions that prior-
itize action over character, readers can identify with and empathize with
these characters. This is partly because, in the case of Alice, she almost
continuously interprets the world she encounters and partly because Collodi never relaxes the narrative pressures on, or the sympathetic narrato-
rial attitude to, his hero. In a way, Alice and Pinocchio are *us* in all their,
and our, individual complexity.

This is not the place for an analysis of *all* postmodern revisions of
the novels (which would probably require a thicker volume entirely devoted
to the subject); in this chapter I shall only mention a few examples of postmodernist revisions in order to give an idea of the variety of approaches
to these texts. I will concentrate on the way Angela Carter and Robert
Coover have deconstructed *both* books, each in their distinctive ways, in
the course of their careers (Disney is obviously the other famous adapter

of both books that immediately comes to mind, but I would not call his work postmodernist, however vague and all-encompassing this term has become).

It is remarkable that Carter's and Coover's versions achieve a form of universality by *de*humanizing or insisting on the "fleshy" humanity of their revised characters; we observe, perhaps dispassionately, Alice and Pinocchio's modern counterparts dealing with aging and gender roles, common morality and hybridity, and struggling to find meaning in their surreal worlds, struggles which become impersonal, abstract, quests. To these quests the reader on the one hand tends to react with detachment (even revulsion) rather than empathizing with the characters, while on the other hand, he or she can find the existential insecurity of the refashioned characters a familiar feature of modern reality.

Alice, a Postmodernist Icon

Alice's appeal and dissemination is not an exclusively postmodern and/or contemporary phenomenon, as sequels, imitations and parodies started to be published in the Victorian period and continued well into the 1930s and beyond (Siegler 1997). Both Modernist and Surrealist writers were equally attracted to *Alice*: Dusinberre, for example argues that

> in *The Voyage Out* Woolf writes from a sensibility in which a contempt for reverence to art [...] originates in Alice's polite but determined refusal to see her world in terms dictated by the Duchess, Humpty Dumpty, the Mad Hatter, the Walrus or even the Carpenter [73].

If the *Alice* books are not in themselves postmodernist, they can be seen, as Jan Susina suggests, as a "proto-hypertext" (143); Susina suggests that it is rather *Sylvie and Bruno* "Carroll's most ambitious, if not most deeply flawed, literary work" [...] which "set out a path for post-modernist writers" (126–127). The legacy of *Alice* survives, in children's literature, particularly in picturebooks: Nikolajeva and Scott note that "the play with the signifier and the signified [had] occurred already in the works of Lewis Carroll" and that "an increasing number of contemporary picturebooks make use of this device" (200). Jaques and Giddens devote a remarkable chapter to the textual afterlives of *Alice*, and argue that until recently, new versions "have tended to address one type of reader, or the other, [adult or child] but not both" (154), but the era of "crossover texts" has blurred this distinction.

Brooker has investigated the contemporary presence and the meaning of *Alice* in comic books, graphic novels, fan clubs, computer games, cyberpunk science fiction, to name just a few of the media that have made Alice as a character and *Alice* as a set of books relevant to the concerns of our century. As Israel has put it succinctly, "no one can keep their hands off Alice, but no-one can hold on to her either" (280).

McHale in *The Cambridge Introduction to Postmodernism* (2015) identifies 1966 as the year in which *Alice* "underwent a significant reorientation" (53) as a key text for postmodernist works that were not specific adaptations of Carroll's text, but which incorporated elements from it into their own "postmodernist schema," such as Thomas Pynchon's 1966 novel *The Crying of Lot 49*, an exemplary postmodern text. As McHale suggests, the *Alice* books are a fundamental feature of postmodernist fiction:

> So ubiquitous are allusions to *Alice* in postmodern novels [...] that the presence of *Alice* might almost be considered a *marker* of literary Postmodernism. If *Alice* appears, the novel is likely to be postmodernist[...]. Indeed, so ubiquitous are *Alice* allusions that one might legitimately wonder whether there are *any* novels that we generally regard as "postmodern" that do *not* allude somehow or other to *Alice*[...]. Postmodern *Alice* is Postmodernism in a nutshell [2015: 53, 61].

In a similar vein, more recently, Marco Minghetti has built a website project on humanistic management which centers on *Alice* as the prototype for Postmodernism and a model for contemporary media. Alice's opening sentence in Carroll's book, for example, is seen to prefigure blogs and social networks (he argues "What is Facebook, if not a book with images and conversations?") as well as to voice the thought of the "Digital Native," who cannot conceive of a form of communication *without* images and/or conversations.

In the last few decades *Alice* has been fantastically popular as a *hypotext* (Genette 11) for narrative, and especially postmodernist, revisions. Hollingsworth wonders what other story space is quite like *Alice*'s, "unfolding with an elusive, improvisational necessity—punctuated [...] by disjunctive movements from one discrete space to another" (xvii–xviii) while McHale has noted that "narrativizing *Alice*" has often meant imposing a narrative cohesion on the picaresque world of the disjointed episodes of the originals, in the attempt to counteract, paradoxically, the "antinarrative tendencies of Carroll's *Alice*" (2015: 58).

One can identify a few recurring types of narrative engagement with the *Alice* books, one of the most popular being the sequel. There are novels that use a pastiche of Carroll's style, plot devices and characters, to expand its scope by providing further adventures of Alice (e.g., Gilbert Adair's *Alice Through the Needle's Eye*, 2012); or retellings in which Alice or other characters revisit Wonderland after the first original journey. Gregory Maguire's *After Alice* (2015) is about Ada (only mentioned in Carroll's text as having longer ringlets than Alice), who goes looking for her friend Alice after she has gone missing. She inadvertently falls down the rabbit hole and spends the rest of the story in pursuit of her friend in Wonderland, encountering many of the characters that Alice has already come across in her journey, like the Pigeon (and some new ones, like the tin dancer):

> "If you please, my name is Ada."
> "Adder! I knew it! And a very fat adder at that. You shall find no mercy from *me*!"
> At this the little bird began to fly in Ada's face, beating and shrieking.
> "I'm not an adder, please! I'm a girl."
> The bird returned to a branch and cocked her head to look with one eye, then twisted about to look with a second. "*Another* girl? I'm not sure I believe you. The serpent said she was a girl, too, but I never saw a girl with such a long neck. I imagine she thought *she* was being the neck of the woods. She was only drawing attention to herself in an unseemly fashion, if you ask me" [Maguire 80–81].

This tendency to retrace Alice's adventures is not limited to print narrative, of course: in Tim Burton's film *Alice in Wonderland* (2010) a 19-year-old Alice returns to Wonderland (or Underland, as it is called) as a distraction and possibly an escape from an arranged marriage—she embarks on a quest to slay a monster and reinstate the White Queen.

Other novels mix the fictional universe of *Alice* with pseudo-biographical recreations of the relationship between Alice Liddell and Lewis Carroll. Katie Roiphe's *Still She Haunts Me* (2002), for example, speculates on the nature of their relationship and tries to "explain" the mystery of the rift with the Liddells (see Brooker 182–194). David Slavitt's 1984 novel *Alice at Eighty* is the fictional exploration of a series of encounters between Alice Hargreaves née Liddell and two grown-up women who had also been Lewis Carroll's favorite photographic models when they were little girls. More recently, in 2015, and following the 150th anniversary of the publication of *Alice's Adventures in Wonderland*, Alice Liddell's great-granddaughter, Vanessa Tait, has written *Looking Glass House*, a novel about the friendship between Lewis Carroll and young Alice Liddell, told from the viewpoint of the family governess, Mary Prickett. Similarly, John Logan's 2013 play *Peter and Alice* imagines the encounter between the eighty-year-old Alice Hargreaves and Peter Llewellyn Davies, the real-life Peter Pan, at a Lewis Carroll exhibition in 1932. *The Looking Glass Wars* fantasy series (2004–2007), by Frank Beddor, with its spin off *Hatter M* (2006–2015), also renegotiates the relationship between Alice and Lewis Carroll as in the Prologue Alyss complains that Carroll's transcription of the story she told him is incorrect:

> She skipped ahead, turned page after page. The Pool of Tears, the caterpillar, her aunt Redd: it had all been twisted into nonsense.
>
> "I admit that I took a few liberties with your story," Dodgson explained, "to make it ours, as I said I would." [...]
>
> The grinning Cheshire cat. The mad tea party. He'd transformed her memories of a world alive with hope and possibility and danger into make-believe, the foolish stuff of children. He was just another in a long line of unbelievers and this—this stupid, nonsensical book—was how he made fun of her. She had never felt more betrayed in all her life.
>
> "No one is ever going to believe me now!" she screamed. "You've ruined everything! You're the cruelest man I've ever met, Mr. Dodgson, and if you had believed a single word I told you, you'd know how very cruel that is! I never want to see you again! Never, never, never!" [Beddor 3].

Apart from the opening premise about Carroll having intentionally distorted her story, the first novel of the *Looking Glass Wars* series goes back to when Alyss Heart's mother, the Queen of Wonderland, is beheaded by her sister, Redd. Alyss is forced, on her seventh birthday, to flee into the Pool of Tears and escape to another world: Victorian London, where she is befriended by Lewis Carroll and adopted by the Liddell family. When, a few years later, Alyss returns to Wonderland, she finds that Redd has turned her happy, carefree home into a nightmare of Dark Imagination and injustice. Alyss remembers how to use White Imagination to regain the throne and eventually leads her people to victory.

Kali Israel has analyzed a number of novels based on the *Alice* books but set in the modern world in which adolescents or young women deal with several pathologies (such as Cathleen Schine's first novel *Alice in Bed*, 1985) including eating disorders: these novels use "Carroll's Alice's struggles with bigness and littleness and the power of looking glasses" (Israel 268) to tell stories about anorexia and the control of bodies. The *Alice* books have also been interpreted as voicing concerns about the transitions of the female body: Flegar and Wertag, for example, have argued that Alice acts precociously for her age, "making her adventures reflect the transitions of an adolescent," and that "Alice goes through a process called an *identity crisis*" (215). So it is not surprising that transformative appropriations of *Alice* by women writers should often connect the girl character's change of size with the experience of the female body changing in adolescence: Alice Duncan, the protagonist of Lisa Dierbeck's 2003 novel *One Pill Makes you Smaller* is only 11 but looks much older and seductive having already reached puberty at the age of nine. Like Coover's Alice, she feels uncomfortable with her growing body, but also she needs to fend off unwanted sexual male attention. In her analysis of further recent postmodernist adaptations of *Alice* which focus on Alice's female identity Siegler concludes that these retellings "demonstrate that present-day writers [...] continue to find an empowering cultural icon in this idealized 'dream-child' of a fussy Victorian mathematician and to appropriate the imaginative space of her fantasy wonderlands" (2005: 143).

Postmodernist *Pinocchio*: Between Cyborg and Fractured Fairy Tale

Like the *Alice* books, *Pinocchio* started to be rewritten, adapted and amplified not long after its publication, in novels that see Pinocchio (or an invented relative of his: brother, sister, cousin, son) embark on a series of new adventures (from Africa to the moon) and the fascist *Pinocchiate* have attracted considerable critical attention (see Curreri 2011, and Aroldi). As character and book and archetype of the human/non-human paradox, Pinocchio has often been transferred from his nineteenth-century original location into our technological and media-obsessed age.

Wunderlich and Morrissey in *Pinocchio Goes Postmodern* (2002) have identified many characteristics of the book which facilitate postmodernist adaptations, such as its "indeterminacy, a hallmark of postmodern fiction [...] the slipperiness of Pinocchio's self" (169): his multiple identities as humanoid, animal, and man-made construct have triggered innumerable transformations over cultures and languages (for *Pinocchio*'s transformation, adaptations and remediations in contemporary culture see, among others, Bettetini; Pezzini and Fabbri; Beckett 2004 and 2006; Dedola and Casari; Paruolo 2017). As Katia Pizzi has explained, Pinocchio is at the same time "a quintessentially nineteenth century creature" (1) and a symbol of a modern fluid identity—a "postmodern, posthuman icon[...]. Pinocchio's robotic, stiff and yet bendable body, his hybrid nature between mechanical and human, render him an ancestor of the Futurist Cyborg" (2). Jaques remarks that *Pinocchio* "invites post-human readings" (213): this archetypical agent of transformation moves between the animate and the inanimate, between the (dead?) substance of wood and living flesh—and lies between his double human and mechanical identity, with a typically postmodernist quality of in-betweenness between body and machine (Braidotti 214).

Stefano Benni's play *Pinocchia* (1999) has thoroughly exploited the mechanical potential of Pinocchio as a posthuman icon. In the play, Collodi's puppet is transformed into a female robot operated by a chip—Geppetto buys the robot girl and establishes a different, but always highly conflictual, relationship with her, as the robot (played by the actress Angela

Finocchiaro in the original production) can grow and change from a young daughter to a rebellious teenager, and from a lover to a mother figure. In this world of reality shows and illusory fame, Geppetto is finally discovered to be a clone (for an analysis of the play see Gören). In a similar vein, Steven Spielberg's movie *A.I. Artificial Intelligence* (2001) has a human mother read to the robot David a page from *Pinocchio*—he is substituting for her son Martin who has been placed in suspended animation until he can be cured of a rare disease. When Martin gets better and returns home, after a series of incidents and misunderstandings in the family, the robot is abandoned by his "mother" in the woods. The paradox is that although this robot, just like the puppet Pinocchio, cannot mature and grow up, he has feelings like any other (real) child, as he has been programed to love a human unconditionally and permanently. This is a world in which robots appear to have deeper feelings than humans (for a discussion of the movie see Morrissey 2004).

The mystery of Pinocchio's creation has been compared to Mary Shelley's *Frankenstein* (see Klopp 2006 and 2012) and recently, Ausonia's graphic book *Pinocchio, storia di un bambino* (2014) has used a strategy of inversion to produce a highly disturbing version of the book. In a world of wooden puppets Pinocchio is the only one made of flesh, a flesh that has been assembled by his cruel butcher father and that is always in danger of rotting. Pinocchio has been made without a nose, but a nose grows every time he tells the truth, which is, basically, all the time, while the puppets lie constantly. Lying is what puppets do to avoid taking responsibility—in this society telling the truth is dangerous and a crime, and Pinocchio is not believed when he tells the judge that he has been beaten up, raped, exploited, tortured and disfigured. His only happy time is spent in the Land of Toys, where puppets are still young and innocent and have not learnt yet how to lie. Ausonia's truthful Pinocchio is a melancholic loser, and the ending, in which the puppets rummage through his flesh to find out why he is behaving in this way is a sort of vivisection—the defeat of the individual by a totalitarian and warlike society.

Another example of a postmodernist *Pinocchio* for an adult audience, is Canadian Michael Kenyon's *Pinocchio's Wife* (1992), retold by the shape-changing Fairy—but there is no feminist message here as one might expect, although the Fairy seems to have adapted very well to the North American way of life: "Never thought I'd leave Italy. Never wanted to. Economically expedient, the publisher said, and gave me a Hollywood address[...]. A free spirit, unfettered, I explored the continent. I took up aerobics" (Kenyon 101–102).

The typical narrative voice of classic fairy tales is an extradiegetic narrator; changing the narrator's voice and have a character tell the story in the first person may give the reader a limited perspective on the story, but also provides the unique opportunity to enter a character's consciousness, and access the motivations behind his or her behavior. Unlike the elusive Fairy of Collodi's book, Kenyon's Fairy is an external observer of a grown-up Pinocchio's strained relationship with his Canadian wife (who is having an affair with Lampwick) and of Geppetto's loneliness in a nursing home. She is also aware of her literariness, that she was created by Collodi, who has recast her as a mother, and has been given her an actress's body and fame by Disney. She often talks about the animators, and the music that seems to underscore every moment of Pinocchio's life in the novel, the "Disney's demiurges," as she calls them. It is a very interesting (and very postmodern) narrative experiment on fictionalized lives, but one that cannot rely on a happy ending as the characters live in an ordinary world of solitary meals, infidelity, sexual ambiguity, and nursing homes (where Geppetto dies, waiting in vain for his son's visit). Questions of sexual identity are central: Pinocchio's homoerotic tendencies are at the heart of marital discord (Wunderlich and Morrissey 188).

Postmodern retellings of *Pinocchio* for a young audience are—obviously—not as dark and distressing. As Beckett has noted, "*Pinocchio* is exploited for a ludic purpose in an endless array of children's books that fracture the fairy tale only to retain one or two elements and discard the rest" (2004: 114). Self-referential texts explicitly de-familiarize the young reader using narrative techniques which we tend to associate with fiction written exclusively for adult readers, such as irony, pastiche, superimposition of narrative voices, boundary breaking and so on. As these texts can hardly imply an audience already equipped to deal with such techniques, especially if the audience is still consolidating primary reading skills, self-referential texts can actually serve as "postmodernist primers," a playful introduction to the more complex texts the reader might have to face as an adult (Tosi 2006b: 74). Lane Smith and Luigi Malerba are two of the authors who have used Pinocchio's story as a starting point to produce what can be defined as children-friendly postmodern versions of Collodi's tale.

Lane Smith is the illustrator of Scieszka's *The Stinky Cheese Man and Other Fairly Stupid Fairy Tales* (1992), a collection of retold fairy tales for a child audience which uses typically postmodern foregrounding and boundary-breaking techniques. He is the author and illustrator of *Pinocchio the Boy* (2002), a sequel to Collodi's book that starts when the Blue

Fairy grants the puppet his wish. The joke is that Pinocchio is completely unaware of the transformation (the Fairy changed him while he was asleep) and therefore, when he wakes up, continues to behave like a puppet. When he complains, to a girl who befriends him, that he can no longer talk to the Cricket, or that his father has lived in a fish, she thinks he is slightly disturbed. Even Geppetto does not recognize him as a boy, until the Fairy explains everything (and is told off by her daughter: "next time you change a puppet into a kid, you might want to wake him up first"). *Pinocchio con gli Stivali* (1988) by Luigi Malerba, is a fairy-tale salad (a term coined by Gianni Rodari in *A Grammar of Fantasy* to describe a fictional jumble of fairy-tale characters) addressed to a child audience, which starts at the end of chapter 35 of Collodi's book, when the protagonist decides that he does not intend to become a well-behaved boy (Beckett 2004). So he tries to find himself a role in a different tale but the characters are very conservative types (the wolf in "Little Red Riding Hood," for example, does not want to exchange places with him) and want to stick to their preordained plots—some, like Cinderella's prince, even treat him with contempt, as a parvenu who wants to intrude in a much older and more famous story. In the end this narrative rebel does manage to interfere in "Puss in Boots" and as a consequence he is kicked out of the story and sent back to chapter 36 and his transformation into a boy.

In the same ironic and playful vein, in 1995 Umberto Eco retold *Pinocchio* only with words starting with P (a tautogram which would be challenging to translate in another language). The title is, of course, *Povero Pinocchio*. Disney's Pinocchio, sporting an improbable Tyrolean costume and American accent, is also a character in the Dreamworks fairy-tale salad film *Shrek* (2001) and its sequels. This is a typical case where parody has a fantastically comic effect: in the first *Shrek*, Pinocchio is sold to Lord Farquaad by Geppetto for 5 shillings (recalling the 5 golden coins given to Pinocchio by Mangiafoco), and he is called by one of the guards "the possessed toy." In *Shrek 2* (2004) the fairy godmother turns him into a real boy but then he is hit by a blast of magic that turns him back into a puppet, and in *Shrek 3* (2007) he replies with comic ambiguity to Prince Charming's interrogation about whether he knows the whereabouts of the ogre Shrek: "It wouldn't be inaccurate to assume that I couldn't exactly not say that it is or isn't almost partially incorrect." One of the running jokes in *Shrek 2* is his lying about his ambiguous sexual identity and wearing women's underwear.

Just as with the *Alice* books, references to *Pinocchio* are everywhere, not just in books, but in advertising, jokes, cartoons and toys. Collodi's novel has been retold and updated across different media platforms—theme parks, theatre adaptations, graphic novels, and artistic installations, and in different languages (see Paruolo 2017). (The Internet Movie database, IMDb, at the time of writing, lists Pinocchio's appearance in 128 movies and TV series. Alice appears in 103). The issues of identity that were crucial in the original books are translated into other cultural and generic contexts thus taking on different implications and nuances.

Fragmented identities and alienation from the self and especially from one's body are common experiences in both Carter's and Coover's fiction. As I discussed in chapter 5, both Alice and Pinocchio are forever trying to locate (and stabilize) their identities, in a world that encourages change and mutability, and they are in constant danger of being downgraded to lower forms on the animal scale. Their identity as iconic bodies in flux parallels their shifting identities in revisions and remediations.

Angela Carter and Robert Coover

Despite the abundance of experimental, and postmodern revisions of *Alice* and *Pinocchio*, there are not many authors who, like Disney, have engaged with both *Pinocchio* and *Alice*. Coover and Carter refashion Alice and Pinocchio's destinies in different ways but end up exploring very similar aspects of these books. As Robert Coover recalls in an article:

> Angela Carter and I first encountered one another in the landscape of the tale, somewhere between *Pricksongs & Descants* and *Fireworks*, published a year or so apart, discovering therein an immediate affection for one another's imaginations. We corresponded for two years before we actually met and became lifelong (alas, not so long) friends, and in that time confirmed that we shared much as writers and differed little, if at all, and thus what either of us might write might seem a message or a tribute to the other [1998: 242].

According to the classic study by McHale, the "dominant" of postmodern fiction is *ontological* (unlike the modernist dominant, which is epistemological)—the shift is "from problems of knowing to problems of modes of being[...]. Other typical postmodernist questions bear either on the ontology of the literary text itself or the ontology of the world which it projects" (1989: 10). It is therefore not surprising that these authors have put the question of identity, of characters as "beings," at the heart of their rewriting of *Alice* and *Pinocchio*. They defamiliarize the books by exploring their characters' fragmented identities, set in precariously-built fictional worlds in which the reader is left "wondering" about the consistency of their actions. Both authors challenge clear notions of genre and gender and raise questions about the unity of the subject.

What is most interesting in this context about their work on Collodi and Carroll is the way in which they have shifted the emphasis from nationality to other concepts of identity. While the original texts tend to suppress the subtexts of sexuality (in a more complex way than referring to Alice's neck or Pinocchio's nose, of course) these postmodern experiments have put a fragmented and complex sexual identity at the center of their revisions. For both characters "Growing Up" has become a form of disillusionment: the essentially exuberant and exploratory bodily metamorphoses the characters have to undergo in Collodi's and Carroll's texts have become grotesque, and the result of often shocking negotiations with gender roles. For all their erratic progress, the original adventures of Alice and Pinocchio are ultimately philosophically, culturally, and politically coherent; in their postmodern manifestations, both reader and characters are disoriented and forced to look in vain for some organizing principle; the narrative world has become a web of intertextual allusion and experimental narrative stances.

Alice, *the Gothic and the Female Puppet Paradigm*

The effect of Angela Carter's "carnival of rewriting is to shift the narrative focus onto transformations, metamorphosis and exchanges of identity" (Sage 173). Her engagement with *Alice* and *Pinocchio* is less direct than Coover's—while he writes sequels, she uses the intertextual references to Carroll's character in surreal settings, in novels and tales placed at the intersection of genres, in which the conventions of fairy tale and classic Gothic fiction often interact. Alice is an important subtext in much of Carter's fiction, and the motifs of mirrors as reflectors of female identity and blurred boundaries between the real world and the world beyond the mirror are pervasive. Jacqueline Pearson's observation about the novel *Several Perceptions*, that it presents "an apparently chaotic world and narrative may come into a newly, though perhaps ironically, clear form when we see it through the prism of its main intertext, *Alice's Adventures in Wonderland*"(ix), can also be applied to most novels by Carter: the fragmentation and disorientation of the self that Alice experiences in Wonderland (Suchan 82) becomes a sort of primary imprinting for several female characters in her writing.

"Wolf Alice" is the last tale in *The Bloody Chamber* (1979), a collection of revised fairy tales which explore the dark content of the originals, which

Carter published after translating the tales of Perrault and Mme d'Aulnoy—
many of her tales are based on the French versions, although they rely on
many other sources (Collodi, it may be remembered, wrote *Pinocchio* after
translating Perrault's tales, see "Collodi's translation of Perrault" in chapter
4). Carter's tale, based on the legend of a girl raised by wolves (who has
been treated unkindly by the nuns she has been living with, and now lives
with the Duke, a werewolf), is blended with allusions to "Little Red Riding
Hood." The oscillation between the human and the bestial is present in
other tales of the collection, notably "The Lady of the House of Love,"
about a female vampire, or the retellings of "Beauty and the Beast" which
project a transgressive, unorthodox and liminal female identity (see Armitt
and Koenen). "Wolf Alice," in which the girl explores both herself and the
mysterious human world that surrounds her, challenges and deconstructs
clear notions of the human and the feral: "Nothing about her is human
except that she is *not* a wolf; it is as if the fur she thought she wore had
melted into her skin and become part of it, although it does not exist"
(Carter 1979: 119).

As I mentioned in chapter 4, Carroll's Alice has been seen to have
animal characteristics: Auerbach, for example, argues that "the more sinister and Darwinian aspects of animal nature are introduced into Wonderland by the gentle Alice in part through projections of her hunger onto
Dinah and the 'nice little dog' [...] and in part through the semi-
cannibalistic appetite her songs express" (37). And of course her world
revolves around the issue of size, and the way eating and drinking can
affect her body, and make her more vulnerable or powerful in relation to
the other characters. Hybridity triumphs: Alice can be perceived as serpent
and a little girl: Wonderland is a world "of human and animal interchange-
ability" (Lovell-Smith 46). Like Carroll's protagonist, Carter's Wolf Alice
constantly slips between categories. She learns to recognize herself as
human by looking at her reflection in the mirror, and then by the cyclical
appearance of her menses, which gives her a sense of time. It is when she
grasps the bi-dimensional structure of the mirror that her beast nature
begins to change. However, the way she kindly attends to the Duke after
he has been attacked by humans, is typically animal as she licks his wounds
and helps *him* become human. After her ministrations, he can finally project his image on the mirror, which until then had refused to reflect it
(and this has been seen as a reference to Carroll's own photographic
artistry—see Schanoes 2012 and 2014): the Duke enters humanity only
when he can see himself in the mirror. Wolf Alice parallels the Duke's
shifting between animal and human nature—they are both outcasts; after

the girl, "pitiful as her gaunt grey mother" (Carter 1979: 126), has helped the Duke heal, they appear to have embraced an ambivalent form of humanity. Carter's Alice complicates Carroll's construction of the child and its relationship with the animal world: "In creating a series of constantly shifting women, constantly shifting wolves, Carter offers an alternative to the dominant myth of singularity" (Lau 92).

"Alice in Prague or the Curious Room," which Carter dedicated to the Czechoslovakian film director and animator Jan Svankmajer and his own experimental movie *Alice* (1987) has no plot and the scant dialogues are totally surreal. It reads like an assemblage of parts, a Renaissance wunderkammer like the one in possession of Rudolf II King of Bohemia and Hungary (1552–1610), who is one of the characters in the tale. The other characters are the Renaissance magus Dr. Dee and his assistant Kelly, and the Mannerist Italian painter Giuseppe Arcimboldo, who worked in Prague from 1562 to 1587 (it is interesting that Carter's work, as well as Coover's, has been called "mannerist" as well as "postmodernist" [see Frankova and Bond] as if she were borrowing Arcimboldo's knack for assembling parts in his paintings—Arcimboldo is famous for painting imaginative still-life portraits of people made entirely of objects such as fruits and vegetables, flowers, fish, and books). Unsurprisingly, in a tale in which thingness is so important, lists of objects related to the *Alice* books abound, among them "a raven and a writing desk" (Carter 1994: 125). In this fictional world Carter's analogical thinking—a world of allusion (to Shakespeare, John Donne, Wittgenstein and many others) which can be very rewarding for the literary critic/sleuth—parallels alchemy, the discipline that has as a founding principle cosmic analogy (and which Dr. Dee was believed to master). It is a world of literary, magical and natural transformation:

> a series of multi-layered, intertextually saturated language games, the reader's subsequent vertigo becomes a "laboratory" in which the alchemical processes of Carter's aesthetic occur, where the ideological forces of language momentarily surface and interpellate the reader [Ryan-Sautour 76].

The sudden arrival of Carroll's Alice in Dr. Dee's crystal glass, instead of the angels that he is expecting to summon, is totally unaccounted for: she grows and shrinks with food and drink given to her by a very bemused Dr. Dee and an ever more bemused Kelly, who is just a trickster and does not believe in magic ("Kelly continued to mumble: 'There must be some rational explanation'" Carter 1994: 133).

Alice continues to ask the men mathematical riddles (taken from Carroll's own *Tangled Tale*) which they cannot answer as they would probably need a logical nineteenth-century mind in order to be able to do so. Alice's frustration grows, but the ending is open:

"How did they do it?" she repeated, now almost with desperation, as if, if they only could stumble on the correct reply, she would be precipitated back, diminutive, stern, rational, within the crystal ball and thence be tossed back through the mirror to "time will be," or, even better, to the book from which she had sprung [Carter 1994: 138].

Carter's late sixteenth-century Prague hosts a court that believes in Wonder, in collecting rarities from the natural world (like a mermaid, or a falling star), in speaking with angels, in the transformative power of alchemy, and in magic. The enigmatic nature of Carter's tale, in which anachronism, the inversion of cause and effect, and the animation of the inanimate are the norm, may be interpreted as yet another investigation of the theme of identity. This enigmatical tale could be about, among other things, the clash of sixteenth-century identity and nineteenth-century identity, but this contrast raises endless questions. Are our identities constructs in which the past and the future continuously change places, spaces where we animate things, summon memories, or resurrect the dead to have mental conversations with them? Is the human brain a wunderkammer, a "curious room" full of incongruent articles taken from the most disparate sources, an "organ" that is the quintessence of intertextuality? Alice needs a logical reply to her riddles, but she will not find it. The tale seems to suggest that we all host an Alice in our mental wunderkammer, which often we let out of our personal crystal balls, and let her grow so that she asks uncomfortable questions to which we may not have a ready reply.

Carter's allusions to *Pinocchio* are again in terms of gender, as they tend to concentrate on the place of the feminine in Gothic-like settings, and female hybrid identities. The novel *The Magic Toyshop* (1967) seems to be more concerned with the notion of free will and determinism. The orphan Melanie, who is sent with her brothers to live at her uncle Philip's (a Mangiafoco-type puppeteer who has nothing of the sentimental nature of the original), is ordered to impersonate a puppet in her uncle's theatrical scenario. She has to act in "Leda and the Swan," clearly a sexual fantasy of her uncle's, and the central scene is the grotesque surrogate coupling of the woman-as-puppet and a huge wooden swan puppet. During the "rape" Melanie "was hallucinated: she felt herself not herself, wrenched from her own personality" (Carter 1967: 166). The puppeteer transforms her into an object, in the same way that he has transformed his own wife into a silent puppet (she has not spoken since her wedding day). The scene in which Melanie plays the puppet revives her earlier memory of a present her Uncle Philip sent her many years before, a jack-in-the-box with a caricature of her face which scared her as a child. In the course of the novel Melanie is precipitated, like Alice, into an underworld of uncanny replicas and patriarchal sadism—she grows surrounded by life-sized puppets that her uncle adores, and by his family, which he ties to him by strings of fear (Gamble 71). Growing up is connected with metamorphosis and rites of passage: she has to come to terms with what she will decide to become—either a silenced object like her aunt ("poor women [...] planets round a male sun" [140]) or someone with agency. In the novel, artificial doubles are often preferred to real-life originals: "You overacted," Philip complains after Melanie's performance as Leda, "You were melodramatic. Puppets don't overact" (167). Although *The Magic Toyshop* uses some stock fairy-tale motifs, and has grotesque moments, the novel is basically realist (although Peach disagrees: "the novel has more in common with 'magic realism' than 'realism'" [75]).

With the tale "The Loves of Lady Purple" Carter moves towards a more experimental form of fiction in which it is extremely difficult to distinguish between identities and their origins. Lady Purple is a life-sized marionette who must act "The Notorious Amours of Lady Purple, the Shameless Oriental Venus." It is not clear whether she has started her lustful career as a woman and has been transformed into a puppet afterwards, crystalized in the mechanical repetition of her bizarre and destructive sexual voracity, or whether as a puppet she enacted a role on stage. But when her creator, the puppeteer called the Professor, kisses her before he puts her to bed, she comes to life and drains her maker's blood. And then she walks towards the village brothel to start the cycle of sexual excess and outrage again, as if the male-dominated society could not offer her any other role to play:

> Whether she was renewed or newly born, returning to life or becoming alive, awakening from a dream or coalescing into the form of a fantasy generated in her wooden skull by the mere repetition so many times of the same invariable actions [...] she could not escape the tautological paradox in which she was trapped; had the marionette all the time parodied the living or was she, now living, to parody her own performance as a marionette? [Carter 1974: 37–38].

At the crossroads of the picaresque and Gothic horror, this tale is a commentary on gender and simulacra, a reversal of the equation puppet= female submission that we find in *The Magic Toyshop*, and a cross-gender revision of *Pinocchio* which reflects on the nature of transformation, female exploitation, and "revenge" against one's creator. In this tale the Gothic undertones of *Pinocchio* are exploited to the full—if Pinocchio is "resurrected" after he is hung at the end of chapter 15, Lady Purple is punished by the debasement from human into puppet, and her change back into a human body does not come as a reward for her good deeds. Resurrected in all her depravity by killing her creator, she just won't be packed away: "Here Carter uses paradox and irony to show how Lady Purple represents male fears of the vampiric femme fatale and patriarchy's necrophilic desire to make women into inanimate dolls" (Wisker 130).

Robert Coover: Exploding Child and Adult Identities

In 1971, with *La Vita Nova*, the visionary novelist Luigi Compagnone set his version of *Pinocchio* (an adaptation of as well as a commentary on the original novel) in contemporary Naples. He denounces the corruption and the ills of Italian society in a *tour de force* where the past and the present coexist, the Blue Fairy is Medea, the puppeteer Mangiafoco is Dr. Freud, and characters from history and literature (from the Sun King Louis XIV to Karl Marx) are mixed with the defamiliarized characters of Collodi's novel. Pinocchio's social climbing from beggar into rich, ruthless and exploitative entrepreneur in a capitalistic society is rewarded with a human transformation, which coincides with Geppetto's death (for a detailed reading of *La Vita Nova* see Paruolo 2003). Twenty years later, Robert Coover, with *Pinocchio in Venice* (1991) provided yet another postmodern *tour de force* in an Italian city with symbolic associations remarkably different from the Tuscan setting of the original. Coover moves Pinocchio's story from Tuscany to Venice, which allows him to explore the book's darker suggestions in its labyrinthine space (Wunderlich and Morrissey 182).

As Bell has observed, "this novel's extravagance makes Rabelais look like a junior reader" (34). In the manner of many sequels and fan fiction, it provides an answer to the question "What happens to Pinocchio after he has become a boy?" It is also an updating of Collodi's book, which starts from an old Pinocchio, now a famous professor of Art in the United States—Professor Pinenut—who goes back to his native Italy to finish his autobiography (called "Mamma"). He embarks on a journey during which he revisits, disastrously, the episodes of his textual life as a puppet (following Collodi rather closely), only this time the Fox and Cat steal his precious computer with the un-backed-up Mamma files, as well as his money. Coover recontextualizes passages, events and characters from *Pinocchio* and imaginatively fills in some narrative gaps, as for example, when Pinenut recalls his own sexual initiation by the Fairy.

Many fairy tales and fantasies have to do with death, and *Pinocchio* and *Alice* are no exception (see chapter 5). In these books the depiction of fear, death and loss of identity, distortions and dystopias are pervasive: but if traditional folk and fairy tales are concerned with death, Coover's rewriting of *Alice* and *Pinocchio* deals with aging and the body's decay.

Professor Pinenut's memories of his puppet days are traumatic. It is as if he had experienced hunger, pain, violence, near-death as a human being instead of as a resilient wooden puppet and we are told that Geppetto was spiteful and mean, as when he didn't want Pinocchio to save him from the shark's belly: "You, you little spunk, you sap, you sucker, you nutless wonder! You twist of tinder fungus! You're a thorn in my side! A splinter in my eye! A sprit up my ass! One step closer, knothole, and I'll make toothpicks out of you!" (Coover 1991: 112).

But Pinocchio is not the only one to have unhappy memories. We learn that Eugenio, the boy that Pinocchio thinks he has killed with a volume on arithmetic in the "Battle of the Books" (chapter 27), was raped by the Omino. It turns out that the little man who took children to the Land of Toys, has used some of them as his sexual toys. Coover makes the subtext of sexual predation that lurks in the cruel child thief of the original novel explicit, and makes Eugenio the Omino's heir, not only of his substance, but also of his tricks and power over the city. Eugenio is a ruthless Venetian merchant, the most powerful man in Venice, and behaves like a mafia boss (he dies at the end, squashed, once again, but this time by a computer that Pinenut throws out of the window in frustration, after having realized that Eugenio's gang has removed his files). It is only the Puppet Brigade, a terrorist gang and an updated version of the puppet theater, that tries to counteract Eugenio's power. They immediately recognize Pinocchio (again) as one of them, and Pinocchio realizes that when he met the puppets in Collodi's book, that had been "the happiest night of his life" (Coover 1991: 138).

Very self-centered and self-referential, totally defenseless against Venetian swindlers, Pinenut, a Nobel laureate, exemplifies the gullible tourist in a city that unfortunately knows a thing or two about fleecing visitors. Venice is the conflation of all the dystopian spaces of Collodi's *Pinocchio*: it is, at the same time, *il Paese dei Balocchi*, *il Paese di Acchiappacitrulli*, and *l'Isola delle Api Operose*. But it is also the quintessential city where death, corruption and ambivalence interact: not just Thomas Mann's Venice, but also Joyce's Dublin, and even Dante's Purgatory and Prufrock's London (these are only some of the texts and spaces that Coover alludes and responds to in his fiction). Venice is "the city of endless illusion" (Coover 1991: 185) and the place where the real "Campo dei Miracoli" (field of miracles) is to be found (Santa Maria dei Miracoli, the church overlooking the eponymous *Campo* in Venice, is one of the most exquisite examples of early Renaissance art). As Seaboyer notes,

> Venice is the perfect setting, too, for Coover's virtuoso exegesis of Bakhtinian dialogism. Coover places himself in a long line of literary thieves of language in the construction of his text, and raids the history of western literature, art, architecture, and philosophy, much as Venice raided the Eastern Mediterranean in its self-construction as a legible, urban text. *Pinocchio in Venice* is like the façade of San Marco, a collage of disparate bits and pieces that are nonetheless of a piece [244].

At the beginning of the novel, Professor Pinenut is over a century old, and in his search for the self and for the meaning of his existence, he finds himself reverting to the puppet he was—to his wooden core. In this endless transformation his body is equated to the body of Venice, and its wooden encrusted foundations under water, as when he falls into a canal: "He has come at the end to the beginning, to the very foundations of this mysterious enterprise and of his own as well: back to the slimy ooze and the ancient bits of wood, driven deep, holding the whole apparition up" (Coover 1991: 155). Robbed and arrested with his pants down, all dignity lost, his appendages starting to fall off and apparently rotting, he is confused and alienated: he even ends up "embedded in molded pizza dough [...] and now, six cooks all helping at once, they ease him on backwards on a little trolley into the bread oven" (Coover 1991: 270–271). This is a parody and a rewriting of the incident in Collodi's book where Pinocchio is coated in flour and almost fried in chapter 28. But in Coover this takes an extra meaning as the chapter is entitled "Cooked in Love" ("cotto" in Italian means having a crush, or being in love), and Pinenut indeed is burning with love for his ex-student Bluebell, one of the many reincarnations of the Blue Fairy. In the book this is a widespread strategy—that of literalizing Italian proverbs and idioms in English—but one that only a bilingual reader can appreciate. Professor Pinenut's social and physical degradation is a prelude to his own Easter regeneration, after the Carnival craze (everyone wears a mask), when, on the verge of death he is finally reunited with the Blue Fairy. In the course of his Venetian adventures, Pinenut starts questioning both his humanity and his puppet identity. But this exploration of human nature is performed in a hallucinatory context and with a lot of scatological humor, which prevents the reader from being really moved by Pinenut's painful experience of disintegration of identity and body.

In Coover's short story "Alice in the Time of the Jabberwock" (2000), also a sequel as well as a rewriting of Carroll's book, Alice is living Peter Pan's nightmare: she grows up and grows old, in a world in which everything stays the same. Like Pinenut, Alice revisits (but not for the first time, it appears) the places of her memories, like the Tea Party. But this time her pinafore is stained, the steaming cup makes her hot flushes worse and the birthday song that the characters sing to her is cruel and mean: "'Happy birthday to Alice!' they were singing, 'And to her spreading hips! To her varicose veins! And her tender nips!'" (Coover 2006: 85). Frustratingly caught between states (she is flattered by the Knave of Hearts' advances but she cannot stand his rudeness), she questions her "young girl" identity:

> I wake up at night, soaking wet with perspiration, trying to remember who I am or what I am, afraid that Alice isn't going to be Alice anymore. It's as though that pretty little girl has gone away and left me and I'm now just another extinct and imbecile old creature stumbling around crazily in Wonderland [Coover 2006: 102].

The characters reassure her half-heartedly:

> "But what's happening to me?" She bawled. "I can't stop *changing*! *Who* am I? *What* am I?"
> "Why, you are a little girl, of course," snapped the Mad Hatter[...]. "Just like you have always been! As large as life and—"
> "No, no! *Much* larger! Look at me!" [Coover 2006: 78].

Similarly, the parodies of poems that they recite are revealing and crude:

> You are old, mother Alice, and big as a door,
> And all covered in wrinkles and fat!
> [...]
> You are old, Mother Alice, your hair has turned white,
> And your skin is as rough as sandstone! [Coover 2006: 92]

The menopausal Alice feels hideous as she notices her double chin, her flapping upper arms, the spots on the back of her sweaty hands. She has grown bigger in size—once again—but not more powerful, as in this exchange with the Cheshire-Cat:

> "You are hardly invisible," said the Cat with his fixed grin.
> "Because I'm so big and floppy? That's just another way to disappear" [Coover 2006: 99].

The grown-up Alice now thinks with nostalgia about the wood where things have no names, which she calls "the dark wood of forgetfulness" (Coover 2006: 94) and remembers it as a marvelous place where she can lose herself. She has learnt that the very essence of Wonderland is not just madness and death—it is *cruelty* (Coover 2006: 93) and she misses the "real world" of golden afternoons of the aboveground, which appears to have been the Red King's dream (Coover 2006: 71): "after they made me a queen and all the fun was over, though it seemed like more fun for them than it was for me, I kept trying to find the way out" (Coover 2006: 101).

Even the encounter with the butterfly (once the Caterpillar), which tells Alice about the pains and rewards of transformation (the "trials of change" 95) and appears to have come out of its "crisis" triumphant and ready to enjoy every minute of its new life, ends in the bleakest way, with the butterfly being snapped up by a swallow. "Ah well, thought Alice, staring glumly at the abruptly vacated mushroom. Wonderland" (Coover 2006: 95).

Her quest for identity continues, but the transformations she undergoes this time are connected to female middle age: Alice's body has become as grotesque and undignified as that of Professor Pinenut. Both characters, confused and disempowered, have aged badly. Coover deprives them of the vitality, the rebelliousness, and ultimately the charm they used to have. Alice and Pinocchio have changed into pathetic and degraded versions of their younger selves, and revisiting the characters and the episodes of the original texts has become a painful experience, alienated as they are from the fictional worlds they inhabit. Coover's *Pinocchio in Venice* and "Alice in the Time of the Jabberwock" are texts for adults not just because of their explicit language, their middle-aged, or senile, disillusionment, and their exploration of sexuality (that of a puppet-turned-man, or the terrors of an overgrown girl) but because of the viciousness of the characters that surround them, all of whom appear to have deteriorated and become even more corrupt.

Both authors take these characters and these books from the children's world (those critics who believe that *Alice* and *Pinocchio* were never books for children in their complex sub-textuality may feel justified, given the way that postmodern writers for adults have embraced them) and re-used them as patterns for a frustrated quest for a unified self. In Carter and Coover, *Pinocchio* and *Alice*, as texts and characters, become emblematic of typically postmodern, fragmented identities. The dark sides of the originals—those often-savage elements of folk and fairytale which may account for the ways in which *Alice* and *Pinocchio* have transcended their national boundaries—emerge strongly—almost inevitably. These retellings by postmodern writers that I have examined in this chapter emphasize the instability and ambiguity of the original texts and of the unfixed or multiple identities of the original characters. The postmodernist universalization of the quest for identity through fictional characters already accepted as universals adds accessibility to the postmodern project, and further strength to the apparently highly localized characters of Pinocchio and Alice.

7. Childhood, School and Empire in Italy and the UK: Hughes and De Amicis, Henty and Salgari

From Fantasy to Realism: The Age of Empire

Childhood and children's books have always had a symbiotic relationship. Each contributes to the construction of the other, and one of the most revealing ways of understanding how different cultures and nations construct childhood is to reflect on the remarkably different ways in which individual genres are constructed and perceived within different national settings. In the previous chapters of the book, through the comparative analysis of the *Alice* books and *Pinocchio*, I followed the parallel development of the fantasy mode in the countries from which these classics have emerged quite independently. Comparative genre studies investigate the connections between the popularity of a certain genre, or literary theme, in different national cultures and at different periods (O'Sullivan 42–43), and explain the reasons for them. Analyzing the development of a theme, or a genre, or a mode, across national traditions, even when there is no evidence of instances of cross-fertilization, offers a variety of insights into (often unexpected) cultural attitudes to nation, education, and class, and the way that they relate to (in this case) nineteenth-century constructions of childhood. Parallel readings can also often (ironically) be assisted by "Comparative Literature's indiscipline" (Ferris 28–29), and the lack of definition that exists within comparative studies, as the absence of clear

guidelines can afford significant freedom when it comes to the organization and comparison of genres and traditions across national borders. The
aim of this chapter is to encourage, very tentatively, reflection on genres
that in different countries articulate diverse versions of colonialism and
Empire, within a Eurocentric view of the Orient, which, as Said has explained:

> was almost a European invention, and had been since antiquity a place of romance,
> exotic beings, haunting memories and landscapes [...] a mode of discourse with sup-
> porting institutions, vocabulary, scholarship, imagery, doctrines, even colonial bureau-
> cracies and colonial style [1–2].

In this chapter I move on from the fantasy-folktale-bildungsroman
genre triangulation on which *Alice* and *Pinocchio* are based, to an attempt
to contrast two popular genres that can be classified as realistic, and which
in England were aimed primarily, but not exclusively, at a male readership.
School stories and adventure stories became popular at a time (the last
decades of the nineteenth century and the first of the twentieth) when
England and Italy were thinking of themselves as nations in relation to the
polarity of a familiar, local and boundaried educational environment vs.
the "Otherness" and the openness of the spaces of exotic places and the
Empire. In England, in particular, the local and circumscribed functioned
as an educational springboard for those who would then explore, tame,
and control the exotic lands of the colonized. In the middle of the Age of
Empire (Hobsbawm) these genres conveyed radically different notions of
civilization, class, nation and honor, to young Italian and to young English
readers. As in the case of Collodi and Carroll, in the earlier chapters, I
have found it useful in this chapter to contrast the work of specific authors.
I chose those authors who wrote the most typical and recognizable (or
the first) exemplifications of the genre, so that the parallel readings of
works are occasionally reflected (or reinforced, or anticipated—there is
no escaping a degree of circularity) in the temperament and personality
of the authors. When I examine school stories (or, in the case of Italy, stories set in schools, as in Italian there is no equivalent critical term to the
"school story genre" in English) the texts I concentrate on are by Thomas
Hughes and Edmondo De Amicis, and in the adventure stories genre, the
novels of George Henty and Emilio Salgari.

Schoolboys and Citizens

Literary genres are rooted in the cultural, social and educational conditions of the nation that has produced them: in the case of the school

story, we can look at the way the school setting interacts with the representation of children as citizens. Italy's most famous school story, Edmondo De Amicis's *Cuore* (1886) can be seen through the lens of the most influential British example of the school story genre, Thomas Hughes's *Tom Brown's Schooldays* (1857), and vice versa. *Tom Brown's Schooldays*, essentially a liberal text, stands at the head of a genre that is generally associated with an economically based and religiously infused class system. *Cuore*, a non-religious book in a strictly Catholic country was the standard-bearer for a society of multiclass childhoods. In chapter 3 I argued that education is central to both *Le avventure di Pinocchio* and Carroll's *Alice* books: Carroll, in a self-confident high–Victorian world of Empire-building could afford to be satirical about education; De Amicis, writing at a crucial point of the post–*Risorgimento* period, the momentous point of Italian nation-building, was evangelical about it.

Although *Cuore* and *Tom Brown's Schooldays* were not the first children's books in their respective countries to talk about school, they were certainly the first that, quite transparently, subordinated strategies for pupils' character formation to a superior ideal of their nation's character formation. This happened at a time when the expansion of the Empire, in England, and the unification of Italy required from its younger members a new self-perception and new personal skills. They inspired authors to write other books set in school environments (for Italian imitations of *Cuore* see Boero 1999) although in both books academic skills seem to be less important than depicting the way the microcosm of the school, or the class, attempts to mould the pupils according to the values that are necessary to build a certain idea of the nation: "One might speculate, then, that the capacity of school stories in general for conveying and producing meaning is tied to ideologies of the nation" (Reimer 215).

Similarly, childhoods created by the school story—a matter of class segregation in Britain/England, and trans-class and trans-regional utopian thinking in Italy—can be illustrated by taking *Cuore* and *Tom Brown's Schooldays* together. The Italian state schools of post-unification Italy were built on an ethos of egalitarianism. Having an open heart and the ability "to feel" for others, were seen as the only way for the country to overcome linguistic, economic and social differences: children needed to become compassionate and good-hearted citizens. In contrast, the conventional view of the nineteenth-century English school story is that its core values (muscular Christianity, fair play, loyalty) prepared students for often-ruthless roles in the class-stratified Empire. And yet this is—counter-intuitively—not necessarily the case. Just as different traditions of fantasy affect *Alice* and *Pinocchio*, so issues of religion and class and attitudes to childhood and education affect *Cuore* and *Tom Brown's Schooldays*. An initial thesis might be that *Cuore* and *Tom* are about supporting nationhood, with the Italian novel being egalitarian and inward-looking, focused on social integration and nation-building, and the English one being class-based and implicitly outward-looking towards Empire. National imagology (or stereotypical national representations) might suppose that the Italian book would be religious, and the English one, not. The fact that the reverse is the case, suggests that as with fantasy, national literary images of childhood can be complex and contradictory.

The nineteenth-century school story is identified with the English public (that is, private) school, which was at the core of the British imperialistic enterprise: the accepted narrative of the English school story is that it is essentially an upper- and upper-middle class phenomenon. The public schools were (and are) the rich person's territory, and from Harriet Martineau's *The Crofton Boys* (1841), through *Tom Brown*, the work of Talbot Baines Reed in *The Boys' Own Paper* and the comedies of Frank Richards, there is a paradox of stories about an elite and privileged class being read by a lower class. The occasional scholarship boy appearing in the stories may provide a veneer of democracy, but more often, as in Rudyard Kipling's *Stalky and Co* (1899) the "other" were the *nouveaux riches* who needed to be put in their place.

Cuore is the *other* nineteenth-century Italian children's literature classic. Almost as popular as *Pinocchio* (in Italy, at least) and running to many editions and translations, it has always been a controversial work, eliciting ambivalent responses. Several generations of critics and readers have complained about this "sentimental but sadistic tale of submission to family, work, and fatherland [...] the emblem of the petit-bourgeois adaptation to the stuffy, narrow, and insipid Italy of Umberto I" (Stewart-Steinberg 167, 170–171). *Cuore* and *Pinocchio* have often been contrasted, especially regarding their different attitudes to socialization and education, which happens mainly "in the street" for the lower-class puppet and in the city and at school for the middle-class Enrico, the protagonist and main narrator of De Amicis's book. As the Italian historian Arnaldo Momigliano (1908–1987) has put it, "Our generation has grown up with two books: *Pinocchio* and *Cuore*. The former has entertained us, the latter has made us feel guilty" (quoted in Nobile 93, my translation).

Recent revaluations of the book have stressed, for example, the paradoxical relevance of this "outdated" book to Italian schools of today, where immigrant pupils go through similar experiences of social and cul-

tural integration to those gained by the geographically displaced boy from
Calabria emigrating to the North of Italy, or the poorest pupils in *Cuore*'s
class (Nobile 120). As the schoolmaster says emphatically to welcome the
boy from the South newly arrived in Turin, the capital of the newly formed
kingdom of Italy from 1861 to 1865:

> In order that this case might occur, that a Calabrian boy should be as though in his
> own house at Turin, and that a boy from Turin should be at home in Calabria, our
> country fought for fifty years, and thirty thousand Italians died. You must all respect
> and love each other; but any one of you who should give offence to this comrade,
> because he was not born in our province, would render himself unworthy of ever
> again raising his eyes from the earth when he passed the tricoloured flag [De Amicis
> 2011, kindle ed.].

Cuore, as Richter has noted, starts when *Pinocchio* ends, with the puppet's
transformation into a "ragazzo perbene" (Richter 103), a nice little boy, or
a proper boy, who likes going to school—a very different character from
the unreformed and untransformed Pinocchio of most of Collodi's novel.
Cuore was the first Italian novel in which a school, the crowded new school
of the newly unified state, was placed at the center. After *Cuore*, De Amicis
wrote other novels about school, for an adult audience, denouncing the
difficult conditions in which schoolmasters were operating (notably *Il
romanzo di un maestro*, 1890, and *Amore e ginnastica*, 1892). From the
beginning of his writing career he seems to have been interested in a form
of social writing that saw state public education as a project of regeneration for the nation—he joined the Socialist party in 1896. In *Cuore* the
state school is a microcosm in which social classes meet and mix, especially the working classes and the middle classes: the "enlightened" Northern middle classes must support state schools and send their children
there "because they believed in this dream of educational regeneration
for the whole nation" (Boero and Genovesi 12–13, my translation). For De
Amicis, children of all classes must go to the same school as going to
school together means becoming a nation. The school in *Cuore* is crowded
and backward (there are 54 students in Enrico's class), with badly paid
teachers who had chosen what seemed more a mission than a profession,
in order to change a nation with rocketing illiteracy rates (see chapter 3)
into a modern nation with a common language of which few people had
a good command.

   Although it is the most famous of English school stories, and con-
cretized the conventional elements of the genre, *Tom Brown's Schooldays*
is not truly representative of its successors. Hughes was a Christian socialist, if rather rough-and-ready, and would have had little time for the

perfervid evangelism of later school-centered books, such as Frederick Farrar's *Eric, or Little by Little* (1858); his brand of muscular bourgeois Christianity (Grenby 2008: 102) was hugely influential, and ultimately changed the educational climate.

The link between England and Italy in *Tom Brown's Schooldays* is surprisingly direct. When Tom and his friend East successfully challenge the practice of "fagging" (younger boys acting as servants to older boys), their success is held against them, and Hughes reflects that

> if the Angel Gabriel were to come down from heaven and head a successful rise against the most abominable and unrighteous vested interest which this poor old world groans under, he would most certainly lose his character for many years[...]. What can we expect, then, when we have only poor gallant blundering men like Kossuth, Garibaldi [and] Mazzini, and righteous causes which do not triumph in their hands [Hughes 195–196].

When Hughes was writing, Kossuth and Mazzini (who were friends) were in exile in England, and Garibaldi had lately been received as a hero by the working people of Newcastle. (Kossuth bears a similar relationship to Hungarian nationalism as Mazzini does to Italian). The childhood of the English school story, in one of its key moments, was not the right-wing Empire-building monolith that is often portrayed.

The themes of Tom Brown, as Jeffrey Richards put it, "are central to Victorian culture and society [...] *Tom Brown* is first of all a classic exposition of the socialisation of the English public school boy" (Richards 1988: 29). Why does Tom go to school? As his father soliloquizes:

> I won't tell him to read his Bible, and love and serve God; if he don't do that for his mother's sake and teaching, he won't for mine. Shall I go into the sort of temptations he'll meet with? No, I can't do that. [...] Shall I tell him to mind his work, and say he's sent to school to make himself a good scholar? Well, he isn't sent to school for that—at any rate not for that mainly[...]. What is he sent to school for? [...] If he'll only turn out a brave, helpful, truth-telling Englishman, and a gentleman, and a Christian, that's all I want [Hughes 73–74].

Tom Brown, perhaps surprisingly, does not—as many of its successors do—exist in a context of militarism. "Rugby [...] had no military orientation during the years of Thomas Arnold's headmastership" (Bristow 62)—although Hughes does describe a sermon by "the Doctor" (that is, Thomas Arnold) which uses militaristic imagery:

> [It] was brought home to the young boy, for the first time, the meaning of his life—that it was no fool's or sluggard's paradise into which he had wandered by chance, but a battle-field ordained from of old, where there are no spectators, but the youngest must take his side, and the stakes are life and death. And he [...] showed them [...] by every word he spoke in the pulpit, and by his whole daily life, how that battle was to

be fought, and stood there before them their fellow-soldier and the captain of their band. The true sort of captain, too, for a boys' army, one who had no misgivings, and gave no uncertain word of command, and, let who would yield or make truce, would fight the fight out (so every boy felt) to the last gasp and the last drop of blood [Hughes 142–143].

In *Cuore* the pupils do not envisage themselves as future officers in the Empire—but they are the recipient of monthly stories about the behavior of heroic boys during the Wars for Italian Independence; Garibaldi's death is mourned; the pupils watch military parades, grateful to the people who have fought the wars that have freed Italy from foreign domination.

Almost at the beginning of the book, in order to motivate his son, Enrico's father pictures an "army" of pupils, who from every corner of the world, every morning, go to school (De Amicis had been an officer himself—he fought in the third war of Independence and had trained in the "multiregional" royal military school in Turin, the Regia Scuola Militare). As Bacigalupi and Fossati have noted, "the army is a school that you leave with regret after having learnt brotherhood and having opened your mind to what lies beyond your village" (103, my translation). In *Cuore* it is portrayed as a peaceful army who fights, united and inclusive, against the barbarity of ignorance:

> Reflect in the morning, when you set out, that at that very moment, in your own city, thirty thousand other boys are going like yourself to shut themselves up in a room for three hours and study. Think of the innumerable boys who, at nearly this precise hour, are going to school in all countries. Behold them with your imagination, going, going, through the lanes of quiet villages; though the streets of the noisy towns, along the shores of rivers and lakes; here beneath a burning sun; there amid fogs, in boats, [...] in sledges over the snow, [...] over the solitary paths of the mountains, alone, in couples, in groups, in long files, all with their books under their arms, clad in a thousand ways, speaking a thousand tongues, from the most remote schools in Russia [...] to the furthermost schools of Arabia, shaded by palm-trees, millions and millions, all going to learn the same things, in a hundred varied forms. Imagine this vast, vast throng of boys of a hundred races, this immense movement of which you form a part, and think, if this movement were to cease, humanity would fall back into barbarism; this movement is the progress, the hope, the glory of the world. Courage, then, little soldier of the immense army. Your books are your arms, your class is your squadron, the field of battle is the whole earth, and the victory is human civilization. Be not a cowardly soldier, my Enrico. Thy Father [De Amicis 2011, kindle ed.].

And then there is the question of class, pervasive in English society. Of course, Rugby School was (and is) expensive and exclusive—for all the talk in the opening chapters about the yeomen Browns, backbone of England, it appears clear that Tom Brown stops considering the village boys as possible companions as soon as he gets to Rugby (Quigly 55). In *Cuore* the social spectrum goes from the very rich upper-middle class pupils to the very poor ones, who must help their fathers before and after school—Enrico, the protagonist and focalizer (*Cuore* is at the crossroads of the diary, epistolary and short story genres [see Traversetti 1991: 75]) writes mainly about them, and admires their resilience and their determination. There is a clear awareness that the class system will not be eliminated, and that social mobility is out of the question, but there will always be contact and mutual admiration and friendship between the classes.

There is a strange combination of realism and idealization in the way the classes interact. The city offers more contrasts but also more opportunities for the classes to meet—the pupils live in the same *palazzi*, the middle classes on the *piano nobile*, the working classes in the dark attic flats (where the poor pupils sit on the floor and write their homework propping their schoolbooks on a chair). This closeness makes it easier for the poorer to meet the higher classes and be ministered to, after school, as they are only a staircase away.

In the post–*Risorgimento* Italy schoolmasters and schoolmistresses become the paid employees of united Italy—no longer the private tutors of a tyrannical and ignorant aristocracy. In the nineteenth century, together with military service, the elementary school was the most important institution and in the eighties and nineties novels about teachers (mainly from the working class, of course) became very popular. Schoolmasters started to be depicted as the main characters of the post–*Risorgimento* epic, as intellectuals who would provide the link between the world of the illiterate and the world of a superior culture and as the manufacturers of the State that was born from the *Risorgimento* (Casapullo 306; see also Bini). Education was perceived as key for social improvement, and the state school as a utopian space where children of the middle classes, sympathetic and kind, sit next to the children of the working classes. De Amicis tries to soften the resentment between the classes, even as he notices the oppression of the rich over the poor (Cambi 85).

In *Tom Brown,* the teachers are very often, if not the enemy, then in opposition. This was part of Dr. Arnold's plan to induce independence in the boys (see Musgrave 60). As Tom's friend East puts it:

> "Only what one has always felt about the masters is, it's a fair trial of skill and last [sic] between us and them—like a match at football, or a battle. We're natural enemies in school—that's the fact[...]. If we can slip the collar, and do much less without getting caught, that's one to us. If they can get more out of us, or catch us shirking, that's one to them. All's fair in war, but lying" [Hughes 329].

But not in *Cuore.* Teachers are never the enemy and never unkind, and even if they are generally social inferiors to some of the pupils, no one challenges *il maestro*'s moral authority. If the doctor is Tom's hero, the schoolmaster in *Cuore* is more like a lay preacher who teaches the value of "having a heart," which can mean being a good member of the community, and being charitable and sympathetic. However, the tears that flow copiously in this book are not the result of passivity, but the starting point for action and improvement. For *il Maestro Perboni* his pupils are his family, as he emphatically declares at the beginning of the school year:

> I have no family; you are my family. Last year I had still a mother: she is dead. I am left alone. I have no other affection, no other thought than you: you must be my sons [...] show me that you are boys of heart: our school shall be a family, and you shall be my consolation and my pride [De Amicis 2011, kindle ed.].

Paradoxically, the Italian day school (where the students go home every day) is described as being more of a family than the English boarding school—one would expect the opposite to be the case, with teachers as replacement parental figures. But then of course the children in boarding schools were educated to be "sent away," to occupy (eventually) the foreign spaces of the Empire. As Kiberd has noted,

> A culture which taught stoicism out of Roman classics like Seneca, as well as an ideal of heroic state service out of Virgil, might feel a strong necessity to curb the emotional excesses of a parent-child relationship—and the boarding school may have represented one attempt to control a sentiment that might otherwise have caused all stiff upper lips to tremble [57].

In *Cuore* there is a lot of emphasis on gratitude: pupils must be grateful to those who have given their lives for the homeland, to those who love teaching them, to their parents. In other words, they must be grateful to state, school and family. The family is the other powerful source of education—in a day school, school and family collaborate and support one another, schoolmasters teach their pupils to respect their parents, and parents praise and are thankful to their children's teachers (as Enrico's father writes, *Maestro*, after the name of "father" is the most noble, the sweetest name that a man can give another man). As the school story developed in Britain, the war between teachers and pupils became more explicit (Grenby 2008: 94–95), with masters eventually becoming grotesque or comic figures: there is more of a tradition of mocking school teachers in British children's literature than in Italian children's literature.

In Italy, the emotional investment in the children was huge—but the master practices what he preaches: as he does not use corporal punishment, he just corrects by words, and light touches over shoulders: the worst insult is to tell a pupil that he is a coward, or even worse, that he has "no heart." There are tears aplenty even in *Tom Brown*, "but Hughes's depiction of Tom's courage in resisting bullying and in fighting his corner helped to promote an entirely different public school tradition, of self-control and the stiff upper lip" (Richards 1988: 62)—although it might also have produced "emotional stuntedness" in the school story (see Grenby 2008: 101).

What about the bad boys, the boys that drive the substitute teacher crazy, the noisy ones, the one who tease? In *Cuore* they are not given a name—they are an undifferentiated group that does not deserve to be included in the community of good-hearted boys. There are two exceptions, at the opposite ends of the social scale: the upper class Nobis and the working class Franti. Franti in particular represents Absolute Evil with no possibility of redemption—there is really no comparison with the bully Flashman in *Tom Brown's Schooldays*, who is a hangover from the roistering days of pre–Arnold schools, and who leaves the novel on a surprisingly low note (although film versions inflated his status for obvious dramatic reasons). Franti is the villain who refuses to conform to the ideal of the heart, who is not interested in belonging to this brotherhood, the boy who doesn't respect anything and can even laugh at his dying mother. In the end he is expelled. In 1963 Umberto Eco in "Elogio di Franti" [In Praise of Franti] famously celebrated Franti's evil and interpreted his typical wicked smile as a welcome assault on the dominant order, a form of resistance against the militarist-nationalist-sentimental ideology of the book.

In terms of balance of power, the "pedagogical laissez faire principle of the [English] public school" (Petzold 18) contrasts sharply with the teacher-controlled Italian school where being a leader is not that important, and characters are either good (most of them) or bad. According to Boero and Genovesi (73), *Cuore* is not so much a *Bildungsroman* as a representation of Utopia, where it must be clear on which side the pupils must stand—the balance between the obedience of childhood and independence of thought is crushed by benevolent authoritarianism. The paradox is that loving behavior must be imposed: obedience is framed into an act of free will. This is in contrast with the heroes in the English school story, who rebel against bullying but also break the rules and challenge authority, demonstrating independence. In *Cuore*, the power is always on the adult side, benevolent yet ultimately controlling.

Strangely enough in a very Catholic country, but perfectly understandable as the celebration of the new *state* school (the new nation had been born out of an act of pedagogical self-definition against the Catholic Church) *Cuore* eliminates all references to religion; even the festivities that we see celebrated in the school year are civic and not religious (according to the lay ideals of the newly united Italian nation, see chapter 3)—there is no mention of Christmas or Easter. In contrast, the second half of *Tom Brown* is saturated with muscular Christianity, even if it is not, as many subsequent books in the genre were, in the eighteenth-century tradition of tractarian religious teaching. *Cuore's* readers enter a church only on the occasion of the heroic and undernourished schoolmistress's funeral—and Enrico leaves the church with the exclamation: "Povera maestra, lasciata sola nella chiesa oscura" (De Amicis 1996: 359) [Poor mistress, left alone in that dark church]. The contrast with the narrator's last words about Tom, on his return to Rugby, mourning the Doctor, could not be more striking:

> Here let us leave him—where better could we leave him than at the altar, before which he had first caught a glimpse of the glory of his birthright, and felt the drawing of the bond which links all living souls together in one brotherhood—at the grave beneath the altar of him who had opened his eyes to see that glory, and softened his heart till it could feel that bond. And let us not be hard on him, if at that moment his soul is fuller of the tomb and him who lies there, than of the altar and Him of whom it speaks. Such stages have to be gone through, I believe, by all young and brave souls, who must win their way through hero-worship, to the worship of Him who is the King and Lord of heroes [Hughes 376].

There are obvious connections between school stories and adventure stories in England, and it has been noted that fiction at the end of the century is characterized by a "hardening of what is meant by manliness" (Reynolds 50)—if schoolboys are occasionally permitted to display some emotion, and even occasionally androgynous traits, heroes of the Empire are instructed in more aggressive models of masculinity. As Nelson has put it, "Henty's boys are concerned not with what they feel but with what they do" (107). It is less easy to find connections between De Amicis's *Cuore* and Salgari's adventure novels, although these authors were both based in Turin and had similar cultural connections to the city. However, what they have in common is the construction of imaginative worlds that are equally devoid of any religious references (in a way they are godless universes) and heroes in which masculinity is not incompatible with a capacity to feel, and a passionate nature.

Adventure Stories, Pirates and Imperial Literature for Boys

The Canadian critic Perry Nodelman has observed that "a defining characteristic of children's literature is that it intends to teach what it means for girls to be girls and boys to be boys." As a consequence, he argues, "a fairly large proportion of children's literature consists of books specifically for boys or girls" (2008: 173). While the gendering of children's books was evident from the first commercial example in Britain, John Newbery's *A Little Pretty Pocket-Book* (1744), which was sold with a Ball and a Pincushion to please male and female readers, this was perhaps never truer than in Britain in the nineteenth century. Children's books were written and marketed for two distinct audiences: there were domestic, waif, and fantasy novels, primarily for girls—thus identifying the female with the concept of a protected childhood—and adventure stories primarily for boys, deriving from the principles of manly behavior inculcated in school stories (and in the actual British public schools). In *Tom Brown* rugby football is described as a way to prepare for war—as if sport were a safe "war simulator": "My dear sir, a battle would look much the same to you, except that the boys would be men, and the balls iron" (Hughes 116). The metaphor of war as sport, and the notion that sport can introduce very effectively public school boys to the rules of war, were pervasive in popular culture of the 1890s, a culture that was "saturated with nationalistic and militarist ideas" (see Robert MacDonald 18).

To a great extent, the boys' adventure story became progressively synonymous with the ideas of imperialism and Empire, and with deep-rooted ideas of British masculinity. Even when the British Empire is not specifically mentioned—as with R. M. Ballantyne's pioneering *The Coral Island* (1855)—adventure stories were imbued with the ideas and ideals that underpinned Empire: the physical and moral superiority of the British (boy) over other races, the British right of conquest, and often pious declarations of religious responsibility and high-principled codes of behavior. It is not easy for readers today to recognize that the Victorians made a distinction between Empire and imperialism—a distinction clearly made by the British Prime Minister, W. E. Gladstone, in a speech in 1881: "While we are opposed to imperialism, we are devoted to empire" (quoted in Eldridge 17). Imperialism was seen as the rapacious acquisition of territory for territory's sake: Empire was a far nobler concept. As Lord Curzon (Viceroy of India 1899–1905) put it, in Empire the British had found "not merely the key to glory and wealth but the call to duty and the means of service to mankind" (quoted in Richards 1989: 73–74. For other, often contradictory, interpretations of these terms see Wallace and Slemon 75–78). With the Education Acts from 1870 onwards providing a wide readership, and the mutation of the evangelical "muscular Christianity" tradition, the sea-story, and the exotic adventure story into imperialistic channels, a tide of boys' adventure stories, more or less concerned with empire, was unleashed (see Dunae). Among the many prolific (male) authors were R. M. Ballantyne, Lt. Col. F. S. Brereton (a sample title is *With Rifle and Bayonet* [1900]), and W. H. G. Kingston, who edited a penny weekly with a characteristic title, *The Union Jack: Tales for British Boys*. (Other similar publications included *Pluck* [1894–1916], the *Boy's Own Paper* [1879–1967], *Chums* [1892–1934], and *Young England* [1880–1937]). Kingston was succeeded as editor of *The Union Jack* by G. A. Henty, described by one of his colleagues as "the most imperialist of all the Imperialists I ever encountered" (quoted in Butts 2008: 152). Formulaic plot lines and stereotypical characters (the hero with his faithful companion, for example) were a staple feature of adventure novels of this period (see Butts 1992), and the "Henty formula" was a further refinement of this tendency to privilege these stories of survival and final reward.

Emilio Salgari and G. A. Henty were prolific writers of adventure stories—but although their books apparently cover much the same quasi-historical material, they teach very different attitudes to colonial power and race. As with Collodi and Carroll, their nations had distinct priorities and self-perceptions when it came to stories of the Empire. Salgari and Henty were the bestselling authors of the age in their respective countries, and were particularly active in the last two decades of the nineteenth century and the beginning of the twentieth, although when Salgari was at the peak of his popularity Henty had already entertained English youth for a couple of decades, and the English adventure tradition was thriving, with writers such as Robert Louis Stevenson and H. Rider Haggard, among many others. Henty's lifetime, 1832–1902, almost coincides with the reign of Queen Victoria, while Salgari was born one year after the unification of Italy, in 1862 (and died in 1911): thus their dates of birth and death appropriately span the periods that were most relevant to the establishment (or the consolidation) of national identity in England and Italy. Salgari belonged to the first generation of Italians who had been born in a united Italy, and his work also coincides with several significant events connected to Italy's early colonial phase. Both Henty and Salgari came from a journalistic background, and started their careers as writers of adult fiction, but they became very popular among the young (initially Salgari had no idea that his most affectionate readers would include teenagers; later, like Henty, he contributed to boys' magazines). Neither author is very popular with children or teenagers today—Salgari is mainly read by adults and in the last few decades has aroused considerable and steady critical interest.

Henty, who had studied classics at Cambridge, was very well travelled and as a war correspondent had been in the midst of events, from the Crimean War to the Italian Wars of independence (in 1859 he was in Italy helping to organize the hospitals of the Italian legion), to Paris in the years of the Commune, and from Spain to India. He had been at the opening of the Suez Canal, he had met Stanley, and had been a silver mining surveyor in Sardinia, among many other things (his first biography, by Manville Fenn, was appropriately subtitled "The Story of an Active Life"). Salgari never completed his education but was a voracious reader of Jules Verne, Thomas Mayne Reid, James Fenimore Cooper, Alexander Dumas (see Palermo) and in 1899 even published a pirated translation of Haggard's *King Solomon's Mines*, entitled *Le caverne dei diamanti*, under a pseudonym (Pozzo 2007: 111). Unlike Henty, he did not travel, but he built for himself an entirely fictional life as a seafarer and an experienced world traveler, which fooled every one at the time: he even fought a duel to prove that he had not lied about his past and that the title of "Capitan Salgari" he boasted of, was authentic. (It was not. He had not passed the final exams at the end of the second year of the "Regio Istituto Nautico" in Venice). However, he won the duel, so no further evidence was required (Gonzato 77–86). As Arpino and Antonetto have put it, "no man like Emilio could be more obstinate, coherent, self-deluded in devising the character of the tempestuous, fearless mariner exploring the oceans" (36, my translation). Born and bred in peripheral Verona, he was an avid reader of the bulletins of the "Società Geografica Italiana" which charted the explorations of adventurers and scholars alike. He was a friend of missionaries who had come back from Africa with news about the Mahdi uprising in Sudan, and took advantage of every instance in which the exotic world of overseas came to his part of Italy: from the disappointing exhibition of Buffalo Bill on tour in Verona, to the mariners and captains he would interview in the port of Genova (Gonzato 134). In Spadolini's words, "Salgari's books pointed Italian youths towards those mysterious and far-away horizons which coincided with all the splendor of imperialism" (1972b: 219, my translation). Salgari's novels are full of exotic descriptions; as I shall discuss later, his protagonists are never Italian (as Henty's are invariably trustworthy English)—they are natives, or Europeans gone native. That is why they are so fascinating, because they are *different* and unpredictable, and they move in a mysteriously dangerous and alien natural world.

Both authors had an element of the hack writer in them as they wrote three or four novels a year—and ended up writing more than 80 novels each (Arnold 84), as well as many short stories. Henty used to dictate his stories to a secretary who was then occasionally asked to fill in the gaps with information on historical battles (Butts 2008: 152)—extensive research (more of a military kind for Henty) was a pre-requisite for both these authors' work. Salgari wrote his books while chain-smoking in a corner of his crowded living room, full of notebooks, magazines, and encyclopedias (he told a friend "When I take a rest, I am in the library to research and gather information" [Arpino and Antonetto 88, my translation]). He struggled all his life to support his large family; he was overwhelmed by debts, and shortly after his wife was taken to a mental institution, he killed himself (like his father and later his son) by what resembled a Japanese ritual suicide (self disembowelment with a knife), a kind of melodramatic death that one would not be surprised to find in his novels.

While a good number of Salgari's and Henty's novels were translated into several other languages shortly after publication (Salgari, for example, has always been very popular in South America) I have been able to find only four translations of Henty into Italian (the earliest two were published in the 1920s in the periodical *Il romanzo illustrato per i ragazzi*). As for Salgari, translations into English are very recent—the first novel was translated in the United States (*The Tigers of Mompracem*) as late as 2003 so that children of Hispanic parents who had known and enjoyed the Spanish translations as children, could read it in English (Gruppi 270). Lawson Lucas suggests that this lateness was because England already had a rich native adventure tradition, and because Salgari's criticism of colonial practices could not attract publishers at a time in which imperialism was a dominant ideology (Lawson Lucas 2005: 48). Salgari's books articulate very different views of Empire and adventure, encourage different values and offer very different constructions of heroism as well as representations of relationships between colonizers and natives, from Henty and other English authors of adventure stories.

The time and space range of the Henty novels is astounding; from pre–Christian times to very recent periods of history such as the Indian Mutiny and the Crimean War: 25 of his books were based on incidents in recent imperial history (Huttenback). His most popular books had British lads as protagonists and it is noticeable that his heroes leave from England, embark on a number of breathtaking and perilous adventures abroad, and then regularly go back to their homeland (Guy Arnold distinguishes between Henty's Indian stories, the African stories and the American stories, but of course there are other novels that escape this convenient albeit not terribly nuanced categorization). Huttenback repeats the well-established critical view that

> Life was uncomplicated for Henty[...]. The difference between right and wrong, virtue and vice was always clearly discernible. To Henty [...] imperialism was the achievement of greathearted and noble men acting mightily in a most worthy cause. That he was a dull and repetitive writer did not disturb his readers [75].

One of Henty's most quoted passages, the Preface to *St George for England* (1882) (his books generally start with a patronizing address to his readers: "My Dear Lads"), helps to sum up the pride of a generation and the mystique of the Empire:

> You will learn from tales like this that determination and enthusiasm can accomplish marvels, that true courage is generally accompanied by magnanimity and gentleness, and that if not itself the very highest of virtues, it is the parent of almost all the others[...]. The courage of our forefathers has created the greatest empire in the world around a small and in itself insignificant island; if this empire is ever lost, it will be by the cowardice of their descendants [*St George for England*, in Henty, kindle ed.].

And of course, "many people in Britain encountered the Empire through imperial imagery circulated by the mass media as [much as] as they did through more tangible types of connection" (Thompson 6).

Representations of class were key in establishing correspondences between hierarchical structures in the homeland and in the territories of the Empire: Henty's books, inevitably, provide a distillation of the prejudices, the doctrines and the dogmas of his age (Richards 1989: 73). All this did not escape the attention of the author of a letter addressed to a magazine for boys, *The Captain* (the boys' equivalent of *The Strand* magazine) in May 1908. The letter, written by R. van Eeghen, whom Arnold describes as a "refreshingly vituperative foreigner" (23), was headed "Concerning Englishmen":

> There is no doubt that the immortal Henty and his hosts of imitators have made the British nation the most conceited people on this earth. It is the plotless trash of authors who shelter themselves behind the section of the library catalogue entitled "Books for Boys," which has given the average young Englishman that very excellent opinion of himself which he now enjoys[...]. After fourteen or fifteen years' perusal of "piffle" written apparently for his edification, the young Englishman leaves home and country with the very firm idea in his head that he, personally, is equal to two or more Frenchmen, about four Germans, an indefinite number of Russians and any quantity you care to mention of the remaining scum of the earth [...] Henty and Co. have done more to endanger the Empire than the blundering of many statesmen whom we could name [quoted in Arnold 22–23].

Salgari's literary geography is as wide as Henty's (with the exception of European settings, which Salgari does not use) and it is equally difficult to try and classify it. He set a lot of his novels in the places of the British Empire, especially India, Borneo and the Indian Archipelago, places of conflict of civilizations, in which Europeans are contrasted with the imaginary representation of an exotic Orient (Traversetti 1989: 42). Unlike Henty, Salgari wrote his novels mainly in adventure cycles with the same cast of characters, the most famous being the Indo-Malayan pirate cycle, with Sandokan as its protagonist (in this case the Indian cycle and the Malayan cycle were brought together to form a new series), the Black Corsairs cycle, set in the Caribbean from the end of the seventeenth century and the first half of the eighteenth, and the cycle set in the American Far West (in one of these books, *La Sovrana del campo d'oro* [The Queen of the Golden Field], Buffalo Bill makes an appearance).

While in Britain in the last two decades of the nineteenth century, imperialist ideology was the orthodoxy and most British subjects believed that a nation that had reached the apogee of civilization was entitled to various forms of colonial control, in Italy attitudes to colonialism were different and more complicated. In general, Italy was the European country, with the exception of Germany, that had held her colonial possessions for the shortest period: the Italian Overseas Territories were one of the smallest, poorest, and least advantageous of all (Labanca 8). The "failure" of Italian colonialism caused intense political and diplomatic frustration: the first Italian colony, the port of Assab (1882) had only 160 inhabitants, and Italy's subsequent attempts to join "the scramble for Africa" were much haunted by the tragic defeat in Adwa, in 1896, of the Italian invading army by the Ethiopian forces under Emperor Menelik II. The high illiteracy rates, suffrage restrictions (in 1867 only 6.7 percent of male population could vote), and a "substantially anti-colonial political context" (Labanca 222, my translation), had proved formidable obstacles to colonial propaganda among the masses—the Italian colonial enterprise in West Africa had been largely unpopular. Thus Italy's late arrival in the colonial arena is possibly the reason why Italian writers did not produce any imperial literature of the Kipling or Haggard kind, although the fin-de-siècle fascination with exoticism was certainly present in popular culture and in the arts. If for England and France colonial discourse helped define and shape national identities as it was trying to define the natives as Other, in Italy it was only later, with Fascism, that the colonial enterprise was used to reinforce a less radicated Italian national identity. The first fascist and colonial "Pinocchiate" (see chapter 2) started to be written only in the second and third decades of the twentieth century (Curreri, only recently, has uncovered what he has called "Salgarian Pinocchiate," three short stories written by Bettino d'Aloja in 1928, with a similar structure to Collodi's book, but set in India, Malaysia and Ceylon, in which "a sort of dislocated but not banal fidelity to Collodi's original, is projected onto a Salgarian map" [Curreri 2017: 98, my translation]).

It is not by chance that Salgari's "romanzi d'Africa," distributed all through his career, and not organized in cycles, avoid the settings of the Italian unfortunate colonial enterprises. In contrast, De Amicis had been quite a traveler for his age: he had been to Morocco in 1874 with a diplomatic delegation, but in his report he shows "an ingenuity not yet tainted by any imperialist rhetoric" (Botto 77): he mentions the *risotto alla milanese* and the *maccheroni al sugo* (dishes, respectively, from the North and the South of Italy) which their cook had served under a tent in the presence of the Spanish and American consuls. The still unstable Italian identity, unsurprisingly, appeared to be cemented by the awareness of the difference between Italian food and local exotic foods (Botto 78).

A lot has been written about the so called "Henty formula" (Butts 2008, Huttenback, Bratton and many others), an *ars combinatoria* of typical characters, story patterns and recurring themes, which centers around a young British hero of about sixteen, who as a consequence of some family misfortune (generally a parent's death) needs to make his fortune in the world and ends up in the center of the story's historical action (often with a "follower" of the lower class). Because of his (often military) exploits, courage, resourcefulness (which leads him to rescue somebody in danger, often a girl), loyalty and "pluck" (to which Green adds "Dash [...] and lion-heartedness, not obedience, duty and pity" [220]), he distinguishes himself, is noticed by an important commanding officer or historical figure and is rewarded or promoted. This mixture of history and adventure (Arnold 39) ends with future settlement in England and marriage. As Lawson Lucas has noted, even when they face obstacles and danger, "these fellow countrymen heroes give the reader a sense of security, even of familiarity" (2005: 51).

This idealized male hero is offered to the readers as Everyman—"the hero is constructed to be emulated" (Johnson 210) so that literature is very transparently used as imperial propaganda in which character is built along lines contributory to imperial ambitions (Ashley xv). It is also very clear that the heroes are positioned as a touchstone of British virtue against which the colonized people must be measured: "Henty's work is built upon notions of 'the other': the other nation, the other race, or the other army, in an aggressive polarization" (Kelen and Sundmark 164).

So, in the African novels, such as *By Sheer Pluck* (1884), which is set during the third Anglo-Ashanti war of 1873–1874, Henty shares the European assumption that the black Africans were idle and had to be taken care of (Kossi Logan). In a much quoted passage from this book, we find a summary of all the ideas of superiority that pervaded contemporary Western thought:

> They are just children. They are always laughing and quarrelling. They are good-natured and passionate, indolent, but will work hard for a time, clever up to a certain point, densely stupid beyond. The intelligence of an average negro is about equal to that of a European child of ten years old. [...] Living among whites their imitative faculties enable them to attain a considerable amount of civilization. Left alone to their own devices they retrograde into a state little above their native savagery [*By Sheer Pluck*, in Henty, kindle ed.].

But the most villainous and most detested "race" of all for Henty is the Boers, whom he describes in the three South African novels as "unsavoury in appearance as they were brutal in manners": they wash only four times a year and are "altogether without education, and very many Boers are scarcely able to sign their names" (*With Buller in Natal*, 1901, in Henty, kindle ed.).

Although Salgari uses national stereotypes as convenient shorthand and inevitably mentions ethnicity when he introduces a new character, the underlying assumption is that of a substantial equality between the races. It is clear that heroism and nobility are not the prerogative of the white—rather, the contrary seems to be the case (and yet, Salgari's heroic natives may well signal his implication in Orientalist ideology, and in particular, his fascination with the myth of the noble savage, as the ideal receptacle for projections of the ideals of courage, altruism, and virility).

If in England emulation and reader identification were encouraged by Henty's heroes who were instructing their readers in culturally desirable masculine traits, in Italy there was more concern about youths' identification with the *adult* heroes of Salgari's novels. In his edition of Salgari's tales of "Prateria, giungla e di mare" [Prairie, jungle, and sea], Ponchiroli reports that teachers and parents at the time were worried that Salgari may go to the young readers' heads, and inflame their imaginations with the stories of passionate pirates and exalted corsairs. In his fiction, characters come from all the races and corners of the world—for Salgari is color blind and firmly anti-racist when it comes to his heroes. Salgari's most famous heroes are often dispossessed natives, like the aristocrat Sandokan turned pirate after the British have exterminated his family. Similarly, Salgari always chooses the rebel cause against the colonial oppressor, as in many novels

The characters who are personally and morally good are also politically good, and vice versa; moreover, the politically bad are in power, the politically good are subjugated. From Salgari's second novel [...] onward, it is clear in many different situations, political and otherwise, that his sympathies always lay with the "underdog," the person or people who had been wronged, abused, vanquished [Lawson Lucas 1996: 160].

It follows that in Salgari's most famous cycle of novels, set in India and Borneo, the climate of colonialism is brought to the foreground, and oppressors are inevitably British, embodied by the historical Lord Brooke, the White Rajah of Sarawak. But Salgari's firmly anti-jingoistic stance is a little more nuanced than one might expect and does not depend exclusively on national stereotypes, but on the nature of the specific conflict. For example, in *Le Stragi delle Filippine* (1897) he sides with the Filipino rebels against Spanish rule while in *La Capitana dello Yucatan* (1899), set during the Spanish-American war of 1898, his sympathies are with the Spaniards defending Cuba against the aggressive policy of the USA. In both cases his sympathies go to the rebels, or the disempowered and the oppressed.

There is no deep psychological complexity in Salgari's characters (Tropea 51): his heroes are always right; they are brave and honorable and are ready to give their lives for "a good cause." This could be a trait that he shares with Henty, if it were not for the fact that in most cases Salgari supports the cause of the downtrodden (generally), natives who want to free themselves from a powerful oppressor. There is no anti–British sentiment *per se* in the Italian novels, although in the 1920s Salgari was revalued (and totally misunderstood) as an author who had heralded (anti–British) fascist values and therefore recommended for this reason to young readers (see Lawson Lucas 1990). Salgari, who declared "soffro lo spleen degli inglesi" [I suffer from the spleen of the English] to describe his tormented and melancholic nature (Pozzo 2000: 101), sometimes made use of national stereotypes to ridicule characters in his novels—and these could be British. For example, Lord Wylmore, in the Far West cycle, is an arrogant as well as splenetic English aristocrat who is obsessed with killing American buffalos and speaks with a comic simplified English in order to be understood by the natives.

Similarly, inter-racial and inter-class marriages are not uncommon— Sandokan falls in love and marries a British girl, Marianna, who joins her pirate husband's cause; the prince-pirate's best friend, the Portuguese Yanez, marries an Indian princess; and the Bengalese Tremal-Naik marries British Ada, Marianna's cousin. Salgari is not overtly concerned with class either—Yanez is ostensibly working class, but he is the best friend of a

Malayan prince (they call each other "brother") and at the end of his adventures rules Assam with his wife Surama, the true heiress to the Assam kingdom. In the same way as the new nation for De Amicis is an interclass utopia, in Salgari's novels class is largely irrelevant. As Lawson Lucas has put it, "in his novels social classes do not exist. Aristocrats, except for the Black Corsair, are never considered as special or superior beings by birth or rank. [...] They are judged on the basis of their actions, not on the basis of their social position" (2000: 95). Consistently, the Italian writer refrains from any judgment connected to the superiority of one race over another, although he occasionally allows the narrator to balance the strong anticolonial hatred of his native heroes with simplified historical analysis, as in the Conclusion to *The Pirates of Malaysia* (1896) in which "the great improvements introduced by that wise, brave, energetic man" [Lord Brooke] (Salgari 2014b: 246) are pointed out. He seems to have a special sympathy for characters of "mixed blood" and casts half Indians as commanders of British ships (Ambrosini 11). A classic example of Salgari's class/race blindness, again in *The Pirates of Malaysia,* is the recognition scene in which Sir James Guillonk realizes that the woman the pirate Tremal-Naik is in love with, Ada Corishant, is his niece and that his other niece, Marianna, had been Sandokan's late wife (English ladies in this series have a thing for pirates). Hostilities are stopped at once and in a surreal moment Lord Guillonk even asks his ex enemy to call him uncle: "Call me uncle, Sandokan[...]. You are my nephew after all" (Salgari 2014b: 168). In the rest of the novel the pirates hatch a plot against Lord Brooke, but gallantly reassure their "uncle" that they do not expect him to change his allegiances:

> "Do you have a plan?" asked Lord Guillonk.
> "Our fate rests with Pangeron Macota[...]. Find him and tell him that the Tigers of Mompracem will help him execute his plans. My pirates will land there, take command of his insurrection, attack our prison, and set us free."
> "But I'm British, nephew," said his lordship.
> "I am not asking you to play any part in this, Uncle James. You cannot conspire against one of your own countrymen" [Salgari 2014b: 169].

Again, the fact that Salgari's heroes are not Italian, can make it safer and less complicated to represent inter-racial marriages. His ideal of miscegenation is projected onto other ethnicities and nationalities, with a member of the mixed couple who is typically English (or British).

As for Henty, he obviously believes in hierarchies of class and race. His politics were deeply right-wing: in *Out With Garibaldi: A Story of the Liberation of Italy* (1901) he admires Cavour (as a moderate), and Garibaldi (as a romantic), but strongly disapproves of Mazzini (as a republican). The boy-heroes of his books are generally from the middle-classes and the public schools—cementing a close relationship between these elite schools, the military and the expanding state.

Possibly because Salgari's heroes are older, there is more romance in his books than in Henty's—Henty's heroes have a highly reserved attitude to women: females are strictly marginalized, generally relegated to domestic spaces and romantic encounters are very few, and reassuringly mild. In Salgari's Indo-Malayan cycle, women (or, rather, girls) are all astonishingly beautiful, a beauty that provokes emotion and turmoil in the manly heroes, and innocently seductive (see Beseghi, and Neiger). These girls are thrown in the middle of adventure, and although they tend to faint at moments of crisis (Marianna and Ada die conveniently soon after marriage so that they can free their husbands to continue their adventures, as it were) they speak the same passionate language as men, as in this exchange between Marianna and Sandokan in *Sandokan: The Tigers of Mompracem* (1883–1884):

> "No, Sandokan, I won't drive you away. I love you too much, *because you are brave, you are powerful, and you are as devastating as the hurricanes that upset the oceans*"[...].
>
> "Mine! You are mine!" he exclaimed jubilantly. "Tell me, my adored one, what can I do to make you happy? Nothing is impossible. If you wish to be a queen, I'll topple a sultan and give you his throne. If it's riches you desire, I'll ransack the temples of India and Burma and shower you with diamonds and gold; say the word and I'll become an Englishman[...]. Tell me your desires. Ask me the impossible and I'll do it. For you, I could lift the world and hurl it through the night sky" [Salgari 2014a: 59, the passage in italics is my translation as it was omitted in the English edition].

This is the language of melodrama, at a time when Verdi and Puccini were also exploring exotic locations in their operas (Salgari renamed his wife Ida, *Aida*).

Sandokan is possibly the hero that has established the firmest hold on the imagination of Salgari's readers (and viewers, thanks to a very popular 1976 TV adaptation in Italy). Many critics have also noted connections between the pirate and the flesh and blood hero of the age, Garibaldi. Sandokan, in a way, can be seen to embody the same ideals of freedom and justice, and the same personality traits of heroism, fearlessness and a desire for social change as Garibaldi. Both noble adventurers, after having operated in exotic spaces (Garibaldi was called the "Hero of Two Worlds" because of his military enterprises in Brazil and Uruguay, fighting alongside the local rebels, as well as in Europe) and after a lifetime of battles, they retired to their islands, Mompracem and Caprera:

> Deep down, even Garibaldi, as he presented Southern Italy to the rest of the country
> [...] imposed an ideal of brotherhood which was very difficult to achieve in reality.
> Garibaldi and Salgari were certainly alien to any kind of racism and, one with the
> sword and the cannon, the other with the pen and a rickety writing desk, they made
> Italy [Manzi 19, my translation].

Once again, while Salgari, the armchair traveler, could meet the Italian
national hero only in the character produced by his imagination, Henty
had met him in person and admired him as a man and as a commander:
"He welcomed me in the heartiest manner [...] the Garibaldini [...] are,
simply, without exception, the finest material for soldiers that I ever saw
(quoted in William Allan 75).

Salgari's India "is an India that does not belong to any specific time
but at the same time it is of all times" (Singh 67): it is a well-documented
compendium of costumes, folklore, religion, musical instruments, animals,
trees and flowers, which are sprinkled in his novels and make the exotic
and the strange, credible and fascinating. India and Malaysia are at the
center of Salgari's emotional world—as Traversetti has argued (1989: 42),
the Italian writer stages the Great Exhibition of the Exotic. His descriptions are catalogues of "items" with evocative and foreign names: an abundance of unusual plants and all sorts of dangerous animals inhabit forests
and jungles. Salgari is a visual collector of natural wonders. Similarly, Sandokan's crew is composed of an accumulation of the different ethnicities
of the Malayan archipelago. In terms of language, while Henty intersperses
his direct and generally factual dialogues with Indian colloquialisms
(Naidis 52), Salgari is credited with introducing words that are not easily
understandable from their context but are incredibly atmospheric and
replete with natural, sensual abundance, as in this description in *I misteri
della giungla nera* (1887):

> It was a magnificent night in August, a veritable tropical night. The air was tepid,
> sweet, elastic, embalmed by the sweet scent of jasmine, of *sciambaga*, of *mussenda*
> and of the *nagatampo*[...]. Swarms of marabou storks were flying over the stream,
> alighting on each bank, at the feet of the coconut trees, the banana trees and the
> tamarind [italics and translation are mine, from Salgari 2010, kindle ed.].

The mysterious terms in italics are distorted Hindi words which Salgari
may have found in a French encyclopedia and misspent while copying
(Mancini 67–69). But in a way it does not terribly matter to establish that
sciambaga is really *michelia champaka*, a plant of very sweet-smelling flowers, because when we read, we already know.

Visions of the British Empire provided a dramatic background for
many of Henty's boys' adventures—his Indian novels, for example, chart

the progression of the British expansion in India from the eighteenth century to 1900. The popularity of these novels "impressed a whole generation of English-reading schoolboys (and presumably some adults) with his special image of British India" (Naidis 50): in these novels British superiority towards the Indian natives and the benefits of British presence in India are never questioned, although Henty is not blind to the inadequate imperial policies in India (Arnold 100). In the *Tiger of Mysore* (1896), set in the 1790s, during the Anglo-Mysore wars, Indian indolence is contrasted with English valor—the Rajah stresses the value of an English education as well as that of having some English blood:

> We in India have courage; but it is because our princes and nobles are brought up in indolence and luxury that the English, though but a handful in point of numbers, have become masters of such wide territories[...]. Your grandmother was an Englishwoman, and I want to see that, with the white blood in your veins, you have some of the vigour and energy of Englishmen [*Tiger of Mysore*, in Henty, kindle ed.].

Henty's *Times of Peril. A Tale of India* (1881) belongs to the subgenre of the Victorian mutiny novel. This tradition is characterized by the suppression of marginal voices and absence of dissent in the construction of British colonial identity: this ideological cohesion becomes even more noticeable in fiction addressed to a young audience (Nicora 2005: 38). In the novel the Indian Mutiny (renamed in Indian historiography as India's first War of Independence) is described, in all its military as well as gory details, as a threat to the English and their families, in line with the official colonial interpretation and the general sentiment of shock and horror which the carnage had aroused only a few years before. The passage is about British soldiers entering a house in Cawnpore after a massacre of civilians:

> The floor was deep in blood; the walls were sprinkled thickly with it. Fragments of clothes, tresses of long hair, children's shoes with the feet still in them—a thousand terrible and touching mementos of the butchery which had taken place there met the eye[...]. Soldiers picked up the bloody relics—a handkerchief, a lock of hair, a child's sock sprinkled with blood—and kept them to steel their hearts to all thoughts of mercy [*Times of Peril*, in Henty, kindle ed.].

This official version of events (which often took the form of sensationalist accounts) never showed the British public the carnage of the Indian population that followed. As Sharpe explains, real evidence of systematic mutilation, rape and torture during the Mutiny could not be found. However, narratives of sexual assaults, censored in Henty's novel and displaced, in the quoted passage, to the violence on children, were very common and appeared to sanction the use of colonial violence: "upon recapturing Delhi, the British army was reported to have massacred anywhere from twenty-five thousand to thirty thousand of its inhabitants" (Sharpe 233).

In Salgari's novels, the British Empire is often the background to other conflicts, as in *Le due tigri* [The Two Tigers] (1904) which is about the final confrontation between Sandokan ("the Tiger of Malaysia") and his arch-enemy, the evil Suyodhana ("The Tiger of India"), who is the head of the bloodthirsty Thugs, the cruel followers of the Goddess Kali (not all Indians are good in Salgari). In the course of the novel Sandokan and his followers find themselves in the middle of the 1857 Indian Mutiny, and they decide to remain neutral although Yanez would like to join the rebels. As it happens, they act as witnesses of the events (Sandokan is often the focalizer in the Malayan cycle). It is not surprising that Salgari would take the opportunity to fill this gap and show the Mutiny from the Indian perspective (Salgari does not distinguish between the English and the British—for him they are all *Inglesi*). In the "Conclusion" the narrator describes the barbarous repression of the mutiny, although he is never as graphic as Henty:

> The Delhi massacre lasted for three days, a terrible tragedy that tore a cry of indignation from all Europe and even England herself. The Indians, fully aware of the fate that awaited them, battled for every inch of ground, fighting desperately[...]. *On the 20th Dehli was entirely in the hands of the English. Terrible scenes and unheard-of bloodshed followed, scenes that were worthy of the savages of Polynesia, not of civilised people, of Europeans.* The city was ransacked. Thousands upon thousands of Indians were murdered by troops drunk with gin and bloodlust, without regard for age and gender. The brave men who had fought to free India from the British fell, many after killing their wives and children with their very hands so they would not fall victim to the victors' cruelty. On the 24th, Sandokan and his companions, after having obtained General Wilson's permission, left the devastated city [Salgari 2009, Kindle ed. the passage in italics is my translation—it was omitted in the English edition].

In contrast, the way the Indian mutiny was represented and explained in England in war reports as well as in popular culture necessarily reinforced national identity as an iconic moment in the imperial enterprise, which had a powerful impact on collective imagination. And, as we have seen, the involvement of English women and children in the siege was used to arouse strong emotions and desire for revenge (see Nicora 2007 and Galli-Mastrodonato). This way of focusing on the suffering of the colonizers and ignoring the much more bloodthirsty British reaction was the common denominator in the Eurocentric way the Mutiny was conceptualized and explained. Salgari provides a different point of view, although the (censored) reference to the savages of Polynesia can indicate that one of the standard associations between non–European natives and savagery was also ingrained in Salgari's mind. Salgari was a man of his time, too, so his anti-colonialism is not monolithic—in the Far West cycle, for example, even if the awareness of the genocide of the Native Americans emerges clearly in the series, he describes the "Red Indians" as either savage on the prairies ("redskin" women can be very savage too, and scalp their prisoners) or, when they have moved to villages, partly responsible for their unfortunate destiny, because "the Indian did not submit to the hard law of work: he did not want to dig the soil and make it fertile with his sweat [...] some of them lead a sad existence, put aside in their villages, getting drunk every time they capture an animal and can sell their skin" (Salgari 1905: 96, my translation).

The Henty British boy hero and the Salgari native man hero could not be more different, although they obviously share loyalty, bravery and "pluck." And, of course, a strong moral code: characters are either unambiguously good or unambiguously bad—no fascinating villains are allowed to exist in their fictional universes.

Constructions of the British Empire clearly resonated in a radically different way in the two authors and in their fiction. Salgari, born in economically and culturally backward Italy, with a fragile and relatively recent identity as a united nation could look at the Empire with the eyes of the excluded, easily identifying with of the underdog's perspective under the weight of colonial oppression. Henty was a highly efficient and unrepentant "imperial apologist," and could not escape the racism and self-confidence of the British Empire at its most virulent, at a time in which contemporary classifications of race placed the Anglo-Saxons at the top, and especially the manly boys, with their stiff-upper-lip stoicism, and an underlying belief in athleticism, discipline, and pursuit of Christian ideals.

After Salgari's death, a piece of paper was found in his notes, with drawings of Oriental characters and scribbled on with these sentences: "I was 23 when I was made prisoner by the pirate Sandokan" and "I am Sandokan's slave and companion" (quoted in Arpino and Antonetto, my translation 35)—a form of neurotic identification with his heroic characters. In letters to his wife he would sign as "selvaggio Malese" [savage Malay]. Writing was possibly a form of compensation for not travelling (or the equivalent of today's armchair travel) (Lawson Lucas 1993: 88) but his stories can offer their readers, in the space of a few pages "the world as spectacle and prodigy" (Traversetti 1989: 42).

Henty was showing his lads the world of Empire—asking them to identify with the civilizing mission of a nation that self-represented itself as superior economically, culturally, politically, and racially; Salgari was not asking his readers to follow him on the map of desire of Italian colonial aspiration, but he was asking them to imagine the magic landscapes of adventure. Had he wanted to imitate Henty's patronizing openings, he would probably have written: "My dear Lads, we may not have the colonies, but I can show you the world," or words to that effect.

From *Alice* and *Pinocchio*, and their points of departures, Oxford and Florence, through the international world of translation and adaptation, the fabulous journeys of compared children's literatures have taken us to far-off destinations, to the exotic worlds of Empire, to the colonial outposts where Italians and the British were defining their national identity in their relationship with different populations, foreign spaces, languages, and customs.

Appendix: "Strange Meeting in Wonder-Tuscany"
by Peter Hunt

Alice was growing very tired of sitting next to her sister (who was flirting with a very handsome Italian boy) and trying to understand this strange language, and trying to eat all this strangely-shaped food.

The sun was shining and it was very hot, and the fizzy drink that she had been drinking made her feel drowsy, and nobody was taking any notice of her. Alice longed to be in the shade of the tall trees that lined the white road, so she slipped off her chair and tiptoed in among the leaves of the lower branches. There was a little path and she followed it for a while, until she was startled by a voice near her shoulder, which said "Chi sei?"

Alice stopped and looked around: there was a large Cricket sitting on a branch. Oh, dear, Alice thought, more nonsense, but she said, politely, in the only phrases of Italian that she had learned: "No capisco. Ho solo parla Inglesi," which, she thought, should be good enough for anyone.

"Bene," said the Cricket. "I shall talk to you in English. May I ask where you are going?"

But Alice had become a wise little girl after her experiences, so she said, "You may certainly ask, Sir, but I am not certain that I can answer, because I don't know."

The Cricket nodded its head. "I meant to say, are you running away and making someone worry about you?"

Alice thought of saying, "If you meant to say it, why didn't you say it," but the Cricket *had* said it now, so she replied, for she was an honest little girl, "I'm only going for a walk, and I don't think anyone will worry about me."

The Cricket seemed to be a little concerned about this, and said, "Nevertheless, I think that I should give you a present," and he held out a small wine-glass. "Don't worry," he went on, seeing Alice's look. "If you drink this, you will be able to understand what everyone is saying."

Alice took the glass. "But I can understand what you say already," she said.

"That's because I'm a Cricket," said the Cricket, "and cricket is the most English thing there is."

This didn't seem quite right to Alice, but she was feeling thirsty, so she drank from the glass, and at once the birds that had been saying "cip cip" began to say "cheep, cheep."

The Cricket smiled at her, said "Buona fortuna," and disappeared. This was nothing new to Alice so she walked on down the path, and around a corner she found herself in a farmyard, with a small house, and outside it was a dog-kennel. As she came up to it there was a scuffling noise, and something came rapidly out of the kennel, with a chain around its neck, saying "Bark, bark, bark"; stumbled over her foot, turned a somersault, and crashed into a tree.

"Are you all right?" said Alice, much concerned, but the boy—at least she thought it was a boy—merely got up and dusted himself down.

"I'm alright," he said. "It helps being made of wood. You don't feel things," and he burst into tears.

"But if you don't feel things," Alice said, "why are you crying?"

"I don't know," said the wooden boy. "Perhaps I'll stop," and he stopped.

Alice thought that she had not seen a more curious figure all day. He seemed to have been burned around the legs, and bitten around the arms, and his nose and ears seemed to be longer than one might have expected. She remembered her manners.

"Good afternoon," she said. "My name is Alice. Who, or what, are you?"

"My name is Pinocchio," said the thing. "And I'm a very famous puppet. Everyone has heard of me."

This didn't seem to be absolutely true, but Alice went on, "If you are very famous, why are you in a dog-kennel?"

"Oh, that," said the puppet, casually. "Well, I was hungry and so I went to pick some grapes, and I got caught in a trap, and for punishment the nasty farmer said I had to be a watch dog."

"But why," said Alice, who liked to make sure that she understood things properly, "are you saying 'bark, bark'? If you are a watch dog, you should say 'tick tock.'" (She was secretly very pleased with this reply.)

"I'm saying 'bark, bark' because I'm made of a tree," said Pinocchio. He burst into tears again.

"But don't you have a mother and father who could come and rescue you?" said Alice, who found these displays of emotion somewhat embarrassing.

"I have a Papa," Pinocchio sobbed. "He made me, but I ran away, and then he gave me an alphabet book so that I could go to school, but I sold it so I could go to a play."

Alice's eyes had grown very large. "But why did you do such an awful thing?"

Pinocchio stopped crying and laughed and kicked his legs in the air. "Because I wanted to!" he said.

"But you can't just do anything you want," Alice said, gravely.

"I can," said the puppet. "Because I'm very clever." He ran around at the length of his chain, turning somersaults.

"But if everyone did everything they wanted, then the world would be very confused," Alice said, thinking carefully.

"That wouldn't matter," said Pinocchio. "As long as I'm alright." He suddenly stopped and looked around. "Have you seen a Fox and a Cat?" he said.

"I've seen a Caterpillar and a Cheshire-Cat, but no Fox. Why?"

"They've been chasing me. Is anybody chasing you?"

"No," Alice said. "Nobody ever chases me. What a curious idea. Why are the Fox and the Cat chasing you?"

"They want to steal my money," said the puppet, "and then they'll probably hang me from a tree until I'm dead."

This didn't seem a very comfortable arrangement to Alice. "Why don't you just go home?" she asked.

"I really, really want to," said the puppet, bursting into tears again. "My poor papa is waiting for me, heartbroken. I let him down about buying my school book and I have been a wicked and disobedient boy."

"In that case," Alice said (she was becoming rather tired of this conversation), "let me take that collar off and you can go home."

She undid the collar, and the puppet jumped up. "Look how clever I am," he shouted. "I've managed to get away!" and he ran off into the wood without a word of thanks.

Alice was used to this kind of behavior, and she was not very surprised when, a few seconds later, a villainous-looking Fox and Cat ran past her and disappeared into the wood.

Alice gazed at the spot where they had vanished, and walked slowly on. "What a strange thing to worry about," she thought. "Why, anybody can just pick up a school book anywhere, and I can't imagine anyone waiting for me," and she walked calmly back along the path. The birds had stopped cheeping and were singing "cip cip" again.

She sat under a tree and watched her sister, who was still flirting, and she was about to doze off when she saw a cloud of dust coming along the road. It was Pinocchio, and he skidded to a halt when he saw her.

"Alice! Quando ti vedrò di nuovo?," he shouted, and started running again.

And Alice, quite forgetting that she had nothing in common with the puppet, and didn't even speak his language, waved back and shouted "Molto presto, Pinocchio!" and waved and waved until he was out of sight.

Chapter Notes

Chapter 1

1. "vide una bella camerina ammobiliata e agghindata con una semplicità quasi elegante" (Collodi 1993: 280).

Chapter 3

1. "I veri poveri, in questo mondo, meritevoli di assistenza e compassione, non sono altro che quelli che, per ragione d'età o di malattia, si trovano condannati a non potersi più guadagnare il pane col lavoro delle proprie mani" (Collodi 1993: 168).

Chapter 4

1. "'Metti giudizio per l'avvenire, e sarai felice.'

A questo punto il sogno finì, e Pinocchio si svegliò con tanto d'occhi spalancati.

Ora immaginatevi voi quale fu la sua meraviglia quando, svegliandosi, si accorse che non era più un burattino di legno: ma che era diventato, invece, un ragazzo come tutti gli altri" (Collodi 2009: 279–280).

2. "C'era una volta...

—Un re!—diranno subito i miei piccoli lettori.

No, ragazzi, avete sbagliato. C'era una volta un pezzo di legno.

Non era un legno di lusso, ma un semplice pezzo da catasta, di quelli che d'inverno si mettono nelle stufe e nei cami-netti per accendere il fuoco e per riscaldare le stanze" (Collodi 1993: 19).

3. "Pinocchio, non dar retta ai consigli dei cattivi compagni: se no, te ne pentirai!—

Povero Merlo, non l'avesse mai detto! Il Gatto, spiccando un gran salto, gli si avventò addosso, e senza dargli nemmeno il tempo di dire *ohi* se lo mangiò in un boccone, con le penne e tutto.

Mangiato che l'ebbe e ripulitasi la bocca, chiuse gli occhi daccapo e ricominciò a fare il cieco come prima.

—Povero Merlo,—disse Pinocchio al Gatto—perché l'hai trattato cosi male?

—Ho fatto per dargli una lezione. Così un'altra volta imparerà a non metter bocca nei discorsi degli altri" (Collodi 1993: 81).

4. "Finora questa fatica di girare il bindolo,—disse l'ortolano,—l'ho fatta fare al mio ciuchino: ma oggi quel povero animale è in fin di vita[...]. Appena che Pinocchio fu entrato nella stalla vide un bel ciuchino disteso sulla paglia, rifinito dalla fame e dal troppo lavoro. Quando l'ebbe guardato fisso fisso, disse dentro di sé, turbandosi:

—Eppure quel ciuchino lo conosco! Non mi è fisionomia nuova!

E chinandosi fino a lui, gli domandò in dialetto asinino:

—Chi sei?—

A questa domanda, il ciuchino aprì gli occhi moribondi, e rispose balbettando nel medesimo dialetto:

—Sono Lu...ci...gno...lo...

E dopo rinchiuse gli occhi e spirò.
—Oh! Povero Lucignolo!—disse Pinocchio a mezza voce: e presa una manciata
di paglia, si rasciugò una lacrima che gli
colava giù per viso" (Collodi 1993: 275).

5. "...una stanzina terrena, che pi-
gliava luce da un sottoscala" (Collodi 1993:
29).

6. "Ma si può dire che partisse a tas-
toni, perché fuori dell'osteria c'era un buio
cosi buio, che non ci si vedeva da qui a li"
(Collodi 1993: 90).

7. "Appena dette queste ultime parole,
il Grillo-parlante si spense a un tratto,
come si spegne un lume soffiandoci sopra,
e la strada rimase più buia di prima" (Collodi 1993: 91).

8. "Quest'idea di trovarsi solo, solo,
solo in mezzo a quel gran paese disabitato,
gli mise attorno tanta malinconia, che stava
lì lì per piangere" (Collodi 1993: 165).

9. "un po' di pane, magari un po' di
pan secco, un crosterello, un osso avan-
zato al cane, un po' di polenta muffita, una
lisca di pesce, un nocciolo di ciliegia[...].
Oh! Che brutta malattia è la fame!" (Collodi 1993: 42).

10. "Ora che ho perduto te e il mio
babbo, chi mi darà da mangiare?[...]
Sarebbe cento volte meglio che morissi
anch'io!" (Collodi 1993: 156).

11. "c'è più dignità a morir sott'acqua
che sott'olio" (Collodi 1993: 254).

12. "Mi fareste il piacere di dirmi se in
quest' isola vi sono dei paesi dove si possa
mangiare, senza pericolo di essere man-
giati?" (Collodi 1993: 165).

13. "Entrati nell'osteria, si posero tutti
e tre a tavola, ma nessuno di loro aveva
appetito. Il povero gatto, sentendosi grave-
mente indisposto di stomaco, non potè
mangiare altro che trentacinque triglie
con salsa di pomodoro e quattro porzioni
di trippa alla parmigiana: e perché la trippa
non gli pareva condita abbastanza, si
rifece tre volte a chiedere il burro e il for-
maggio grattato! La Volpe avrebbe spilluz-
zicato volentieri qualche cosa anche lei,
ma siccome il medico le aveva ordinato
una grandissima dieta, così dové conten-
tarsi di una semplice lepre dolce e forte
con un leggerissimo contorno di pollastre
ingrassate e di galletti di primo canto.
Dopo la lepre si fece portare per tornagusto

un cibreino di pernici, di starne, di conigli,
di ranocchi, di lucertole e d'uva paradisa;
e poi non volle altro[...]. Quello che mangiò
meno di tutti fu Pinocchio. Chiese uno
spicchio di noce e un cantuccino di pane,
e lasciò nel piatto ogni cosa. Il povero figliolo col pensiero sempre fisso al Campo dei
miracoli, aveva preso un'indigestione an-
ticipata di monete d'oro" (Collodi 1993:
86–87).

14. "c'erano quattro marionette più
vispe e più graziose di quelle che si vedono
sui teatrini alle grandi fiere di Padova e di
Sinigaglia" (Collodi 2002: 159).

15. "Allora si affacciò alla finestra una
bella Bambina, coi capelli turchini e il viso
bianco come un'immagine di cera, gli occhi
chiusi e le mani incrociate sul petto, la
quale, senza muover punto le labbra, disse
con una vocina che pareva venisse dall'altro mondo:
—In questa casa non c'è nessuno. Sono
tutti morti.
—Aprimi almeno tu!—gridò Pinocchio
piangendo e raccomandandosi.
—Sono morta anch'io.
—Morta? e allora che cosa fai costí alla
finestra?
—Aspetto la bara che venga a portarmi
via" (Collodi 1993: 100–101).

16. "bisogna sapere che la Bambina dai
capelli turchini, non era altro in fin dei
conti che una bonissima Fata che da più
di mill'anni abitava nelle vicinanze di quel
bosco" (Collodi 1993: 107).

17. "ora mi ritrovi donna; tanto donna,
che potrei quasi farti da mamma"; "vi chi-
amerò la mia mamma. Gli è tanto tempo
che mi struggo di avere una mamma come
tutti gli altri ragazzi" (Collodi 173, 174).

Chapter 5

1. "Intanto s'era levato un vento im-
petuoso di tramontana, che soffiando e
mugghiando con rabbia, sbatacchiava in
qua e in là il povero impiccato, facendolo
dondolare violentemente come il battaglio
d'una campana che suona a festa. E quel
dondolio gli cagionava acutissimi spasimi,
e il nodo scorsoio, stringendosi sempre
più alla gola, gli toglieva il respiro.
A poco a poco gli occhi gli si appan-
narono; e sebbene sentisse avvicinarsi la

morte, pure sperava sempre che da un momento all'altro sarebbe capitata qualche anima pietosa a dargli aiuto. Ma quando, aspetta aspetta, vide che non compariva nessuno, proprio nessuno, allora gli tornò in mente il suo povero babbo ... e balbettò quasi moribondo: —Oh babbo mio! se tu fossi qui!... —E non ebbe fiato per dir altro. Chiuse gli occhi, aprí la bocca, stirò le gambe e, dato un grande scrollone, rimase lí come intirizzito" (Collodi 1993: 105).

2. "E allora avvenne una scena, che parrebbe incredibile, se non fosse vera. Avvenne, cioè, che Pinocchio e Lucignolo, quando si videro colpiti tutti e due dalla medesima disgrazia, invece di restar mortificati e dolenti, cominciarono ad ammiccarsi i loro orecchi smisuratamente cresciuti, e dopo mille sguaiataggini finirono col dare in una bella risata. E risero, risero, risero, da doversi reggere il corpo" (Collodi 1993: 232).

3. "Diventò bianco come un panno lavato, e non disse altro che queste parole:—O mamma mia, aiutatemi ... perché muoio!" (Collodi 1993: 187).

4. "...tenero e untuoso come una palla di burro, con un visino di melarosa" (Collodi 1993: 218).

5. "Sciagurato figliolo! E pensare che ho penato tanto a farlo un burattino per bene!" (Collodi 1993: 11).

6. "—Numi del firmamento! Sogno o son desto? Eppure quello laggiù è Pinocchio!...

—È Pinocchio davvero—grida Pulcinella.

—È proprio lui—strilla la signora Rosaura, facendo capolino di fondo alla scena[...].

È il nostro fratello Pinocchio![...] Pinocchio, vieni quassù da me,—grida Arlecchino,—Vieni a gettarti tra le braccia dei tuoi fratelli di legno" (Collodi 1993: 67).

7. "Oramai è scritto nei decreti della sapienza, che tutti quei ragazzi svogliati che, pigliando a noia i libri, le scuole e i maestri, passano le giornate in balocchi, in giochi e divertimenti, debbano finire poi col trasformarsi in tanti piccoli somari" (Collodi 1993: 229).

8. "Si piegarono tutti e due carponi a terra, e camminando con le mani e coi piedi, cominciarono a girare e correre per la stanza. E intanto che correvano, i loro bracci diventavano zampe, i loro visi si allungarono e diventarono musi e le loro schiene si coprirono di un pelame grigiolino chiaro, brizzolato di nero[...]. Il momento più brutto e umiliante fu quello quando sentirono spuntarsi di dietro la coda. Vinti allora dalla vergogna e dal dolore, si provarono a piangere e a lamentarsi del loro destino. Non l'avessero mai fatto! Invece di gemiti e di lamenti, mandavano fuori dei ragli asinini: e ragliando sonoramente, facevano tutti e due in coro: j-a, j-a, j-a" (Collodi 1993: 233).

9. "Molte frustate da levare il pelo" (Collodi 1993: 238).

10. "Pinocchio andò incontro fin dai primi giorni a una vita durissima e strapazzata" (Collodi 1993: 235).

11. "Andò subito in cerca di uno specchio, per potersi vedere; ma non trovando uno specchio, empì d'acqua la catinella del lavamano e, specchiandovisi dentro, vide quel che non avrebbe mai voluto vedere: vide, cioè, la sua immagine abbellita di un magnifico paio di orecchi asinini." (Collodi 1993: 130)

12. "Dopo andò a guardarsi allo specchio, e gli parve di essere un altro. Non vide più riflessa la solita immagine della marionetta di legno, ma vide l'immagine vispa e intelligente di un bel fanciullo coi capelli castagni, con gli occhi celesti e con un'aria allegra e festosa come una pasqua di rose" (Collodi 1993: 280).

13. "I ragazzi dovrebbero sapere che un buon medicamento preso a tempo può salvarli da una grave malattia e fors'anche dalla morte" (Collodi 1993: 117).

14. "Mentre si disperava a questo modo, fece l'atto di volersi strappare i capelli, ma i suoi capelli, essendo di legno, non potè nemmeno levarsi il gusto di ficcarci dentro le dita" (Collodi 1993: 23).

15. "Un vestituccio di carta fiorita, un paio di scarpe di scorza d'albero e un berrettino di midolla di pane" (Collodi 1993: 55).

16. "Tutti se la passavano bene. Il più ricco di loro chiedeva l'elemosina" (Collodi 1993: 30).

17. "I burattini non crescono mai. Nascono burattini, vivono burattini, e muoiono burattini" (Collodi 1993: 174).

18. "Pinocchio, alla presenza del giudice, raccontò per filo e per segno l'iniqua frode, di cui era stato vittima; dette il nome il cognome e i connotati dei malandrini, e finì con chiedere giustizia.

Il giudice lo ascoltò con molta benignità: prese vivissima parte al racconto: s'intenerì, si commosse: e quando il burattino non ebbe più nulla da dire, allungò la mano e suonò il campanello[...].—Quel povero diavolo è stato derubato di quattro monete d'oro: pigliatelo dunque e mettetelo subito in prigione—" (Collodi 1993: 134–135).

19. "In questo caso avete mille ragioni— disse il carceriere; e levandosi il berretto rispettosamente e salutandolo, gli aprì le porte della prigione e lo lasciò scappare" (Collodi 1993: 137).

20. "Appena entrato in città, Pinocchio vide tutte le strade popolate di cani spelacchiati, che sbadigliavano dall'appetito, di pecore tosate che tremavano dal freddo, di galline rimaste senza cresta e senza bargigli, che chiedevano l'elemosina d'un chicco di granturco, di grosse farfalle, che non potevano più volare, perché avevano venduto le loro bellissime ali colorite, di pavoni tutti scodati, che si vergognavano a farsi vedere, e di fagiani che zampettavano cheti cheti, rimpiangendo le loro scintillanti penne d'oro e d'argento, oramai perdute per sempre" (Collodi 1993: 128).

21. "Le strade formicolavano di persone che correvano di qua e di là per le loro faccende: tutti lavoravano, tutti avevano qualche cosa da fare. Non si trovava un ozioso o un vagabondo, nemmeno a

cercarlo col lumicino." (Collodi 1993: 167– 168)

22. "Non ti vergogni? Invece di fare il bighellone per la strada, vai piuttosto a cercarti un po' di lavoro, e impara a guadagnarti il pane!" (Collodi 1993: 170).

23. "Si passano baloccandosi e divertendosi dalla mattina alla sera" (Collodi 1993: 213).

24. "Il giovedì non si fa scuola: e ogni settimana è composta di sei giovedì e di una domenica. Figurati che le vacanze dell'autunno cominciano col primo di gennaio e finiscono con l'ultimo di dicembre" (Collodi 1993: 212).

25. "Domani finisco di essere un burattino e divento un ragazzo come te, e come tutti gli altri" (Collodi 1993: 212).

26. "Era già da cinque mesi che durava questa bella cuccagna di baloccarsi e di divertirsi le giornate intere, senza mai vedere in faccia né un libro né una scuola" (Collodi 1993: 225).

27. "Lì non vi sono scuole: lì non vi sono maestri: lì non vi sono libri" (Collodi 1993: 212).

28. "I più vecchi avevano 14 anni, i più giovani ne avevano 8 appena. Nelle strade un'allegria, un chiasso, uno strillo da levar di cervello![...] Chi rideva, chi urlava, chi chiamava, chi batteva le mani, chi fischiava, chi rifaceva il verso alla gallina quando ha fatto l'ovo: insomma, un tal pandemonio, un tal passeraio, un tal baccano indiavolato, da doversi mettere il cotone negli orecchi per non rimanere assorditi" (Collodi 1993: 223–224).

Works Cited

Abate, Michelle Ann. 2011. "The Queen Had Only One Way of Settling All Difficulties ... 'Off with His Head': *Alice's Adventures in Wonderland* and the Anti-Gallows Movement." *Papers: Explorations in Children's Literature* 21.1: 33–56.

Abbadie Clerc, Christiane. 1991/2002. "Pinocchio dall'altra parte dello specchio. Letture contro le buone maniere." In *Pinocchio Esportazione*, edited by Giorgio Cusatelli, 101–112. Roma: Armando Editore.

Adair, Gilbert. 2012. *Alice Through the Needle's Eye: The Further Adventures of Lewis Carroll's Alice.* London: Picador.

Ahlberg, Allan, and Janet. 1990. *Peepo!* London: Viking.

_____. 1999. *The Jolly Postman and Other People's Letters.* London: Puffin Books.

Alderson, Brian. 1995. "Introduction." In *The Water Babies* by Charles Kingsley. Oxford: Oxford University Press. vii–xl.

Aldrich, Thomas Bailey. 1870/1976. *The Story of a Bad Boy.* New York: Garland.

Allan, Robin. 1999. *Walt Disney and Europe: European Influences on the Animated Feature Films of Walt Disney.* London: John Libbey.

Allan, William. 1974. "G.A. Henty." *Cornhill Magazine* 1082: 71–100.

Allen, Brigid, ed. 1994. *Food: An Oxford Anthology.* Oxford: Oxford University Press.

Ambrosini, Richard. 2007. "Emilio Salgari e la 'grande' tradizione del romanzo d'avventura inglese." In *Emilio Salgari e la grande tradizione del romanzo d'avventura*, edited by Luisa Villa, 5–30. Genova: ECIG.

Anderson, Benedict. 1983/1991. *Imagined Communities. Reflections on the Origin and Spread of Nationalism.* London: Verso.

Anstey, F. 1882/1911. *Vice Versa, or: A Lesson to Fathers.* London: Smith Elder.

Armitt, Lucie. 1997. "The Fragile Frames of *The Bloody Chamber.*" In *The Infernal Desires of Angela Carter: Fiction, Femininity, Feminism*, edited by Joseph Bristow and Trev Lynn Broughton, 88–99. London: Longman.

Arnold, Guy. 1980. *Held Fast for England: G.A. Henty Imperialist Boys' Writer.* London: Hamish Hamilton.

Aroldi, Piermarco. 1994. "I parenti terribili." In *La fabbrica di Pinocchio: Le avventure di un burattino nell'industria culturale*, edited by Gianfanco Bettetini, 97–114. Torino: Nuova Eri.

Arpino, Giovanni, and Roberto Antonetto. 1982. *Vita, tempeste, sciagure di Salgari, il padre degli eroi.* Milano: Rizzoli.

Ashley, Leonard R.N. 1999. *George Alfred Henty and the Victorian Mind.* San Francisco: International Scholar Publications.

Asor Rosa, Alberto. 1975. *Storia d'Italia. Vol. IV, Dall'Unità a oggi.* Torino: Einaudi.

Attebery, Brian. 1992. *Strategies of Fantasy.* Bloomington: Indiana University Press.

Auerbach, Nina. 1973. "Alice and Wonderland: A Curious Child." *Victorian Studies* 17: 31–47.

Auerbach, Nina, and U.C. Knoepflmacher, eds. 1992. *Forbidden Journeys: Fairy Tales and Fantasies by Victorian Women Writers*. Chicago: University of Chicago Press.

Ausonia [Francesco Ciampi] 2014. *Pinocchio: Storia di un burattino*. Novara: Lineachiara.

Avanzini, Alessandra. 2011. *Il viaggio di Alice. Una sfida controcorrente*. Milano: Francoangeli.

Avery, Gillian. 1994. *Behold the Child: American Children and Their Books, 1621–1922*. London: Bodley Head.

_____. 2000. "British and Irish Fairy Tales." In *The Oxford Companion to Fairy Tales*, edited by Jack Zipes, 66–77. Oxford: Oxford University Press.

Bacchilega, Cristina. 1997. *Postmodern Fairy Tales: Gender and Narrative Strategies*. Philadelphia: University of Pennsylvania Press.

Bacigalupi, Marcella, and Piero Fossati. 2000. *Da plebe a popolo. L'educazione popolare nei libri di scuola dall'Unità d'Italia alla Repubblica*. Milano: Università Cattolica.

Bacon, Martha. 1973. "Puppet's Progress: *Pinocchio*." In *Children and Literature: Views and Reviews*, edited by Virginia Havilland, 71–77. Glenview, IL: Scott Foresman.

Bakewell, Michael. 1996. *Lewis Carroll: A Biography*. London: Heinemann.

Bakhtin, Mikhail. 1984. *Rabelais and His World*. Bloomington: Indiana University Press.

Ballantyne, Robert Michael. 1855/1990. *The Coral Island*, edited by Dennis Butts. Oxford: Oxford University Press.

Barberi Squarotti, Giorgio. 1976. "Gli schemi narrativi di Collodi." In *Studi Collodiani, Proceedings of the Conference of the Fondazione Nazionale "Carlo Collodi" (Pescia, 5–7 October May 1974)*, 87–108. Pistoia: Cassa di Risparmio di Pistoia e Pescia.

Barrie, J.M. 1911/1999. *Peter Pan in Kensington Gardens*, and *Peter and Wendy*, edited by Peter Hollindale. Oxford: Oxford University Press.

Beauvoir, Simone de. 1949/1997. *The Second Sex*. London: Vintage.

Beckett, Sandra. 2004. "Le pantin persistent et protéiforme: réécritures de *Pinocchio*." *Quaderni d'Italianistica* 25.1: 43–67.

_____. 2006. "Recycling *Pinocchio* for Contemporary Audiences." In *Approaches to Teaching Collodi's* Pinocchio *and Its Adaptations*, edited by Michael Sherberg, 112–118. New York: Modern Language Association of America.

Beckett, Sandra, and Maria Nikolajeva, eds. 2006. *Beyond Babar. The European Tradition in Children's Literature*. Lanham, MD: Scarecrow Press.

Beddor, Frank. 2006. *The Looking Glass Wars*. New York: Penguin.

Beer, Gillian. 1983. *Darwin's Plots: Evolutionary Narrative in Darwin, George Eliot and Nineteenth-Century Fiction*. Abingdon-on-Thames: Routledge.

_____. 2016. *Alice in Space: The Sideways Victorian World of Lewis Carroll*. Chicago: University of Chicago Press.

Belardelli, Giovanni, Cafagna, Luciano, Galli della Loggia, Ernesto, and Sabbatucci, Giovanni. 1999. *Miti e storia dell'Italia unita*. Bologna: Il Mulino.

Bell, Elizabeth Ly. 2012. "Robert Coover and the Neverending Story of *Pinocchio*." *The Review of Contemporary Fiction* 32.1: 32–46.

Beller, Manfred. 2007. "Italians." In *Imagology: The Cultural Construction and Literary Representation of National Characters*, edited by Manfred Beller and Joep Leerssen, 194–200. Amsterdam: Rodopi.

Beller, Manfred, and Joep Leerssen. 2007. "Foreword." In *Imagology, The cultural construction and literary representation of national characters*, xiii–xvi. Amsterdam: Rodopi.

Benni, Stefano. 2007. "Appunti per una conferenza tenuta a Napoli per l'Arn il 7 luglio 2007." http://www.lostraniero. net/archivio-2007/34-ottobre/204-alice-e-pinocchio.html.

_____. 2013. *Pinocchia*. In *Teatro 2*, 8–64. Milano: Feltrinelli.

_____. 2016. *La bottiglia magica*. Milano: Rizzoli.

Berman, Ruth. 2003. "Alice as Fairy-Tale and Non Fairy-Tale." *The Carrollian— The Lewis Carroll Journal* 11: 51–62.

Bertacchini, Renato. 1961. *Collodi narratore*. Pisa: Nistri-Lischi.

_____. 1964. *Collodi educatore*. Firenze: La Nuova Italia.

_____. 1981. "Epifanie e segni del paesaggio nelle "Avventure di Pinocchio." In *C'era una volta un pezzo di legno*. *La simbologia di* Pinocchio, *Proceedings of the Conference of the Fondazione Nazionale "Carlo Collodi" (Pescia, 24–25 May 1980)*, 113–141. Milano: Emme.

_____. 1983. *Le avventure ritrovate: "Pinocchio" e gli scrittori italiani del Novecento*. Pescia: Fondazione nazionale Carlo Collodi.

_____. 1993. *Il padre di Pinocchio. Vita e opere del Collodi*. Milano: Camunia.

_____. 2015. *Le fate e il burattino. Carlo Collodi e l'avventura dell'educazione*. Bologna: Edizioni Dehoniane Bologna.

Bertoni Jovine, Dina. 1965. *Storia dell'educazione popolare in Italia*. Milano: Laterza.

Beseghi, Emy. 1992. "Jolanda e le altre. Figure femminili nell'opera di Emilio Salgari." In *La valle della luna. Avventura, esotismo, orientalismo nell'opera di Emilio Salgari*, edited by Emy Beseghi, 123–144. Firenze: La Nuova Italia.

Bettetini, Gianfranco, ed. 1994. *La fabbrica di Pinocchio: Le avventure di un burattino nell'industria culturale*. Torino: Nuova Eri.

Bhabha, Homi K. 1990. "Introduction: Narrating the Nation." In *Nation and Narration*, edited by Homi K. Bhabha, 1–7. Abingdon-on-Thames: Routledge.

Bini, Giorgio. 1989. "La maestra nella letteratura: Uno specchio della realtà." In *L'educazione delle donne. Scuole e modelli di vita femminile nell'Italia dell'Ottocento*, edited by Simonetta Soldani, 331–362. Milano: Franco Angeli.

Blackman, Lisa. 2006. *The Body: Key Concepts*. Oxford: Berg.

Blamires, David. 1989. "The Early Reception of the Grimms' *Kinder-und Hausmärchen* in England." *Bulletin of the John Rylands University Library of Manchester* 71: 63–77.

Blount, Margaret. 1974. *Animal Land: The Creatures of Children's Fictions*. London: Hutchinson.

Blythe, Lucy Helen. 2014. *The Victorian Colonial Romance with the Antipodes*. London: Palgrave Macmillan.

Boero, Piero. 1999. "La Linea del cuore." In *Alla frontiera. Momenti, generi e temi della letteratura per l'infanzia*, edited by Pino Boero, 11–25. Torino: Einaudi.

Boero, Piero, and Carmine de Luca. 2009. *La letteratura per l'infanzia*. Bari: Laterza.

Boero, Piero, and Giovanni Genovesi. 2009. *Cuore. De Amicis tra critica e utopia*. Milano: Francoangeli.

Bond, Barbara. 2004. "Postmodern Mannerism: An Examination of Robert Coover's *Pinocchio in Venice*." *Critique: Studies in Contemporary Fiction* 45.3: 273–292.

Borghese, Lucia. 1986. "Storia della ricezione delle fiabe grimmiane in Toscana e della loro prima traduzione italiana." In *Interni e Dintorni del Pinocchio. Atti del Convegno "Folkloristi Italiani del tempo del Collodi"*, edited by Pietro Clemente and Mariano Fresta, 49–58. Pescia: Editori del Grifo.

Botto, Margherita. 1998. "Due Italiani nel Rif. L'Africa nella 'letteratura industriale' da De Amicis a Salgari." *Italies Narrativa* 14: 71–88.

Braidotti, Rosi. 2006. *Metamorphoses: Towards a Materialist Theory of Becoming*. Cambridge: Polity.

Bratton, J. S. 1981. *The Impact of Victorian Children's Fiction*. London: Croom Helm.

Briggs, Katherine. 1963. "The Influence of the Brothers Grimm in England." *BruderGrimm Gedenken* 1: 511–524.

Bristow, Joseph. 1991. *Empire Boys: Adventures in a Man's World*. London: HarperCollins.

Brome, Richard. 1640/1963. *The Antipodes*. London: Arnold.

Brooker, Will. 2005. *Alice's Adventures: Lewis Carroll in Popular Culture*. London: Bloomsbury Academic.

Buckle, Thomas. 1857–1861/1902. *History of Civilization in England*. London: Longmans.

Bulwer-Lytton, Edward. 1834/1842. *The Last Days of Pompeii*. Leipzig: B. Tauchniz.

Burstyn, Joan. 1984. *Victorian Education and the Ideal of Womanhood*. New Brunswick, NJ: Rutgers University Press.

Butler, Judith. 1986. "Sex and Gender in

Simone de Beauvoir's Second Sex." *Yale French Studies* 72: 35–49.

Butler, Samuel. 1872/1985. *Erewhon*, edited by Peter Mudford. London: Penguin.

Butts, Dennis. 1992. "The Adventure Story." In *Stories and Society: Children's Literature in Its Social Context*, edited by Dennis Butts, 65–83. London: Macmillan.

———. 2008. "Exploiting a Formula: The Adventure Stories of G.A. Henty (1832–1902)." In *Popular Children's Literature in Britain*, edited by Julia Briggs, Dennis Butts, and M.O. Grenby, 149–163. Farnham: Ashgate.

Butts, Dennis, and Peter Hunt. 2013. *How Did Long John Silver Lose His Leg? And Twenty-Six Other Mysteries of Children's Literature*. Cambridge: Lutterworth Press.

Byatt, A.S. 2002. "Queen of Hearts and Minds." *The Guardian* 14 December 2002. https://www.theguardian.com/books/2002/dec/14/classics.asbyatt.

Calendoli, Giovanni. 1994. "Pinocchio nella storia dei burattini e delle marionette." In *Pinocchio sullo schermo e sulla scena*, edited by Giuseppe Flores D'Arcais, 125–137. Milano: La Nuova Italia.

Calvino, Italo. 1956/1983. "Introduzione." In *Fiabe Italiane*. Milano: Mondadori, 7–67.

———. 1991/2000. *Why Read the Classics?* New York: Vintage.

Cambi, Franco. 1985. *Collodi, De Amicis, Rodari. Tre Immagini d'infanzia*. Bari: Dedalo.

Cambon, Glauco. 1973. "*Pinocchio* and the Problem of Children's Literature." *Children's Literature* 2: 50–60.

Cammarata, Adele. 2015. "Italians Love Alice!" In *Alice in a World of Wonderlands: The Translations of Lewis Carroll's Masterpiece*, edited by Jon A. Lindseth and Alan Tannenbaum, 310–315. New Castle, DE: Oak Knoll Press.

Campbell, Lori M. 2010. *Portals of Power: Magical Agency and Transformation in Literary Fantasy*. Jefferson, NC: McFarland.

Canepa, Nancy. 1999. *From Court to Forest: Giambattista Basile's* Lo Cunto de li Cunti *and the Birth of the Literary Fairy Tale*. Detroit: Wayne State University Press.

———. 2006. "Talking (with) Animals. *Pinocchio* and Dialogicity." In *Approaches to Teaching Collodi's* Pinocchio *and Its Adaptations*, edited by Michael Sherberg, 57–94. New York: Modern Language Association of America.

Carpenter, Humphrey. 1985. *Secret Gardens: The Golden Age of Children's Literature*. London: George Allen and Unwin.

Carroll, Jane Suzanne. 2011. *Landscape in Children's Literature*. Abingdon-on-Thames: Routledge.

Carroll, Lewis. 1885. *A Tangled Tale*. London: Macmillan.

———. 1887. *A Game of Logic*. London: Macmillan.

———. 2009. *Alice's Adventures in Wonderland and Through the Looking-Glass*, edited by Peter Hunt. Oxford: Oxford University Press.

Carter, Angela. 1967. *The Magic Toyshop*. London: Virago.

———. 1968. *Several Perceptions*. London: Heinemann.

———. 1974. "The Loves of Lady Purple." In *Fireworks*, 23–38. London: Quartet Books.

———. 1979/1995. "Wolf Alice." In *The Bloody Chamber*, 119–126. London: Vintage.

———. 1990/1994. "Alice in Prague or the Curious Room." In *American Ghosts and Old World Wonders*, 121–139. London: Vintage.

Casapullo, Rosa. 2012. "Maestri e maestre nella prosa letteraria dell'Ottocento." In *La nazione tra i banchi. Il contributo della scuola alla formazione degli italiani tra Otto e Novecento*, edited by Vittoria Fiorelli, 305–318. Catanzaro: Rubbettino.

Castoldi, Massimo, ed. 2016. *Piccoli eroi. Libri e scrittori per ragazzi durante il ventennio fascista*. Milano: FrancoAngeli.

Cech, John. 1986. "The Triumphant Transformations of *Pinocchio*." In *Triumphs of the Spirit in Children's Literature*, edited by Francelia Butler and Robert Rotert, 171–177. Hamden, CT: Library Professional.

Citati, Pietro. 1979. "La fata dai capelli turchini." In *Il velo nero*, 214–220. Milano: Rizzoli.

Clark, Anne. 1979. *Lewis Carroll: A Biography.* London: Dent.

Clemente, Pietro. 1986. *"Pinocchio e le fiabe di Perrault."* In *Interni e Dintorni del Pinocchio. Atti del Convegno "Folkloristi Italiani del tempo del Collodi,"* edited by Pietro Clemente and Mariano Fresta, 199–214. Pescia: Editori del Grifo.

Cocchiara, Giuseppe. 1952/1981. *History of Folklore in Europe.* Philadelphia: Institute for the Study of Human Issues.

Coetzee, J.M. 1986. *Foe.* Johannesburg: Rovan.

Cohen, Morton. 1995. *Lewis Carroll: A Biography.* New York: Macmillan.

Collingwood, Stuart Dodgson. 1899a. *The Lewis Carroll Picture Book.* London: T. Fisher Unwin.

_____. 1899b. *The Life and Letters of Lewis Carroll.* London: T. Fisher Unwin.

Collodi, Carlo. 1875/2002. *I racconti delle fate,* edited by Giuseppe Pontiggia. Milano: Adelphi.

_____. 1877/1988. *Giannettino.* Torino: Petrini.

_____. 1880. *Il Viaggio per l'Italia di Giannettino. Parte prima (L'Italia superiore).* Firenze: Paggi.

_____. 1883/1993. *Le Avventure di Pinocchio,* edited by Fernando Tempesti. Milano: Feltrinelli.

_____. 1886. *Il Viaggio per l'Italia di Giannettino. Parte terza (L'Italia meridionale).* Firenze: Paggi.

_____. 1890. *La lanterna magica di Giannettino.* Firenze: Bemporad.

_____. 1995a. "Il ragazzo di strada." In *Carlo Collodi. Opere,* edited by Daniela Marcheschi, 179–188. Milano: Mondadori.

_____. 1995b. "Sangue Italiano." In *Carlo Collodi. Opere,* edited by Daniela Marcheschi, 238–343. Milano: Mondadori.

_____. 1996. *The Adventures of Pinocchio,* edited and translated by Ann Lawson Lucas. Oxford: Oxford University Press.

Compagnone, Luigi. 1971. *La vita nova di Pinocchio.* Firenze: Vallecchi.

Cook, Chris, ed. 2005. *The Routledge Companion to Britain in the Nineteenth Century.* Abingdon-on-Thames: Routledge.

Cook, Elizabeth. 1976. *The Ordinary and the Fabulous,* 2nd ed. Cambridge: Cambridge University Press.

Coover, Robert. 1991. *Pinocchio in Venice.* New York: Grove Press.

_____. 1998. "Entering Ghost Town." *Marvels & Tales* 12.1: 231–238.

_____. 2000/2006. "Alice in the Time of the Jabberwock." In *Alice Redux: New Stories of Alice, Lewis, and Wonderland,* edited by Richard Peabody, 71–104. Arlington: Paycock Press.

Croce, Benedetto. 1966. *La letteratura della nuova Italia,* vol. V. Bari: Laterza.

Crompton, Richmal. 1922. *Just—William.* London: George Newnes.

Curreri, Luciano, ed. 2011. *Pinocchio in camicia nera. Quattro "pinocchiate" fasciste.* Cuneo: Nerosubianco.

_____. 2017. *Play it Again, Pinocchio. Saggi per una storia delle "pinocchiate."* Bergamo: Moretti and Vitali.

Cusatelli, Giorgio. 1983. "Filologi e fiabe: le vicende grimmiane in Italia," In *Studi di Cultura francese ed europea in onore di Lorenza Maranini,* edited by Giorgetto Giorgi, Aurelio Principato, Elisa Biancardi, and Maria Cecilia Bertoletti, 529–535. Fasano: Schena.

D'Angelo, Marco. 2002. "Lettore avvisato, burattino salvato. Strategie seriali." In *Le avventure di Pinocchio tra un linguaggio e l'altro,* edited by Isabella Pezzini and Paolo Fabbri, 75–94. Roma: Meltemi.

Darton, F.J. Harvey. 1932/1982. *Children's Books in England: Five Centuries of Social Life,* 3rd ed., revised by Brian Alderson. Cambridge: Cambridge University Press.

D'Aulnoy, Marie-Catherine [M.me D'Aulnoy]. 1697. "L'oiseau bleu" https://fr.wikisource.org/wiki/L%E2%80%99Oiseau_bleu_(Aulnoy).

Day, Barry, ed. 2009. *The Essential Noël Coward Companion.* London: Methuen Drama.

D'Azeglio, Massimo. 1867. *I Miei ricordi.* Firenze: Barbera.

De Amicis, Edmondo. 1892/1960. *Il Romanzo di un maestro.* Milano: Garzanti.

_____. 1892/1971. *Amore e ginnastica.* Torino: Einaudi.

_____. 1886/1996. *Cuore.* In *Edmondo De*

Amicis. *Opere Scelte*, edited by Falco Portinari and Giusi Baldissone, 103–375. Milano: Mondadori.

_____. 2011. *Cuore: An Italian Schoolboy's Journal: A Book for Boys.* Translated by Isabel Hapgood. Whitefish, MT: Kessinger Publishing.

Decollanz, Giuseppe. 1976. "Educazione e politica nel *Pinocchio*." in *Studi Collodiani*, 169–187. Fondazione Nazionale Carlo Collodi. Pistoia: Cassa di Risparmio di Pistoia e Pescia.

Dedebas, Eda. 2011. "Christina Rossetti's *Speaking Likenesses*: Different Forms of Travel in Victorian Children's Literature." *Extravío. Revista Electrónica de literatura comparada* 6: 53–68.

Dedola, Rossana. 2002. *Pinocchio e Collodi.* Milano: Bruno Mondadori.

Dedola, Rossana, and Mario Casari, eds. 2008. *Pinocchio in volo tra immagini e letterature.* Milano: Bruno Mondadori.

de la Mare, Walter. 1971. "On the Alice Books." In *Aspects of Alice: Lewis Carroll's Dreamchild As Seen Through the Critics' Looking-Glasses, 1865–1971*, edited by Robert Philips, 89–98. New York: Vanguard Press.

Del Beccaro, Felice. 1992. "Il paesaggio in Pinocchio." *Rassegna Lucchese* 9: 67–85 special number: *Omaggio a Pinocchio*.

Demurova, Nina. 1982. "Toward a Definition of *Alice*'s Genre: The Folktale and Fairy-Tale Connections." In *Lewis Carroll: A Celebration—Essays on the Occasion of the 150th Anniversary of the Birth of Charles Lutwidge Dodgson*, edited by Edward Guiliano, 75–84. New York: Clarkson N. Potter.

De Rienzo, Giorgio. 1975. *Narrativa toscana dell'Ottocento.* Firenze: Olschki.

Despinette, Janine. 2002. "Pinocchio presenza francese." In *Pinocchio Esportazione*, edited by Giorgio Cusatelli, 17–26. Roma: Armando Editore.

Detti, Ermanno. 2002. "Introduction." *The Lion and the Unicorn* 26.2:143–149.

Dierbeck, Lisa. 2003. *One Pill Makes You Smaller.* Edinburgh: Canongate.

Domínguez, César, Haun Saussy, and Dario Villanueva. 2015. *Introducing Comparative Literature: New Trends and Applications.* Abingdon-on-Thames: Routledge.

Donaldson, Ian. 1970. *The World Upside-Down: Comedy from Jonson to Fielding.* Oxford: Clarendon Press.

Douglas-Fairhurst, Robert. 2015. *The Story of Alice: Lewis Carroll and the Secret History of Wonderland.* London: Harvill Secker.

Dunae, Patrick. 1980. "Boys' Literature and the Idea of Empire 1870–1914." *Victorian Studies* 24: 105–121.

Dusinberre, Juliet. 1987. *Alice to the Lighthouse: Children's Books and Radical Experiments in Art.* London: Macmillan.

Eco, Umberto. 1963. "Elogio di Franti." In *Diario Minimo*, 81–92. Milano: Mondadori.

_____. 1995. *Povero Pinocchio. Giochi linguistici di studenti bolognesi al Seminario di scrittura di Umberto Eco.* Bologna: Panini.

Ehling, Holger. 2012. *Finding England: An Ausländer's Guide to Perfidious Albion.* London: The Armchair Traveller.

Eldridge, C.C. 1996. *The Imperial Experience: From Carlyle to Forster.* London: Macmillan.

Elick, Catherine. 2015. *Talking Animals in Children's Fiction: A Critical Study.* Jefferson, NC: McFarland.

Ewing, Juliana Horatia. 1886. *Mary's Meadow.* London: SPCK.

Faeti, Antonio. 2011. *Guardare le figure. Gli illustratori italiani dei libri per l'infanzia.* New Edition, Roma: Donzelli.

Falconer, Rachel. 2009. *The Crossover Novel: Contemporary Children's Fiction and Its Adult Readership.* Abingdon-on-Thames: Routledge.

Farrar, Frederic William. 1858/1971. *Eric, or, Little by Little, a Tale of Roslyn School.* London: Hamish Hamilton.

Faustini, Alessandra. 1990. "Le traduzioni italiane dei *Kinder-und Hausmärchen* dei fratelli Grimm." In *La fiaba d'area germanica. Studi tipologici e tematici*, edited by Enza Gini, 57–68. Firenze: La Nuova Italia.

Feldmann, Doris. 1996. "Victorian (Dis)-Enchantments: Fantasy and Realism in the Visions and Revisions of Scrooge and Alice." In *Fantasy in Film und Literatur*, edited by Dieter Petzhold, 112–125. Heidelberg: Universitatsverlag C. Winter.

Fenn, G. Manville. 1907. *George Alfred Henty: The Story of an Active Life*. London: Blackie.

Ferretti, Roberto. 1986. "Gli animali nella narrativa orale e in *Pinocchio*: alcune osservazioni in merito alle esperienze e ai patrimoni fiabistici toscani." In *Interni e Dintorni del Pinocchio. Atti del Convegno "Folkloristi Italiani del tempo del Collodi,"* edited by Pietro Clemente and Mariano Fresta, 215–240. Pescia: Editori del Grifo.

Ferris, Davis. 2011. "Why Compare?" In *A Companion to Comparative Literature*, edited by Ali Bendad and Dominic Thomas, 28–45. Hoboken, NJ: Wiley-Blackwell.

Fiedler, Leslie. 1960. *Love and Death in the American Novel*. New York: Dalkey Archive Press.

Fisher, Margery. 1986. *Classics for Children and Young People*. South Woodchester: Thimble Press.

Flegar, Želika, and Tena Wertag. 2015. "*Alice* Through the Ages: Childhood and Adaptation." *Liber & Liberi* 4: 213–240.

Fox, Kate. 2004. *Watching the English: The Hidden Rules of English Behaviour*. London: Hodder and Stoughton.

Frankova, Milada. 1999. "Angela Carter's Mannerism in Rudolf II's Curious Room." *Brno Studies in English* 25: 127–133.

Freeman, Sarah. 1988. *Mutton and Oysters: The Victorians and Their Food*. London: Gollancz.

Fresta, Mariano. 1986. "L' alimentazione di Pinocchio." In *Interni e Dintorni del Pinocchio. Atti del Convegno "Folkloristi Italiani del tempo del Collodi,"* edited by Pietro Clemente and Mariano Fresta, 133–143. Pescia: Editori del Grifo.

Frey, Charles and John Griffin. 1987. *The Literary Heritage of Childhood: An Appraisal of Children's Classics in the Western Tradition*. Westport, CT: Greenwood Press.

Gabriele, Mino. 1976. "Il burattino e lo specchio." In *C'era una volta un pezzo di legno. La simbologia di Pinocchio*, edited by Gian Luca Pierotti, 43–52. Fondazione Nazionale "Carlo Collodi," Milano: Edizioni Emme.

Gagliano, Maurizio. 2002. "Pulsioni di morte e destini di vita: dal burattino al replicante." In *Le avventure di Pinocchio tra un linguaggio e l'altro*, edited by Isabella Pezzini and Paolo Fabbri, 94–111. Roma: Meltemi.

Galli della Loggia, Ernesto. 1998. *L'identità italiana*. Bologna: Il Mulino.

Galli Mastrodonato, Paola Irene. 2001. "Il 'caso' Salgari e gli studi paraletterari in Italia." *Belphégor: Littérature populaire et culture médiatique* 1.1, November 2001. http://belphegor.revues.org.

Gamble, Sarah. 1997. *Angela Carter: Writing from the Front Line*. Edinburgh: Edinburgh University Press.

Garbarino, Giuseppe. 2014. *Pinocchio svelato. I luoghi, il bestiario e le curiosità nella favola del Collodi*. Empoli: AB edizioni.

Garland, Carina. 2008. "Curious Appetites: Food, Desire, Gender, and Subjectivity in Lewis Carroll's *Alice* Texts." *The Lion and the Unicorn* 32.1: 22–39.

Garland, Sarah. 1984. *The Herb Garden*. London: Frances Lincoln.

Garroni, Emilio. 2010. *Pinocchio uno e bino*. Roma-Bari: Laterza.

Gasparini, Giovanni. 1997. *La corsa di Pinocchio*. Milano: Vita e pensiero.

Gatens, Moira. 1996. *Imaginary Bodies: Ethics, Power and Corporeality*. Abingdon-on-Thames: Routledge.

Gatty, Margaret. 1851. *The Fairy Godmothers and Other Tales*. London: Bell.

Geddes da Filicaia, Costanza. 2012. "La maratona di Pinocchio, eroe dell'Italia postunitaria." In *La letteratura degli Italiani. Rotte, confini, passaggi*, edited by Alberto Beniscelli, Quinto Marini, and Luigi Surdich, 1–8. Atti del XIV Congresso Nazionale dell'Associazione degli Italianisti italiani. Genova: DIRAS.

Gellner, Ernest. 1983. *Nations and Nationalism*. Oxford: Blackwell.

Genette, Gérard. 1982. *Palimpsestes: la l ittérature au second degré*. Paris: Du Seuil.

Genot, Gérard. 1970. *Analyse structurelle de* Pinocchio, Firenze: Industria tipografica fiorentina.

_____. 1976. "Le corps de Pinocchio." In *Studi Collodiani, Proceedings of the*

Conference of the Fondazione Nazionale "Carlo Collodi" (Pescia, 5–7 October May 1974). Pistoia: Cassa di Risparmio di Pistoia e Pescia, 299–313.

Ghiselli, Ettore. 1898. Il fratello di Pinocchio, ovvero le avventure di Pinocchino. Firenze: Bemporad.

Gibbon, Edward. 1776–1789/1854. The History of the Decline and Fall of the Roman Empire. Halifax: Milner and Sowerby.

Gilead, Sarah. 1991. "Magic Abjured: Closure in Children's Fantasy Fiction." PMLA 106: 277–293.

Goldhill, Simon. 2011. Victorian Culture and Classical Antiquity. Princeton, NJ: Princeton University Press.

Goldthwaite, John. 1996. The Natural History of Make-Believe. Oxford: Oxford University Press.

Gonzato, Silvino. 2011. La tempestosa vita di Capitan Salgari. Vicenza: Neri Pozza.

Gordon, Jan B. 1971. "The Alice Books and the Metaphors of Victorian Childhood." In Aspects of Alice, edited by Robert Phillips, 127–150. New York: Penguin.

Gören, Esin. 2010. "Da Pinocchio a Pinocchia: comparando burattino a cyborg/robot." In Variazioni Pinocchio. 7 letture sulla riscrittura del mito, edited by Fabrizio Scrivano, 133–148. Perugia: Morlacchi.

Gottschall, Jonathan. 2012. The Storytelling Animal: How Stories Make us Human. Boston: Houghton Mifflin Harcourt.

Grahame, Kenneth. 1908/2009. The Wind in the Willows, edited by Peter Hunt. Oxford: Oxford University Press.

Graves, Robert. 1957. Poems Selected by Himself. New York: Penguin.

Green, Martin. 1979. Dreams of Adventures, Deeds of Empire. New York: Basic Books.

Grenby, Matthew. 2006. "Tame Fairies Make Good Teachers: The Popularity of Early British Fairy Tales." The Lion and the Unicorn 30.1: 11–24.

_____. 2008. "The School Story." In Children's Literature, 87–116. Edinburgh: Edinburgh University Press.

Grimm, Jacob, and Wilhelm. 1987. "The Maiden Without Hands." In The Complete Fairy Tales of the Brothers Grimm,

edited and translated by Jack Zipes, 118–122. New York: Bantam Books.

Gruppi, Nicoletta. 2007. "Nella lingua dell'Impero: La prima traduzione inglese di Le Tigri di Mompracem." In Emilio Salgari e la grande tradizione del romanzo d'avventura, edited by Luisa Villa, 267–281. Genova: ECIG.

Gubar, Mariah. 2009. Artful Dodgers: Reconceiving the Golden Age of Children's Literature. Oxford: Oxford University Press.

Guillory, John. 1993. Cultural Capital: The Problem of Literary Canon Formation. Chicago: University of Chicago Press.

Halliday, Iain. 2010. Huck Finn in Italian, Pinocchio in English: Theory and Praxis of Literary Translation. Teaneck, NJ: Fairleigh Dickinson University Press.

Hancher, Michael. 1982. "Punch and Alice: Through Tenniel's Looking-Glass." In Lewis Carroll: A Celebration—Essays on the Occasion of the 150th Anniversary of the Birth of Charles Lutwidge Dodgson, edited by Edward Guiliano, 26–49. New York: Clarkson N. Potter.

Hazard, Paul. 1932. Les livres, les enfants, les hommes. Paris: Flammarion.

Henty, G.A. The Collected Complete Works of G.A. Henty. Kindle edition, n.d.

Hillman, David, and Ulrika Maude, eds. 2015. "Introduction" to The Cambridge Companion to the Body in Literature. Cambridge: Cambridge University Press, 1–9.

Hintz, Carrie and Elaine Ostry. 2003. "Introduction" to Utopian and Dystopian Writing for Children and Young Adults. Abingdon-on-Thames: Routledge, 1–19.

Hirsch, Marianne. 1979. "The Novel of Formation as a Genre: Between Great Expectations and Lost Illusions." Genre 12: 293–312.

Hobsbawm, E.J. 1987. The Age of Empire 1875–1915. London: Weidenfeld and Nicolson.

Hollingsworth, Christopher. 2009. "Introduction" to Alice Beyond Wonderland: Essays for the Twenty-First Century, edited by Christopher Hollingsworth, xvii–xxviii. Iowa City: University of Iowa Press.

Honig, Lazaros Edith. 1988. Breaking the Angelic Image: Woman Power in Victorian Children's Fantasy. Westport, CT: Greenwood Press.

Horn, Pamela. 1989. The Victorian and Edwardian Schoolchild. Gloucester: Alan Sutton.

Hughes, Ted. 1997. Tales from Ovid. New York: Faber & Faber.

Hughes, Thomas. 1857/1989. Tom Brown's Schooldays, edited by Andrew Sanders. Oxford: Oxford University Press.

Hunt, Peter. 1987. "Landscape and Journeys, Metaphors and Maps: The Distinctive Features of English Fantasy." Children's Literature Association Quarterly 12: 11–14.

_____. 1996. "'Coldtonguecoldhamcoldbeefpickledgherkinsaladfrenchrolls cresssandwidgespottedmealgingerbeer sodawater….' Fantastic Food in the Books of Kenneth Grahame, Jerome K. Jerome, H.E. Bates and Other Bakers of the Fantasy England." Journal of the Fantastic in the Arts 7: 5–22.

_____. 1997. "Passing on the Past: The Problem of Books That Are for Children and That Were for Children." Children's Literature Association Quarterly 21.4: 200–202.

_____. ed. 2001. Children's Literature: An Anthology 1801–1902. Oxford: Blackwell.

_____. 2009. "Introduction" to Lewis Carroll, Alice's Adventures in Wonderland, edited by Peter Hunt, vi–xlix. Oxford: Oxford University Press.

_____. 2015. "Unstable Metaphors: Symbolic Spaces and Specific Places." In Space and Place in Children's Literature, 1789 to the Present, edited by Maria Sachico Cecire, Hannah Field, and Kavita Mudan Finn, 23–37. Farnham: Ashgate.

_____. 2016. "68—The Key to Through The Looking-Glass." Bandersnatch 171: 8–10.

Huttenback, Robert. 1965. "G.A. Henty and the Imperial Stereotype." Huntington Library Quarterly 29: 63–75.

Huxley, Aldous. 1932/1996. Brave New World. London: Longman.

Hyland, Peter. 1982. "The Ambiguous Alice: An Approach to Alice in Wonderland." Jabberwocky: The Journal of the Lewis Carroll Society 11.4: 104–112.

Incisa di Camerana, Ludovico. 2004. Pinocchio. Bologna: Il Mulino.

Ingelow, Jean. 1869/1964. Mopsa the Fairy. London: J.M. Dent.

Ipsen, Carl. 2006. Italy in the Age of Pinocchio: Children and Danger in the Liberal Era. London: Palgrave Macmillan.

Irwin, W.R. 1976. The Game of the Impossible. A Rhetoric of Fantasy. Champaign, IL: University of Illinois Press.

Israel, Kali. 2000. "Asking Alice: Victorian and Other Alices in Contemporary Culture." In Victorian Afterlife: Postmodern Culture Rewrites the Nineteenth Century, edited by John Kucich and Dianne F. Sadoff, 252–287. Minneapolis: University of Minnesota Press.

Jackson, Rosemary. 1988. Fantasy and the Literature of Subversion. Abingdon-on-Thames: Routledge.

Jaques, Zoe. 2015. Children's Literature and the Posthuman: Animal, Environment, Cyborg. Abingdon-on-Thames: Routledge.

Jaques, Zoe, and Eugene Giddens. 2013. Lewis Carroll's Alice's Adventures in Wonderland and Through the Looking-Glass: A Publishing History. Farnham: Ashgate.

Jefferies, Richard. 1882/1976. Bevis: The Story of a Boy. London: Puffin.

Johnson, Rachel E. 2014. A Complete Identity: The Youthful Hero in the Work of G.A. Henty and George MacDonald. Eugene, OR: Pickwick Publications.

Jones, Laura. 2013. "Writing and Righting History: Henty's Nation." In The Nation in Children's Literature, edited by Christopher (Kit) Kelen and Björn Sundmark, 161–173. Abingdon-on-Thames: Routledge, 161–173.

Jonson, Ben. 1614/1964. Bartholomew Fair. Lincoln: University of Nebraska Press.

Jylkka, Katja. 2010. "How Little Girls are Like Serpents, or, Food and Power in Lewis Carroll's Alice Books." The Carrollian 26: 3–19.

Keene, Melanie. 2015. Science in Wonderland: The Scientific Fairy Tales of Victorian Britain. Oxford: Oxford University Press.

Kelen, Christopher (Kit) and Björn Sundmark, eds. 2013. The Nation in Children's Literature. Abingdon-on-Thames: Routledge.

Kenyon, Michael. 1992. *Pinocchio's Wife.* Ottawa: Oberon Press.

Kiberd, Declan. 2004. "School Stories." In *Studies in Children's Literature 1500–2000,* edited by Celia Keenan and Mary Shine Thomson, 54–69. Dublin: Four Courts Press.

Kincaid, James R. 1973. "Alice's Invasion of Wonderland." *PMLA* 88: 92–99.

Kingsley, Charles. 1863/1995. *The Water Babies,* edited by Brian Alderson. Oxford: Oxford University Press.

Kipling, Rudyard. 1899/1965. *Stalky and Co.* London: Macmillan.

_____. 1906/1961. *Puck of Pook's Hill.* London: Macmillan.

Klingberg, Göte. 1986. *Children's Fiction in the Hands of the Translators.* Lund: Gleerup.

Klopp, Charles. 2006. "'Frankenstein' and Pinocchio, Nineteenth-Century Humanoids." In *Approaches to Teaching Collodi's* Pinocchio *and Its Adaptations,* edited by Michael Sherberg, 28–33. New York: Modern Language Association of America.

_____. 2012. "Workshops of Creation, Filthy and Not: Collodi's *Pinocchio* and Shelley's *Frankenstein.*" In *Pinocchio, Puppets and Modernity: The Mechanical Body,* edited by Katia Pizzi, 63–73. Abingdon-on-Thames: Routledge, 63–73.

Knoepflmacher, U.C. 1986. "Avenging Alice: Christina Rossetti and Lewis Carroll." *Nineteenth Century Literature* 41: 299–328.

_____. 1998. *Ventures into Childland: Victorians, Fairy Tales, and Femininity.* Chicago: University of Chicago Press.

Knuth, Rebecca. 2012. *Children's Literature and British Identity: Imagining a People and a Nation.* Lanham, MD: Scarecrow Press.

Koenen, Anne. 1996. "Vampires of the Senses: The Feminist Fantastic of Angela Carter." *Anglistik and Englischunterricht* 59: 143–161.

Kossi Logan, Mawuena. 1999. *Narrating Africa: George Henty and the Fiction of Empire.* New York: Garland.

Kumar, Krishan. 2003. *The Making of English National Identity.* Cambridge: Cambridge University Press.

Kuznets, Lois Rostow. 1994. *When Toys Come Alive: Narratives of Animation, Metamorphosis, and Development.* New Haven: Yale University Press.

Labanca, Nicola. 2002. *Oltremare. Storia dell' espansione coloniale italiana.* Bologna: Il Mulino.

Labbé, Jacqueline. 1999. "Still She Haunts Me, Phantomwise: Gendering Alice." *The Carrollian: The Lewis Carroll Journal* 3: 19–29.

La Belle, Jenijoy. 1988. *Herself Beheld: The Literature of the Looking-Glass.* Ithaca, NY: Cornell University Press.

Lake, Frederick. 2006. "Folklore and Mythology in the Alice Books." *The Knight Letter. The Lewis Carroll Society of America* 76: 8–12.

Lamb, Charles and Mary. 1976. *The Letters of Charles and Mary Lamb,* edited by Edwin W. Mars. Ithaca, NY: Cornell University Press.

Lapucci, Carl. 1986. "Modi di dire e motti proverbiali come tessuto e come paradigmi narrativi nella storia di Pinocchio." In *Interni e Dintorni del Pinocchio. Atti del Convegno "Folkloristi Italiani del tempo del Collodi,"* edited by Pietro Clemente and Mariano Fresta, 113–122. Pescia: Editori del Grifo.

Lassén-Seger, Maria. 2004. "Exploring Otherness: Changes in the Child-Animal Metamorphosis Motif." In *Change and Renewal in Children's Literature,* edited by Thomas Van del Walt, 35–46. Westport, CT: Greenwood.

_____. 2006. *Adventures into Otherness: Child Metamorphs in Late 20th Century Literature.* Turku, Finland: Åbo Akademi University Press.

Lathey, Gillian, ed. 2006. *The Translation of Children's Literature: A Reader.* Bristol, UK: Multilingual Matters.

_____. 2010. *The Role of Translators in Children's Literature.* Abingdon-on-Thames: Routledge.

Latimer, Dan. 2004. "The 'Golden, Holy Cord of Calculation': Collodi's Second Thoughts on *Pinocchio.*" *The Comparatist* 26: 113–134.

Lau, Kimberley. 2008. "Erotic Infidelities: Angela Carter's Wolf Trilogy." *Marvels & Tales* 22.1: 77–94.

Lavagetto, Mario. 2003. "Pinocchio racconta Pinocchio" in *Lavorare con piccoli indizi*. Torino: Bollati Boringhieri, 265–275.

_____, ed. 2008. *Racconti di orchi, di fate e di streghe. La fiaba letteraria in Italia*. Milano: Mondadori "I Meridiani," 2008.

Lavinio, Cristina. 1986. "Fiaba popolare, oralità, vernacolo." In *Interni e Dintorni del Pinocchio. Atti del Convegno "Folkloristi Italiani del tempo del Collodi,"* edited by Pietro Clemente, Pietro and Mariano Fresta, 187–198. Pescia: Editori del Grifo.

Lawson, John, and Harold Silver, ed. 2007. *A Social History of Education in England*. Abingdon-on-Thames: Routledge.

Lawson Lucas, Ann. 1990. "Fascism and Literature: Il caso Salgari." *Italian Studies* 45: 32–47.

_____. 1993. "Salgari, the Atlas, and the Microscope." In *Literature and Travel*, edited by Michael Hanne, 79–91. Amsterdam: Rodopi.

_____. 1996. "Il Fratellino bianco: Race Relations in Salgari's Adventure Novels." In *Other Worlds, Other Lives: Children's Literature Experiences*, edited by Myma Machet, Sandra Olën, and Thomas Van der Valt, 157–172. Pretoria: University of South Africa Press.

_____. 1997. "Nations on Trial: The Case of *Pinocchio* and *Alice*." In *Gunpowder and Sealing-Wax: Nationhood in Children's Literature*, edited by Ann Lawson Lucas, 49–58. Leicester, UK: Troubador.

_____. 1999a. "Enquiring Mind, Rebellious Spirit: Alice and Pinocchio as Nonmodel Children." *Children's Literature in Education* 30.3: 157–169.

_____. 1999b. "Pinocchio and Alice: Animals, Animus and Animation." *BALCL Bulletin* 6: 5–9.

_____. 2000. *La ricerca dell'ignoto. I romanzi d'avventura di Emilio Salgari*. Firenze: Olschki.

_____. 2002. "A Boy for All Seasons: Nation and Ideology in Images from *Pinocchio*." *Spunti e Ricerche* 17: 15–26.

_____. 2003. "Decadence for Kids; Salgari's *Corsaro Nero* in Context." In *Children's Literature and the Fin de Siècle*, edited by Roderick McGillis, 81–90. Westport, CT: Praeger.

_____. 2005. "Alla conquista di imperi con Salgari, Henty e compagni." In *I miei volumi corrono trionfanti ... Atti del Primo Convegno Internazionale sulla fortuna di Salgari all'estero*, edited by Eliana Pollone, Simona Re Fiorentin, and Pompeo Vagliani, 45–53. Alessandria: Edizioni dell'Orso.

Leach, Karoline. 2009. *In the Shadow of the Dreamchild: The Myth and Reality of Lewis Carroll*, revised ed. London: Peter Owen.

Leerssen, Joep. 1991. "Echoes and Images: Reflections upon Foreign Space." In *Alterity, Identity, Image: Selves and Others in Society and Scholarship*, edited by Raymond Corbey and Joep Leerssen, 123–138. Amsterdam: Rodopi.

_____. 2000. "The Rhetoric of National Character: A Programmatic Survey." *Poetics Today* 21: 2, 267–292.

_____. 2007. "Imagology: History and Method." In *Imagology, The Cultural Construction and Literary Representation of National Characters*, edited by Manfred Beller and Joep Leerssen, 17–32. Amsterdam: Rodopi.

Levy, Michael and Farah Mendlesohn. 2016. *Children's Fantasy Literature: An Introduction*. Cambridge: Cambridge University Press.

Lewis, C.S. 1950/1991. *The Lion, the Witch and the Wardrobe*. New York: HarperCollins.

Lindseth, Jon A. and Alan Tannenbaum, eds. 2015. *Alice in a World of Wonderlands: The Translations of Lewis Carroll's Masterpiece*. New Castle, DE: Oak Knoll Press.

Little, Judith. 1976. "Liberated Alice: Dodgson's Female Hero as Domestic Rebel." *Women's Studies* 3: 195–203.

Lodge, David. 1984. *Small World: An Academic Romance*. New York: Penguin.

Lombello, Donatella. (2009). "La nascita e lo sviluppo della letteratura moderna per l'infanzia. Libri di testo e letteratura per l'infanzia nell'Ottocento in Italia: il *Giannetto* e il *Giannettino*." *The Journal of Linguistic and Intercultural Education* 2.2: 153–163.

Loparco, Fabiana. 2016. *Il Giornale per i Bambini. Storia del primo grande periodico per l'infanzia italiana (1881–1889)*. Pisa: Bibliografia e Informazione.

Lorenzini Paolo [Collodi Nipote] 1954. *Collodi e Pinocchio*. Firenze: Salani.

Lovell-Smith, Rose. 2007. "Eggs and Serpents: Natural History References in Lewis Carroll's Scene of Alice and the Pigeon." *Children's Literature* 35: 27–53.

Lüthi, Max. 1982. *The European Folktale: Form and Nature*. Bloomington: Indiana University Press.

MacArthur, Fiona. 2004. "Embodied Figures of Speech: Problem-Solving in Alice's Dream of Wonderland." *Atlantis* 26: 51–62.

MacDonald, George. 1871/1994. *At the Back of the North Wind*. Ware, England: Wordsworth Classics.

_____. 1872/1994. *The Princess and the Goblin*. London: Penguin (Puffin).

_____. 1883/1994. *The Princess and Curdie*. London: Penguin (Puffin).

MacDonald, Robert. 1990. "A Poetics of War: Militarist Discourse in the British Empire, 1880–1918." *Mosaic: An Interdisciplinary Critical Journal* 23: 17–35.

Maguire, Gregory. 2015. *After Alice*. New York: HarperCollins.

Mancini, Marco. 1997. "'Viaggiare con le parole: l'esotismo linguistico in Salgari." In *Il "caso Salgari"*, edited by Carmine Di Biase, 67–104. Napoli: CUEN.

Mandler, Peter. 2006. *The English National Character: The History of an Idea from Edmund Burke to Tony Blair*. New Haven: Yale University Press.

Manganelli, Giorgio. 1977/2002. *Pinocchio. Un Libro Parallelo*. Milano: Adelphi.

Manguel, Alberto and Gianni Guadalupi. 1999. *The Dictionary of Imaginary Places*. London: Bloomsbury.

Manzi, Elio. 2013. *Geografie salgariane. Ripartire da Mompracem*. Torino: Andrea Viglongo.

Marcheschi, Daniela. 1990. *Collodi Ritrovato*. Pisa: ETS.

_____. 1993. "'Pinocchio' fra letteratura e teatro delle marionette e dei burattini." In *Pinocchio fra i burattini. Atti del Convegno del 27–28 marzo 1987*, edited by Fernando Tempesti, 179–193. Fondazione Nazionale "Carlo Collodi," Firenze: La Nuova Italia.

_____. 1995. "Introduction" to *Carlo Collodi. Opere*. Milano: Mondadori, xi–cxxiv.

_____. 2016. *Il naso corto. Una rilettura delle Avventure di Pinocchio*. Bologna: EDB.

Marchianò, Grazia. 1981. "Pinocchio come sistema metafisico virtuale." In *C'era una volta un pezzo di legno. La simbologia di Pinocchio*, edited by Gian Luca Pierotti, 143–155. Fondazione Nazionale "Carlo Collodi," Milano: Edizioni Emme.

Marciano, Annunziata. 2004. *Alfabeto ed educazione*. Milano: Francoangeli.

Marshall, Cynthia. 1994. "Bodies and Pleasures in *The Wind in the Willows*." *Children's Literature* 22: 58–69.

Martineau, Harriet. 1841/1864. *The Crofton Boys*. Abingdon-on-Thames: Routledge.

Marx, Sonia. 1990. *Le Avventure tedesche di Pinocchio. Letture di una storia senza frontiere*. Pescia: Fondazione nazionale "Carlo Collodi" and La Nuova Italia.

Mascialino, Rita. 2004. *Pinocchio: Analisi e interpretazione*. Padova: Cleup.

Massey, Irving. 1976. *The Gaping Pig: Literature and Metamorphosis*. Oakland: University of California Press.

Mathews, Richard. 2002. *Fantasy: The Liberation of Imagination*. Abingdon-on-Thames: Routledge.

Maurice, Lisa, ed. 2015. "Children, Greece and Rome." In *The Reception of Ancient Greece and Rome in Children's Literature: Heroes and Eagles*. Leiden, Netherlands: Brill. 1–16.

Mavor, Carol. 2008. "For-Getting to Eat: Alice's Mouthing Metonymy." In *The Nineteenth-Century Child and Consumer Culture*, edited by David Denisoff, 95–118. Aldershot: Ashgate.

Mazzoni, Cristina. 2006. "The Short-Legged Fairy: Reading and Teaching *Pinocchio* as a Feminist." In *Approaches to Teaching Collodi's* Pinocchio *and Its Adaptations*, edited by Michael Sherberg, 80–86. New York: Modern Language Association of America.

McEwan, Ian. 2016. *Nutshell*. London: Jonathan Cape.

McGillis, Roderick. 1983. "Fantasy as Adventure: Nineteenth Century Children's Fiction." *Children's Literature Association Quarterly* 8: 18–22.

McGlathery, James M., ed. 1988. *The Brothers Grimm and Folktale*. Champaign: University of Illinois Press.

McHale, Brian. 1989. *Postmodernist Fiction*. Abingdon-on-Thames: Routledge.
_____. 2015. *The Cambridge Introduction to Postmodernism*. Cambridge: Cambridge University Press.
Meek, Margaret. 2001. "The Englishness of English Children's Books." In *Children's Literature and National Identity*, edited by Margaret Meek, 89–102. Stoke-on-Trent: Trentham Books.
Meier, Franz. 2009. "Photographic Wonderland: Intermediality and Identity in Lewis Carroll's *Alice* Books." In *Alice Beyond Wonderland: Essays for the Twenty-First Century*, edited by Christopher Hollingsworth, 117–134. Iowa City: University of Iowa Press.
Meinig, Donald William. 1985. "Symbolic Landscapes: Some Idealizations of American Communities." In *The Interpretation of Ordinary Landscapes*. New York: Oxford University Press, 164–194.
Melchior-Bonnet, Sabine. 2001. *The Mirror: A History*. Abingdon-on-Thames: Routledge.
Mendlesohn, Farah. 2008. *Rhetorics of Fantasy*. Middletown, CT: Wesleyan University Press.
Mengozzi, Dino. 2012. *Corpi posseduti. Martiri ed eroi dal Risorgimento a Pinocchio*. Manduria: Pietro Lacaita Editore.
Michie, Helena. 1987. *The Flesh Made Word: Female Figures and Women's Bodies*. Oxford: Oxford University Press.
Mills, Elliott. 1905. *The Decline and Fall of the British Empire*. Oxford: Alden and Co., Bocario Press.
Minghetti, Marco. "Postmodern Alice." http://www.humanisticmanagement.eu/home/postmodern-alice/.
Mirmina, Emilia. 1976. "La concezione della donna nel capolavoro di Carlo Collodi." In *Studi Collodiani*, Fondazione Nazionale Carlo Collodi, Pistoia: Cassa di Risparmio di Pistoia e Pescia, 405–417.
Montalba, Anthony R. 1849. *Fairy Tales of All Nations*. London: Chapman and Hall. http://www.gutenberg.org/files/34956/34956-h/34956-h.htm.
Montanari, Massimo. 2010. *L'identità italiana in cucina*. Milano: Laterza.
Moretti, Franco. 2000/1987. *The Way of the World: The Bildungsroman in European Culture*. London: Verso.
Morris, Williams. 1890/2003. *News from Nowhere, or, An Epoch of Rest*, edited by David Leopold. Oxford: Oxford University Press.
_____. 1894/1971. *The Wood Beyond the World*. London: Ballantine.
Morrissey, Thomas J. 2004. "Growing Nowhere: Pinocchio Subverted in Spielberg's *A.I. Artificial Intelligence*." *Extrapolations* 45. 3: 249–262.
Morrissey, Thomas J., and Wunderlich, Richard. 1983. "Death and Rebirth in *Pinocchio*." *Children's Literature* 11: 64–75.
Mosley, Leonard. 1987. *The Real Walt Disney*. London: Futura.
Musgrave, P.W. 1985. *From Brown to Bunter: The Life and Death of the School Story*. London: Routledge and Kegan Paul.
Myers, Lindsay. 2012. *Making the Italians: Poetics and Politics of Italian Children's Fantasy*. Pieterlen and Bern, Switzerland: Peter Lang.
_____. 2017. *Un* fantasy *tutto italiano: Le declinazioni del fantastico nella letteratura italiana per l'infanzia dall'Unità al XXI secolo*. Pisa: ETS.
Naidis, Mark. 1964. "G.A. Henty's Idea of India." *Victorian Studies* 8: 49–58.
Neiger, Ada. 1997. "La figura della donna nel ciclo di Sandokan." In *Il "caso Salgari"*, edited by Carmine Di Biase, 175–182. Napoli: CUEN.
Nelson, Claudia. 1991. *Boys Will be Girls: The Feminine Ethic and British Children's Fiction, 1857–1917*. New Brunswick, NJ: Rutgers University Press.
Nesbit, Edith. 1906/1996. *The Story of the Amulet*. New York: Penguin.
Nicholson, Mervyn. 1987. "Food and Power: Homer, Carroll, Atwood and Others." *Mosaic* 20: 37–55.
Nicora, Flaminia. 2005. *Eroi britannici, Sepoys ribelli, l'Indian Mutiny nel romanzo anglo-indiano dal 1857 alla fine del XX secolo*. Torino: l'Harmattan Italia.
_____. 2007. "Patrioti, eroi e avventurieri. Salgari, l'*Indian mutiny* e il romanzo di avventura tra Gran Bretagna, Francia e Italia." In *Emilio Salgari e la grande tradizione del romanzo d'avventura*,

edited by Luisa Villa, 71–78. Genova: ECIG.

Nikolajeva, Maria. 1996. *Children's Literature Comes of Age: Toward a New Aesthetic.* New York: Garland.

_____. 1998. *The Magic Code: The Use of Magical Patterns in Fantasy for Children.* Stockholm: Almqvist and Wiksell International.

_____. 2003. "Fairy Tale and Fantasy: From Archaic to Postmodern." *Marvels & Tales* 17: 138–156.

Nikolajeva, Maria, and Carole Scott. 2001. *How Picturebooks Work.* Abingdon-on-Thames: Routledge.

Nobile, Angelo. 2009. *Cuore in 120 anni di critica deamicisiana.* Roma: Aracne.

Nodelman, Perry. 1985–1989. *Touchstones: Reflections on the Best in Children's Literature.* West Lafayette IN: ChLa Publishers.

_____. 2008. *The Hidden Adult: Defining Children's Literature.* Baltimore: Johns Hopkins University Press.

Orwell, George. 1949/1989. *1984.* New York: Penguin.

Ostry, Elaine. 2003. "Magical Growth and Moral Lessons; or, How the Conduct Book Informed Victorian and Edwardian Children's Fantasy." *The Lion and the Unicorn* 27.1: 27–56.

O'Sullivan Emer. 2001. "Alice in Different Wonderlands: Varying Approaches in the German Translation of an English Children's Classic." In *Children's Literature and National Identity*, edited by Margaret Meek, 11–21. Stoke-on-Trent: Trentham Books.

_____. 2005. *Comparative Children's Literature.* Abingdon-on-Thames: Routledge.

_____. 2006. "Does *Pinocchio* Have an Italian passport? What is Specifically National and What Is International about Classics of Children's Literature." In *The Translation of Children's Literature. A Reader*, edited by Gillian Lathey, 146–162. Bristol: Multilingual Matters.

_____. 2011. "Imagology Meets Children's Literature." *International Research in Children's Literature* 4.1: 1–14.

Padellaro, Nazareno. 1938. "Traduzioni e riduzioni di libri per fanciulli." In *Convegno Nazionale per la letteratura infantile e giovanile, con prefazione manifesto di F.T. Marinetti*, relazioni del convegno [conference proceedings], Roma: Ente Nazionale per le Biblioteche Popolari e Scolastiche, Sindacato Nazionale Fascista Autori e Scrittori, 35–42.

Palermo, Antonio. 1981. *La critica e l'avventura: Serra, Salgari, Il primo Novecento.* Torino, Napoli: Guida.

Panau, Petros and Tasoula Tsilimeni. 2013. "International Classic Characters and National Ideologies: Alice and Pinocchio in Greece." In *The Nation in Children's Literature*, edited by Christopher (Kit) Kelen and Björn Sundmark, 193–206. Abingdon-on-Thames: Routledge.

Panszczyk, Anna. 2016. "The 'Becoming' of Pinocchio: The Liminal Nature of Collodi's Boy-Toy." *Children's Literature* 44: 192–218.

Paolini, Paolo. 1976. "Collodi traduttore di Perrault." In *Studi Collodiani*, Fondazione Nazionale Carlo Collodi, Pistoia: Cassa di Risparmio di Pistoia e Pescia, 445–467.

Parravicini, Luigi Alessandro. 1837/1851. *Giannetto.* Livorno: Antonelli.

Parrish Lee, Michael. 2014. "Eating Things: Food, Animals, and Other Life Forms in Lewis Carroll's *Alice* Books." *Nineteenth-Century Literature* 68: 484–512.

Paruolo, Elena. 2001. "The World of *Pinocchio*: Adventures in Languages and Cultures." In *Hearts of Lightness: The Magic of Children's Literature*, edited by Laura Tosi, 69–100, Venezia: Cafoscarina.

_____. 2003. "Les Pinocchio de Luigi Compagnone." In *Pinocchio. Entre texte et image*, edited by Jean Perrot, 227–240. Pieterlen and Bern, Switzerland: Peter Lang, 227–240.

_____. 2017. *Il Pinocchio di Carlo Collodi e le sue riscritture in Italia e Inghilterra*, Roma: Aracne.

Patriarca, Silvana. 2010. *Italianità. La costruzione del carattere nazionale.* Laterza, Italy: Laterza.

Peach, Linden. 1998. *Angela Carter.* Basingstoke: Macmillan.

Pearson, Jacqueline. 2006. "Foreword" to *Revisiting Angela Carter*, edited by Rebecca Munford, vii–xi. London: Palgrave Macmillan.

Perella, Nicolas J. 1986. "An Essay on *Pinocchio*." *Italica* 63: 1–47.

Perrault, Charles. 1962/1999. *Complete Fairy Tales*. Translated by A.E. Johnson. London: Penguin (Puffin).

Perrot, Jean. 2010. "L'engagement de Carlo Collodi, entre Baroque et Carnaval." In *Writing and Translating for Children: Voices, Images, and Texts*, edited by Elena Di Giovanni, Chiara Elefante and Roberta Pederzoli, 45–60. Pieterlen and Bern, Switzerland: Peter Lang.

Petzold, Dieter. 1990. "Breaking in the Colt: Socialization in Nineteenth-Century School Stories." *Children's Literature Association Quarterly* 15: 17–21.

Pezzini, Isabella and Paolo Fabbri, eds. 2002. *Le avventure di Pinocchio tra un linguaggio e l'altro*. Roma: Meltemi.

Pizzi, Katia, ed. 2012. *Pinocchio, Puppets and Modernity: The Mechanical Body*. Abingdon-on-Thames: Routledge.

Pleij, Herman. 2001. *Dreaming of Cockaigne: Medieval Fantasies of the Perfect Life*. New York: Columbia University Press.

Ponchiroli, Daniele. 1971. "Introduction" to Emilio Salgari, *Avventure di prateria, di giungla e di mare*. Torino: Einaudi, 7–21.

Pozzo, Felice. 2000. *Emilio Salgari e dintorni*. Napoli: Liguori.

_____. 2007. "L' esoterismo 'avventuroso' in Emilio Salgari, Louis Jacolliot, e Henry Rider Haggard." In *Emilio Salgari e la grande tradizione del romanzo d'avventura*, edited by Luisa Villa, 109–123. Genova: ECIG.

Pringles, David, gen. ed. 2006. *The Ultimate Encyclopedia of Fantasy*. London: Carlton.

Propp, Vladimir. 1928/1968. *Morphology of the Folktale*. Austin: University of Texas Press.

Pullman, Philip. 2012. *His Dark Materials*. London: Scholastic.

Pynchon, Thomas. 1966. *The Crying of Lot 49*. Philadelphia: Lippincott.

Quigly, Isabel. 1982. *The Heirs of Tom Brown: The English School Story*. London: Chatto and Windus.

Rackin, Donald. 1991. *Alice's Adventures in Wonderland and Through the Looking-Glass: Nonsense, Sense, and Meaning*. New York: Twayne.

_____. 1997. "Mind Over Matter: Sexuality and Where the 'body happens to be' in the *Alice* Books." In *Textual Bodies: Changing Boundaries of Literary Representation*, edited by Hope Lori Lefkovitz, 161–184. New York: State University of New York Press.

Raeper, William. 1987. *George MacDonald*. Tring: Lion.

Ragionieri, Ernesto. 1969. *L'Italia giudicata 1861–1945, ovvero la storia degli italiani scritta dagli altri*. Bari: Laterza.

Rak, Maria Giovanna. 1993. "Documenti per la storia dei burattini nel secolo XIX." In *Pinocchio fra i burattini. Atti del Convegno del 27–28 marzo 1987*, edited by Fernando Tempesti, 79–97. Fondazione Nazionale "Carlo Collodi," Firenze: La Nuova Italia.

Reichertz, Ronald. 1997. *The Making of the Alice Books: Lewis Carroll's Use of Earlier Children's Literature*. Montreal: McGill-Queens University Press.

Reimer, Mavis. 2009. "Traditions of the School Story." In *The Cambridge Companion to Children's Literature*, edited by Matthew O. Grenby and Andrea Immel, 209–225. Cambridge: Cambridge University Press.

Renan, Ernest. 1990. "What is a Nation." In *Nation and Narration*, edited by Homi Bhabha, 8–22. Abingdon-on-Thames: Routledge.

Reynolds, Kimberley. 1990. *Girls Only? Gender and Popular Children's Fiction in Britain, 1880–1910*. New York and London: Harvester Wheatsheaf.

Reynolds, Kimberley, and Nicola Humble. 1993. *Victorian Heroines: Representations of Femininity in Nineteenth-Century Literature and Art*. New York: New York University Press.

Rhys, Jean. 1966/1968. *Wide Sargasso Sea*. New York: Penguin.

Richards, Jeffrey. 1988. *Happiest Days: The Public School in English Fiction*. Manchester: Manchester University Press.

_____. 1989. "With Henty to Africa." In *Imperialism and Juvenile Literature*, edited by Jeffrey Richards, 72–105. Manchester: Manchester University Press.

_____. 2009. *The Ancient World on the Victorian and Edwardian Stage*. London: Palgrave Macmillan.

Richardson, Brian. 2010. "Transtextual Characters." In *Characters in Fictional Worlds: Understanding Imaginary Beings in Literature, Film, and Other Media*, edited by Jens Eder, Fotis Jannidis, and Ralf Scheider, 525–567. Berlin: De Gruyter.

Richter, Dieter. 2002. *Pinocchio o il romanzo d'infanzia*. Roma: Edizioni di Storia e Letteratura.

Rilli, Nicola. 2008. *Pinocchio in casa sua. Da Firenze a Sesto Fiorentino. Realtà e fantasia di Pinocchio*. Sesto Fiorentino: Metropoli.

Rodari, Gianni. 2000. *The Grammar of Fantasy: An Introduction to the Art of Inventing Stories*, translated by Jack Zipes. New York: Teachers and Writers Collaborative.

Roiphe, Katie. 2002. *Still She Haunts Me*. New York: Delta.

Rörich, Lutz. 1991. *Folktale and Reality*. Bloomington: Indiana University Press.

Rosenthal, M.L. 1993. "Alice, Huck, Pinocchio, and the Blue Fairy: Bodies Real and Imagined." *The Southern Review* 29.3: 486–490.

Rossetti, Christina. 1862/1971. *Goblin Market*. London: Macmillan.

_____. 1874. *Speaking Likenesses*. London: Macmillan.

Roth, Christine. 2009. "Looking Through the Spyglass: Lewis Carroll, James Barrie, and the Empire of Childhood." In *Beyond Wonderland: Essays for the Twenty-First Century*, edited by Christopher Hollingsworth, 23–36. Iowa City: University of Iowa Press.

Rowe, Karen E. 1996. "Feminism and Fairy Tales." In *Folk and Fairy Tales*, edited by Martin Hallett and Barbara Karasek, 325–345. 2nd ed., Peterborough, ONT: Broadview.

Ruskin, John. 1905. "Fairy Stories." In *The Works of John Ruskin*, edited by E.T. Cook, 233–239. London: Allen.

Russell Ascoli, Albert, and Krystyna von Henneberg, eds. 2001. *Making and Remaking Italy: The Cultivation of National Identity around the Risorgimento*. Oxford: Berg.

Ruzza, Carlo. 2000. "Language and Nationalism in Italy: Language as a Weak Marker of Identity." In *Language and Nationalism in Europe*, edited by Stephen Barbour and Catherine Carmichael, 168–182. Oxford: Oxford University Press.

Ryan-Sautour, Michelle. 2012. "The Alchemy of Reading in Angela Carter's 'Alice in Prague or the Curious Room.'" In *Angela Carter: New Critical Readings*, edited by Sonya Andermahr and Lawrence Phillips, 67–80. London: Continuum.

Sage, Lorna. 1992. *Women in the House of Fiction, Post-War Women Novelist*. London: Macmillan.

Said, Edward W. 1995. *Orientalism*. London: Penguin.

Sale, Roger. 1978. *Fairy Tales and After: From Snow White to E.B. White*. Cambridge, MA: Harvard University Press.

Salgari, Emilio. 1883–4/2014. *Sandokan: The Tigers of Mompracem*, translated by Nico Lorenzutti, Rohpress.

_____. 1896/2014. *Sandokan: The Pirates of Malaysia*, translated by Nico Lorenzutti, Rohpress.

_____. 1897. *Le Stragi delle Filippine*. Genova: Donath.

_____. 1899. *La Capitana dello Yucatan*. Genova: Donath.

_____. 1905. *La Sovrana del Campo d'Oro*. Genova: Donath.

_____. 2009. *Sandokan: The Two Tigers*, translated by Nico Lorenzutti, Rohpress.

_____. 2010. *Tutte le avventure di Sandokan, I cicli completi della giungla e dei pirati della Malesia*. Rome: Newton Compton.

Sandis. Dominique. 2006. "Proposing a Methodology for the Study of Nation-(ality) in Children's Literature." In *New Voices in Children's Literature Criticism*, edited by in Sebastien Chapleau, 105–116. Lichfield: Pied Piper Press.

Schacker, Jennifer. 2003. *National Dreams: The Remaking of Fairy Tales in Nineteenth-Century England*. Philadelphia: University of Pennsylvania Press.

Schanoes, Veronica. 2012. "Fearless Children and Fabulous Monsters: Angela Carter, Lewis Carroll, and Beastly Girls." *Marvels & Tales* 26.1: 30–43.

_____. 2014. *Fairy Tales, Myth, and Psychoanalytic Theory: Feminism and Retelling the Tale*. Farnham: Ashgate.

_____. 2017. "Queen Alice and the Monstrous Child: Alice Through the Looking-Glass." *Children's Literature* 45: 1–20.

Schine, Cathleen. 1985. *Alice in Bed.* London: Severn House.

Scieszka, Jon. 1992. *The Stinky Cheese Man and Other Fairly Stupid Tales.* London: Scholastic.

Seaboyer, Judith. 1999. "Robert Coover's *Pinocchio in Venice*: An Anatomy of a Talking Book." In *Venetian Views, Venetian Blinds, English Fantasies of Venice*, edited by Manfred Pfister and Barbara Schaff, 237–255. Amsterdam: Rodopi.

Sendak, Maurice. 1963/2000. *Where the Wild Things Are.* London: Red Fox.

Shakespeare, William. 1995. *Henry V*, edited by T.W. Craik, The Arden Shakespeare. London: Bloomsbury.

Sharp, Evelyn. 1897. *Wymps and Other Fairy Tales.* London: The Bodley Head.

Sharpe, Jenny. 1994. "The Unspeakable Limits of Rape: Colonial Violence and Counter-Insurgency." In *Colonial Discourse and Post-Colonial Theory. A Reader*, edited by Patrick Williams and Laura Chrisman, 221-243. New York: Colombia University Press.

Sigler, Carolyn, ed. 1997. *Alternative Alices: Visions and Revisions of Lewis Carroll's Alice Books.* Lexington: University Press of Kentucky.

_____. 2001. "Was the Snark a Boojum? One Hundred Years of Lewis Carroll Biographies." *Children's Literature* 29: 229–243.

_____. 2005. "Wonders Wild and New: Lewis Carroll's *Alice* Books and Postmodern Women Writers." In *Twice-Told Children's Tales. The Influence of Childhood Reading on Writers for Adults*, edited by Betty Greenway, 133–146. Abingdon-on-Thames: Routledge.

Simonsen, Theresa. 2005. "Modern Educational Ideology in *Alice's Adventures in Wonderland*." *The Carrollian* 16: 13–18.

Simpson, Jacqueline and Steve Roud, eds. 2000. "Introduction" to *A Dictionary of English Folklore*. New York: Oxford University Press, i–vii.

Slavitt, David. 1984. *Alice at Eighty.* New York: Doubleday.

Smiles, Samuel. 1859/2002. *Self-Help.* Oxford: Oxford University Press.

Smiley, Jane. 1991/1992. *A Thousand Acres.* London: Flamingo.

Smith, Louisa. 2004. "Domestic Fantasy—Real Gardens or Imaginary Toads." In *International Companion Encyclopedia of Children's Literature*, edited by Peter Hunt, 447–453. Abingdon-on-Thames: Routledge.

Sorcinelli, Paolo. 1999. *Gli italiani e il cibo. Dalla polenta ai cracker.* Milano: Bruno Mondadori.

Spadolini, Giovanni. 1972a. "Collodi." In *Gli uomini che fecero l'Italia.* Milano: Longanesi, 212–218.

_____. 1972b. "Salgari." In *Gli uomini che fecero l'Italia.* Milano: Longanesi, 219–223.

Spiering, Menno. 2007. "English." In *Imagology, The Cultural Construction and Literary Representation of National Characters*, edited by Manfred Beller and Joep Leerssen, 145–194. Amsterdam: Brill/Rodopi.

Spurling, Cuthbert. 1916. "The Secret of the English Character." *The Contemporary Review* 110: 639–645.

Squarcina, Enrico and Stefano Malatesta. 2012. "La Geografia del 'Viaggio per l'Italia di Giannettino' di Carlo Collodi come strumento per la costruzione nazionale italiana." *Scripta Nova. Revista Electrónica de Geografía y Ciencias Sociales* 16: 418 http://www.ub.edu/geocrit/sn/sn-418/sn-418.htm.

Stapinski, Helene. "I Had Alice in Wonderland Syndrome." *The New York Times* 23 June 2014, http://well.blogs.nytimes.com/2014/06/23/alice-in-wonderland-syndrome/?_r=0.

Stewart-Steinberg, Suzanne. 2007. *The Pinocchio Effect, On Making Italians (1860–1920).* Chicago: University of Chicago Press.

Stych, Franklin Samuel. 1971. *Pinocchio in Gran Bretagna e Irlanda.* Firenze: Quaderni della Fondazione Collodi.

Suchan, James. 1978. "Alice's Journey from Alien to Artist." *Children's Literature* 7: 78–92.

Sullivan, C.W. III. 1992. "Fantasy." In *Stories and Society: Children's Literature in Its Social Context*, edited by Dennis Butts, 97–111. London: Macmillan.

_____. 2004. "High Fantasy." In *Interna-*

tional Companion Encyclopedia of Children's Literature, edited by Peter Hunt, 436–446. Abingdon-on-Thames: Routledge.

Summerfield, Giovanna. 2010. "The Italian Apprentice: Foscolo and Collodi." In *New Perspectives on the European Bildungsroman*, edited by Giovanna Summerfield and Lisa Downward, 61–80. London: Continuum.

Sundmark, Björn. 1999. *Alice's Adventures in the Oral-Literary Continuum*. Lund, Sweden: Lund University Press.

Susina, Jan. 2010. *The Place of Lewis Carroll in Children's Literature*. Abingdon-on-Thames: Routledge.

Swinfen, Anne. 1984. *In Defence of Fantasy: A Study of the Genre in English and American Literature Since 1945*. Abingdon-on-Thames: Routledge.

Syngh, Ghan Shyam. 1980. "L'India perenne di Salgari." In *Scrivere l'Avventura: Emilio Salgari. Atti del Convegno Nazionale*. Torino: Istituto di Italianistica dell'Università di Torino, 66–70.

Tadini, Umberto. 1981. "Il legno delle metamorfosi." In *C'era una volta un pezzo di legno. La simbologia di Pinocchio*, edited by Gian Luca Pierotti, 53–58. Fondazione Nazionale "Carlo Collodi," Milano: Edizioni Emme.

Tait, Vanessa. 2015. *The Looking Glass House*. London: Corvus.

Talairach-Vielmas, Laurence. 2007. *Moulding the Female Body in Victorian Fairy Tales and Sensation Novels*. Farnham, UK: Ashgate.

Tally, Robert T. 2012. "The Way of the Wizarding World: *Harry Potter* and the Magical *Bildungsroman*." In *J.K. Rowling: Harry Potter*, edited by Cynthia Hallett and Peggy Huey, 36–47. London: Palgrave Macmillan.

Tatar, Maria. 1987. *The Hard Facts of the Grimms' Fairy Tales*. Princeton: Princeton University Press.

_____. 1992. *Off with Their Heads! Fairy Tale and the Culture of Childhood*. Princeton: Princeton University Press.

Taylor, Alexander L. 1952. *The White Knight: A Study of C.L. Dodgson*. Edinburgh: Oliver and Boyd.

Taylor, W.C. 1849. "On the Cultivation of Taste in the Operative Classes." *Art Journal* 11: 3–5.

Tempesti, Fernando, ed. 1993. *Carlo Collodi. Pinocchio*. Milano: Feltrinelli.

Thomas, Donald. 1996. *Lewis Carroll: A Portrait with Background*. London: John Murray.

Thompson, Andrew. 2012. "Introduction" to *Britain's Experience of Empire in the Twentieth Century*. Oxford: Oxford University Press, 1–32.

Todorov, Tzvetan. 1970. *Introduction à la littérature fantastique*. Paris: Le Seuil.

Tolkien, J.R.R. 1964/1988. "On Fairy-Stories." In *Tree and Leaf*. Crows Nest, New South Wales: Allen and Unwin, 9–73.

Torpey, Maureen. 2009. "Winterson's Wonderland: *The Powerbook* as a Postmodern Re-Vision of Lewis Carroll's Alice Books." In *Fairy Tales Reimagined: Essays on New Retellings*, edited by Susan Redington Bobby, 111–121. Jefferson, NC: McFarland.

Tosi, Laura. 2006a. "Children's Literature in No-Land: Utopian Spaces and Gendered Utopias in Evelyn Sharp's Fairy Tales." In *Children's Books and Child Readers, Constructions of Childhood in English Juvenile Fiction*, edited by Christiane Bimberg and Thomas Kullmann, 35–46. Aachen, Germany: Shaker Verlag.

_____. 2006b. "The Child Reader in the Text: Intertexuality and Metafiction in Contemporary Versions of Traditional Fairy Tales." *Rivista di Letterature Comparate* 59: 71–90.

_____. 2007a. "Once Upon Many Times: The Literary Fairy-Tale Canon in England." In *Ripensare il canone. La letteratura inglese e angloamericana*, edited by Gianfranca Balestra and Giovanna Mochi, 95–106. Roma: Artemide.

_____. 2007b. *La fiaba letteraria inglese. Metamorfosi di un genere*. Venezia: Marsilio.

_____. 2016. "Bodily Distortion and Loss of Identity in *Alice's Adventures in Wonderland* and *Le Avventure di Pinocchio*." In *Vulnerability: Memories, Bodies, Sites*, edited by Donata Bulotta, 347–369. Perugia: Morlacchi.

Tosi, Laura, and Peter Hunt. 2015. *As Fit*

as a Fish: The English and Italians Revealed. Manningtree, England: Patrician Press.

Traversetti, Bruno. 1989. Introduzione a Salgari. Milano: Laterza.

———. 1991. Introduzione a De Amicis. Milano: Laterza.

———. 1993. Introduzione a Collodi. Milano: Laterza.

Trites, Roberta Seelinger. 2014. Literary Conceptualizations of Growth. Amsterdam, Netherlands: John Benjamins.

Tropea, Mario. 2012. "Dalla parte dei ribelli? L'ideologia anticoloniale di Salgari." In La geografia immaginaria di Salgari, edited by Arnaldo Di Benedetto, 137–152. Bologna: Il Mulino.

Truglio, Maria. 2017. Italian Children's Literature and National Identity: Childhood, Melancholy, Modernity. Abingdon-on-Thames: Routledge.

Tsvetkov, Yanko. 2014. Atlas of Prejudice 2: Chasing Horizons. CreateSpace Independent Publishing Platform.

Tuman, Myron. 1990. "Student Tutoring and Economic Production: Nineteenth-Century British Parallels of Current American Practice." In Culture and Education in Victorian England, edited by Patrick Scott and Pauline Fletcher, 174–182. Lewisburg, PA: Bucknell University Press.

Turiello, Pasquale. 1882/1994. Sul carattere degli Italiani. Roma: Calice.

Twain, Mark. 1876/1993. The Adventures of Tom Sawyer. Oxford: Oxford University Press.

Vagliani, Pompeo, ed. 1998. Quando Alice incontrò Pinocchio. Le edizioni italiane di Alice fra testo e contesto. Torino: Trauben.

Vagnoni, Anna Rosa. 2007. Collodi e Pinocchio. Storia di un successo letterario. Trento: Uniservice.

Van Eeghen, R. 1908. "Concerning Englishmen." The Captain 19: 154.

Vermeule, Blakey. 2010. Why Do We Care About Literary Characters? Baltimore: Johns Hopkins University Press.

Vivarelli, Anna. 2005. All'osteria con Pinocchio. Le ricette di un burattino. Torino: Il Leone verde.

Volpicelli, Luigi. 1963. La verità su Pinocchio. Roma: Armando.

Wakeling, Edward. 2014. Lewis Carroll: The Man and His Circle. London: I.B. Tauris.

Wallace, Jo-Ann, and Stephen Slemon. 2011. "Empire." In Keywords for Children's Literature, edited by Philip Nel and Lissa Paul, 75–78. New York: New York University Press.

Wanning Harries, Elizabeth. 2001. Twice Upon a Time: Women Writers and the History of the Fairy Tale. Princeton: Princeton University Press.

Warner, Marina. 2014. Once Upon a Time: A Short History of Fairy Tale. Oxford: Oxford University Press.

Watkins, Tony. 1995. "Reconstructing the Homeland: Loss and Hope in the English Landscape." In Aspects and Issues in the History of Children's Literature, edited by Maria Nikolajeva, 165–172. Westport, CT: Greenwood Press.

Watson, Victor. 2002. "Introduction" to Coming of Age in Children's Literature, edited by Margaret Meek and Victor Watson, 1–44. London: Continuum.

Weaver, Warren. 2006. Alice in Many Tongues: The Translations of Alice in Wonderland. Mansfield Center, CT: Martino Publishing.

Webb, Jean, ed. 2000. Text, Culture and National Identity in Children's Literature. Helsinki: Nordinfo.

West, Mark I. 1986. "From the Pleasure Principle to the Reality Principle: Pinocchio's Psychological Journey." Proceedings of the Children's Literature Association Conference 1986. West Lafayette, IN: Children's Literature Association, 112–115.

Wilson, Robin. 2008. Lewis Carroll in Numberland. London: Allen Lane.

Wisker, Gina. 1997. "Revenge of the Living Doll: Angela Carter's Horror Writing." In The Infernal Desires of Angela Carter: Fiction, Femininity, Feminism, edited by Joseph Bristow and Trev Lynn Broughton, 116–131. London and New York: Longman.

Woolf, Jenny. 2010. The Mystery of Lewis Carroll: Understanding the Author of Alice's Adventures in Wonderland. London: Hous Books.

Woolf, Virginia. 1971. "Lewis Carroll." In

Aspects of Alice, edited by Robert Philips, 78–80. New York: Penguin.

Wunderlich, Richard, and Thomas Morrissey. 2002. *Pinocchio Goes Postmodern: Perils of a Puppet in the United States.* Abingdon-on-Thames: Routledge.

Yambo [Enrico Novelli] 1902/2006. *Le avventure di Ciuffettino.* Pisa: Campanila.

Zago, Ester. 1988. "Carlo Collodi as Translator: From Fairy Tale to Folk Tale." *The Lion and the Unicorn* 12.2: 61–73.

Ziegler, Georgianna. 2003. "Alice Reads Shakespeare: Charles Dodgson and the Girl's Shakespeare Project." In *Re-Imagining Shakespeare for Children and Young Adults*, edited by Naomi Miller, 107–119. Abingdon-on-Thames: Routledge.

Zipes, Jack. 1987. *The Complete Fairy Tales of the Brothers Grimm.* New York: Bantam Books.

_____. ed. 1999. "Carlo Collodi's *Pinocchio* as Tragic-Comic Fairy Tale." In *When Dreams Come True*. Abingdon-on-Thames: Routledge, 141–150.

_____. 2001. *The Great Fairy-Tale Tradition: From Straparola and Basile to The Brothers Grimm.* New York: W.W. Norton & Company.

_____. 2006. "Towards a Theory of the Fairy Tale as Literary Genre." In *Why Fairy Tales Stick*. Abingdon-on-Thames: Routledge, 1–40.

_____. 2009. *Relentless Progress: The Reconfiguration of Children's Literature, Fairy Tales, and Storytelling*. Abingdon-on-Thames: Routledge.

_____. 2012. *The Irresistible Fairy Tale: The Cultural and Social History of a Genre*. Princeton: Princeton University Press.

_____. 2015. *Grimm Legacies: The Magic Spell of the Grimms' Folk and Fairy Tales*. Princeton: Princeton University Press.

Index